PRAISE FOR

DREW McINTYRE

"Through the years, I've seen firsthand the hard work that Drew McIntyre puts forth both in and out of the ring to be the best. His determination is what gives him the ability to overcome any adversity, and it is what makes him an inspiration to millions of WWE fans around the world."

—Triple H

"I've followed Drew's career for many years. He has had an incredible journey, and now he is on top of the world, kicking ass."

—"Stone Cold" Steve Austin

"WWE is a nonstop climb, with every type of pitfall, obstacle, and barrier imaginable on your way to the top. No one was built for the challenge like Drew McIntyre."

—Shawn Michaels

"Drew is a Goliath with the heart of a David. I'm thrilled to see what he has achieved but more excited for the greatness that lies ahead."

—Bret Hart

"With Drew, it isn't just the mountains climbed and the roads traveled. It's the way he has gone about his business: with humility, passion, and true fire."

—Billy Corgan
of Smashing Pumpkins

A CHOSEN DESTINY

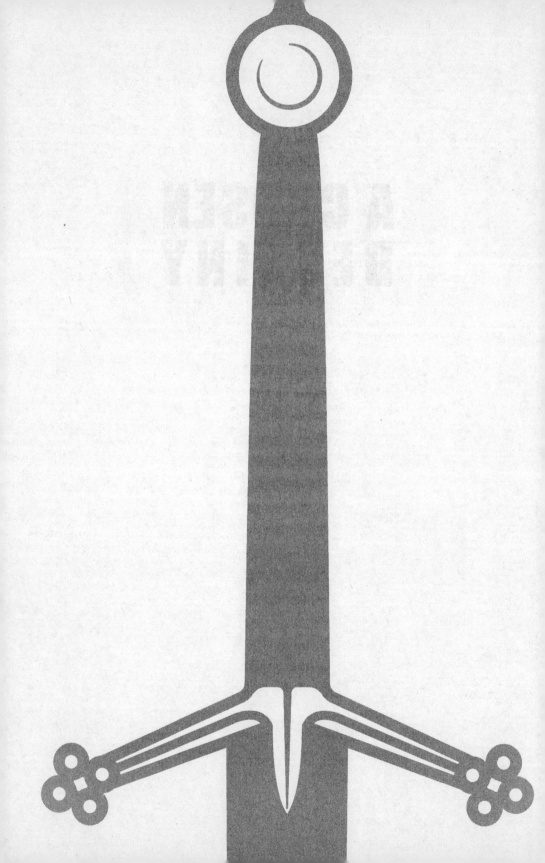

A CHOSEN DESTINY

MY STORY

DREW McINTYRE

WITH SARAH EDWORTHY

G

GALLERY BOOKS

New York   London   Toronto   Sydney   New Delhi

G

Gallery Books
An Imprint of Simon & Schuster, Inc.
1230 Avenue of the Americas
New York, NY 10020

First Gallery Books trade paperback edition February 2022

GALLERY BOOKS and colophon are registered trademarks
of Simon & Schuster, Inc.

For information about special discounts for bulk purchases,
please contact Simon & Schuster Special Sales at 1-866-506-1949
or business@simonandschuster.com.

The Simon & Schuster Speakers Bureau can bring authors
to your live event. For more information or to book an event,
contact the Simon & Schuster Speakers Bureau at 1-866-248-3049
or visit our website at www.simonspeakers.com.

Interior design by Kathryn A. Kenney-Peterson

All insert photos are owned by WWE or courtesy of the author,
except for the following, granted with permission: Page 4,
middle photo © Barry Young; Page 4, bottom photo © Craig Ogston;
Page 5, all images © Irish Whip Wrestling; Page 10,
bottom photo © Moorman Photographics.

Manufactured in the United States of America

10 9 8 7 6 5 4 3 2 1

Library of Congress Cataloging-in-Publication Data is available.

ISBN 978-1-9821-7487-3
ISBN 978-1-9821-7488-0 (pbk)
ISBN 978-1-9821-7489-7 (ebook)

CONTENTS

CONTENTS

A CHOSEN DESTINY

COME ON, MAN, DON'T ARREST ME

APRIL 5, 2020

The dishes are washed. Cats fed. The trash taken out.

We've pulled the bamboo blinds across the big sliding doors that look out across a cluster of palm trees and the lake and switched on some dim lighting. With a large bowl of popcorn, we are now sitting in one of our favorite spots in the world—the big cream leather wraparound sofa that is the heart of our living room. To my left, Kaitlyn is huddled in a huge blanket (she is cold, as usual). On my lap sits a twenty-pound black cat (all the males in our household fall into the heavyweight category). We are not the most outgoing of people. We like to stay inside, happy in our own company, hanging out with our cats, Chaz and Hunter.

It could have been any old evening in front of Netflix. But this was not any old evening. It is fast approaching 7 p.m. on Sunday . . . the second night of *WrestleMania 36*.

With a casual flick of the remote, and a stomach full of butterflies, I am preparing for a surreal but freaking cool out-of-body experience. I am going to watch myself fulfill my destiny "live" on a sixty-inch TV screen.

It counts as an out-of-body experience because I am two distinct selves. One self is me, here, sitting very comfortably, stroking Chaz and picking at popcorn next to my wife, who is not the biggest fan of wrestling, at home in St. Petersburg, in the Tampa Bay area of Florida; my other self is about a hundred miles down the road at the Performance Center in Orlando, where I am about to stalk menacingly into the ring to beat up Brock Lesnar, the most dominant champion in the history of WWE. I am hovering between two dimensions: I am here, but not here. I am happily sitting here in jeans and a black T-shirt, *and* I am the spray-tanned, hairy Scottish Terminator from Claymore Country, restlessly pacing up the locker room, hauling my trademark leather duster over my trunks, soon to be embroiled in the most physically and mentally demanding form of competitive combat known on the planet: a heavyweight world championship match against the evil-chuckling muscle mountain known as the Beast Incarnate.

Crazy, right? Paranormal, even. Which is kind of fitting, as I've always had an interest in supernatural phenomena. Images of my grandmothers flash across my mind: my nana, who showed me the power of the other dimension with a glass whizzing across her Ouija board and who made me promise never to toy with her tarot cards; and Gran, Dad's mum, who would read tea leaves to divine the future, but gave up when she started foreseeing awful things happening to her friends. "Can't you see it? Can't you see it?" she would say, showing us the leaves in the bottom of a cup. No, we never could!

Over the years, I have learned that when you compound the

hard commercial requirements of WWE with the strange reality that television imposes on the world, the results can often be paranormal in ways that would have amazed both of my grandmothers. But this was a situation even more bizarre.

For nineteen years I've been imagining exactly how I would one day wrench the WWE Title from a storied Superstar and shake the title above my head with a roar of triumph, reveling in being the main event of the annual laser-lit, firework spectacle that is *WrestleMania*. I have a whole back catalogue of dream-scenario montages in my head: me taking the big falls, being slammed down onto the canvas, surviving an incredible onslaught before flipping the momentum, powering out of a face-buster and sensationally overcoming my opponent. I drop to one knee to contemplate my victory, then clamber up, climb through the ropes out of the ring, and work my way through the frenzied crowd to find Kaitlyn. I lay the belt on her hands, to acknowledge that the title is something we have achieved together. Maybe get a kiss. The crowd would leap to their feet, the atmosphere is electric . . . And then I wake up.

Never in my overcharged imagination did I think I would experience the biggest match of my life in a time warp, one degree removed, with no fans present.

My sofa-bound self is trying hard to block out the what-could-have-been dream montage: the magical interactive intensity of the fans' surround-sound egging me on to beat the hell out of Brock Lesnar. My audience numbers three: my wife and two cats.

These are surreal times, however, and to be world champion you must stand tall against all challenges. I do—266 pounds and six feet, seven inches with my boots on. People say that few can match Brock Lesnar's imposing, bodybuilder physique, but squaring up to him, eyeball to eyeball, let me tell you: I look down on him.

And six feet, three inches Brock Lesnar is nothing compared
to some of the challenges I have had to overcome. My journey in
wrestling has been . . . complicated, a series of struggles and dis-
appointments, like a giant game of Snakes and Ladders. Ever since
I was fifteen years old, I've heard a word repeated, "potential, potential, potential," ringing in my years. When I was twenty-four, I
was branded the Chosen One by Vince McMahon, the big cheese
who made WWE the global phenomenon it is today. I climbed the
ranks and had the ultimate goal in wrestling in sight, only to slide
back down to the bottom of the reckoning. Let me tell you—this
period, personally, professionally, psychologically, was the lowest
of the lows. But here I am now on the cusp of converting years of
pent-up potential into blockbuster achievement. Thanks to winning a sensational *Royal Rumble* in January, I have earned my shot
at the heavyweight title. If I win—and I sense that is what the
fans really, really want—I will be the first ever British-born WWE
World Champion.

After kicking down every door—as well as a number of my opponents' teeth—I am back near the top of the board. It has been a
long, purposeful climb up the rungs of every ladder in the wrestling
business around the world, and the ultimate prize is once again
within reach . . . And then, just as I ready myself to grasp it, a new
snake slithers across my path, breathing a deadly cloud of invisible
virus particles. The question was, how to bypass it to get to the
top? None of the classic escape moves would rescue me from this
situation. Nor was it something that I could finish off by running
at full speed and booting it smack in the face. I couldn't just pick
up a microphone and cut a brilliant promo to inspire a U-turn in
the mood of the people.

With the spread of COVID-19 confirmed as a global pandemic,

WWE decided the only solution was to follow World Health Organization protocols. So an empty-arena match it would be. It was an irony not lost on some of us that a sport as technically dangerous as wrestling was forced to fall in line with social distancing precautions.

On Planet WWE, we larger-than-life super-strong combatants pride ourselves on prevailing against any objectionable threats that stand in our way, but we were powerless in the face of a global pandemic. The timing was such that those evil spikes of COVID contagion killed off the participatory element of our annual extravaganza, the fans who flock in for *WrestleMania* week, the very lifeblood of WWE. When there are tens of thousands in the arena, the stories in the ring take on their own compelling momentum. For a wrestler, it is absolutely the best feeling in the world: you are improvising in the ring, the crowd is reacting to every move, pulling its collective strings to will the action on. Everyone is on board and strapped in for the emotional roller coaster. And, thanks to COVID-19, I was going to be denied that euphoria, that moment in the sun of the screaming adulation of seventy-five thousand fans? *You have got to be freaking kidding me.*

Owing to the ban on public gatherings, and the introduction of social distancing rules to keep performers safe, we were informed that *WrestleMania* 36 was to be prerecorded behind closed doors at the WWE Performance Center in late March and packaged for pay-per-view and live streaming on April 5 and 6. The dream walk-out at the Raymond James Stadium—home of NFL's Tampa Bay Buccaneers, a host venue for the Super Bowl—was not to be. My big moment was to be staged in a self-contained bubble at WWE's training and developmental facility, the place where wannabe wrestlers train to see if they've got what it takes, not in front of a raucous capacity crowd in the legend-making showcase venue of the "Ray Jay."

My initial reaction—and I am not proud of it—was anger and disappointment, a woe-is-me attitude. After nineteen years of wrestling, of which thirteen were spent away from home, working toward my ambition in America, after turning everything around so that my dream was going to happen and happen on my terms . . . *WrestleMania* was going to be played out in front of *nobody*? I remembered so clearly coming back into the locker room after my segment on *Raw*, and Ricochet drew my attention to the screen, pointing at it and saying, "Oh that's cool." On the screen I saw *Brock Lesnar v Drew McIntyre for the WWE Championship at WrestleMania* and I had to sit down for a second to stay calm. When I heard that Tampa, my American hometown, would be host city for *Mania*, I was grinning from ear to ear. I had earned my heavyweight title shot, in a stadium fifteen minutes from home. Everything had come full circle. It was absolutely perfect. Nothing could possibly go wrong.

Of course it could. The situation made complete sense. It was a typical McIntyre curveball. I have always joked I could be a comic-strip character called Bad Luck Drew. What has ever gone to plan in my life? An unprecedented full-blown global pandemic was the only logical setting in which this *Mania* would ever have happened for me.

But then I dropped the selfish outlook and started to look at the bigger picture. The situation was more significant than my own personal moment in an arena full of screaming people. I was not going to let it faze me. I was going to work hard to make the event unique, a year no one would ever forget. Wrestling is all about unifying people in a collective catharsis. I wanted to flip the negativity and make people feel happy at a time when there was so much suffering and anxiety. How could we be a force for good? Well, we could keep going, stick to the schedule, and give the world an incredible *WrestleMania*, with two days of madness, hilarity, and entertainment, the best sort of escapism during the most difficult time our generation has ever faced.

I may look like Goliath, but mine is a David story. It is about overcoming the odds, doing the impossible, proving a point. We could give everybody a feel-good ending to the event, put smiles on faces . . .

First, I had to win.

ELEVEN DAYS EARLIER.
MARCH 25, 2020.

Returning to the Performance Center, where I'd spent so many days during my time in WWE's third brand, NXT—and realizing this was where *WrestleMania* was going to take place—was weird, just weird. For a start, the taping of the main event (usually the last match on an evening show) was scheduled for midday. Nobody was there, bar a skeleton crew, in accordance with health and safety restrictions. I had the locker room to myself. Instead of the clouds of aroma from self-tan spray, there was a stale smell in the air. The room was so silent and echoey, I played music on my phone to pump me up. I was sitting there trying to remind myself what was going on, what was at stake. In the training room, it was just me, Brian the trainer, and a camera operator at a distance. I stretched and moved around. Not as much as I would have liked, but I remember looking at the clock as I was tying my boots and thinking, I am on the main event of *WrestleMania* in ten minutes and I had better snap into it.

*Come on, Drew! This is your life's work. You are potentially min-
utes from your destiny, you are nearly there!*

The call came that we were going to start a little late. That gave
me time to stretch more, pack in some push-ups, and get mentally primed. When I finally got backstage, which is a very narrow
hallway, I saw Brock in the distance and immediately the buildup
became real. There is no mistaking the ripped silhouette of Brock
Lesnar, the trained fighter who ended Undertaker's streak; he's one
of the most feared, ferocious athletes ever to walk the earth. When
my music hit—a tune I love, despite its not so catchy title of "Gal-
lantry (Defining Moment Remix)" by CFO$—I slipped right into
that moment, fully aware of what this was all about. I was walking
into an empty arena, but I carry so much in my head I could sense
a crowd willing me on, reacting to my entrance of intent. From the
kid who didn't even know where the "hard camera" was in his first
match on *SmackDown*, I was now a man fully aware that millions of
fans around the world were watching down this fixed lens, and I was
going to let everyone in. I was going to emote to them as much as
I could. I was going to spellbind them with the next chapter of my
story and give them a happy ending, my happy ending . . . And that
was all that went through my head during my walk into the ring.

Brock swaggered out to take up my challenge, and I saw the
manic look in his eyes. You know when Brock's into it. You can feel
it. The air bristles with electricity. He generates a force field of
malevolent energy, and he was bringing that into that ring like he
was about to have a brawl in the Ultimate Fighting Championship.
If you could have read my mind, you'd have known I was thinking,
If you pull a funny one out here, Brock, if you pull a fast one, I'll
drop you in a second. That was the stuff that was going through
my head. I worked myself into such a frenzy of aggression that we

could have done that match in a bar, no cameras there. I was so focused and fired up, like I was going into a real fight.

Our match was brief, but he is an absolute beast of a human. He manhandled me at the beginning and went for his German Suplex. The rope was there, and I grabbed it, which he did not expect, and when I felt the jerk, I thought, Wow, there is a reason why this guy's known as The Beast. After I blocked his move, he made sure when he beat me down that I was going over in that German, and I was fully aware, This is a dangerous, dangerous guy. But I was so in the zone, my attitude was: Whatever you do, Brock, I'm getting out of it, I don't care who you are, I don't care how much of a monster you are. And after that trademark Lesnar F-5 when I kicked out of the hold on the count of one, that is a legit look of surprise on his face. I was out there to prove a point. I was out there to have a star-making moment. I wasn't just out there to go along with Mr. Brock, I was going out there for Drew McIntyre.

I have long envisioned these dreams of triumph, but it is insane and overwhelming when they play out and come true. When I won the NXT title in 2017, I remember taking the title out in the hotel room in New York in the quiet of the night, alone, and having a private moment of contemplation. I felt the weight of the title in my hands and thought, Wow, I really did this. If the world had had a sneak peek at me then, that private moment would not have had the same poignancy.

But 2020 was different. If there had been seventy-five thousand people at *WrestleMania* 36 in 2020, the adrenaline would have been through the roof. I would have come backstage after my match to find everyone there, talking, shaking hands, doing high fives, and giving interviews to the media in the locker room. I would have been enjoying every second of it and almost certainly have been the last to leave. The levels of adrenaline coursing around my body would still have been through the roof . . .

After I dethroned Brock Lesnar in the empty Performance Center, I decided to let the world in to see my personal emotions up close. After all, Drew McIntyre is Drew Galloway with the volume switched up high. My victory was the result of overcoming my personal struggles. I was down on my knees, looking at the title, thinking about everything I'd been through on the journey: the sacrifices my wife and family had made, my inspirational mother, whose spirit I carry at every one of my matches, all the torturous grind I've put in to recover from the depths. Here we are, we have done it. And I know I am not dreaming, because Brock Lesnar's prone body is right there.

So much was going through my head. When I snapped to, I saw the floor camera and crawled toward it. Traditionally, it is a very big no-no to turn to that camera and break the fourth wall, but I couldn't help myself. I was alone in the empty Performance Center having won the biggest prize of all and I needed to share my emotions, to tell everybody how I felt. Welling up, I reached out to the camera and said, "Thank you. Thank you for supporting Drew McIntyre, thank you for choosing WWE during this difficult time, it really means the world to me."

My words came straight from my heart.

And that was my *WrestleMania* moment.

After the match, I changed, packed my ring gear into my bag, and drove home. I had brought a smart suit in case I would be asked to do post-match interviews, but due to the unique circumstances and the need to minimize numbers in the Performance Center filming bubble, I had to scurry out hastily so that the subsequent matches could be filmed. I arrived home, showered, and hid the title belt upstairs. With one last look at the glint of prize gold on leather, I put it away in a cupboard in my office and forgot about it.

In the real world, I hadn't officially won the title and I wasn't officially the WWE Champion because our match hadn't yet been streamed, and if it hadn't yet been broadcast, then it hadn't happened. If I'd learned anything from being in this job my entire life, it was this—until it's official, it isn't official. So, the title—that Holy Grail of my life—went into hiding in the back of a cupboard, like a present you put away to bring out for someone at Christmas. Kaitlyn was the only person who knew I had won it. I had conversations with my dad on the phone where he would say over and over, "I know you're not going to tell me, so I'm not going to ask." He'd say that at least six or seven times, and I would keep saying, "Then stop asking, Dad, because I'm not going to tell you! Nothing is official until it is official." Besides, I wanted everyone to enjoy watching the show in "real time."

I did a lot of socially distanced media in the ten days or so between the filming and the streaming of *WrestleMania*, and I had done such an effective job of convincing myself the fight hadn't yet taken place, that I reckon I could have breezed a lie detector test.

Ten days passed in normal lockdown routine. Kaitlyn and I would wake up, eat breakfast, sit on the porch, and have some coffee in the sunshine. I would work through a couple of hours of media work, then go and stretch, do some yoga, have a workout in the gym we had set up in our garage. We would watch a movie, hang out with the cats, and do the household chores. I had been learning to do domestic stuff I should already have known how to do—like laundry and the dishes—which a life on the road had always sort of excused me from. I had started reading a bit. Kaitlyn was trying to coach me to live more in the moment, and not be the serious, driven wrestler 24/7. As a couple, we are well suited to a pandemic lockdown lifestyle, but were those the longest ten days of my entire life? You bet.

◇◇◇◇

APRIL 5, 2020

On the day of *WrestleMania* Sunday I wake up with some flutters of nerves, not to the same degree as if I were preparing for the day of the fight itself, but enough to alert me that today is my day of destiny. I am aware of the buzz on social media triggered by the previous night's show—the first half of this year's "Too Big for Just One Night" edition. Everyone around the world had tuned into *Mania* at home, chatting and commenting online, and the response is unparalleled. My cell phone is popping.

Kaitlyn and I decide to honor the day as if it were in non-COVID times, to get a feel of what it could have been like, so that morning we set off to look at Raymond James Stadium—just a short drive from our house. The whole scenario is odd. The sky is gray and overcast. Rain starts to fall, darkening the deserted streets. We cannot get close to the stadium because it has been closed off and converted into a drive-through COVID-19 testing site. So we head toward Tampa International Airport, which lies on a slight elevation a few blocks to the west. I know from the thousands of times I have landed back home after my three hundred plus days on the road per year that you get a great view of the stadium from there, and Kaitlyn wants to film me with the original *Mania* venue in the background.

The airport is eerie too, with flights grounded and no arrival or departure bustle. We drive into the vast, empty multi-story parking lot. There is nobody around. We head to the top level, and I stand gazing over the wall at the stadium wondering what is going on down there. This is at the very beginning of the pandemic and everything is still a big unknown. Are there lines of sick people? Are people going to turn into zombies? We have no idea. I take a little time to let the significance of the day sink in. I'm enjoying a montage of images from my life whirling in my head when the cops start showing up like they do in the movies, cars swooping in across the parking lot toward us. Kaitlyn and I jump straight back into our car, and the cops pull up behind us, lights flashing, and I'm like, "Come on, man, don't arrest me! I've got to get home and watch *WrestleMania*."

We get away, no problem.

So the clock is counting down, and here I am on the sofa, about to flick the remote, anticipating the climactic moment when the two versions of me align, when Drew Galloway, the man, the husband, the obsessively passionate wrestling fan from a modest apartment in a small town in Scotland, rightfully becomes Drew McIntyre, WWE Champion, the first ever from the United Kingdom to hold the title. My family and friends will watch like the millions of viewers who are also tuning in to Night 2 from all over the world, edgy with anticipation about how things will pan out between me and Brock Lesnar.

I was happy with the way things went when we filmed the match, but until the world has witnessed me become the champion, I cannot let myself believe it is real. And it isn't . . . Unsettling images occasionally barge into my head—I see the ring and hear the referee count "One, two" and I see Roman Reigns or Seth Rollins with the long hair, and "three," and it is Brock who is raising the title. It makes no sense for me to think this way, but we are in uncharted territory. I am so wound up about finally achieving my goal. The outcome is still under wraps, and I have certainly experienced results that changed in the dying seconds when I was winning big matches earlier in my career. Has my longed-for main event match really ended as I remember? Was the finish edited? I sound insane even to myself, but I have been around for a long time.

Until I see my championship match play out against Brock Lesnar on my very own TV screen, nothing is real.

Three hours, four minutes, and thirty-five seconds into the show: the shrill wail of the bagpipes starts and the war drums kick in. My entrance music fires me up. It's a *Braveheart* cry that signals we're going to see a battle, and it was kind of cool to watch Brock Lesnar stalk in under his flaming letters and pace around me with his psycho stare while his advocate Paul Heyman started his wind-up banter on the mic. My sofa-bound self struggles to watch me in the ring—I'm such a perfectionist, I am always thinking I should have done this or that better, but I hold my breath and keep my normal tendency to self-critique at bay.

I see myself take the initiative with a Claymore Kick, but Brock kicks out of the hold. The audacity of my early strike sends him into a frenzy. Three times The Beast tries to finish me off with his trademark fireman's carry face-buster, the F-5. Each one hurts like hell, but I kick out of each hold. From several feet away on the sofa, I see pain wrought on my face; register the heaving of my breath. All the while I am hearing Heyman babbling away with his taunts—"He *can't* keep kicking out"—and I am physically reacting to every move on TV, shadowing on the sofa my actions in the ring, limbs twitching out of pure instinct. Kaitlyn has to move away fast; she is in danger of catching a flying elbow.

And then I see myself plant a final Claymore right between Brock Lesnar's eyes, and my destiny is fulfilled. Kaitlyn whoops and throws the bowl of popcorn in the air and we sit with corn kernel confetti cascading around us.

I finally exhale. Nothing was official until that three count. It is awesome, just incredible. I really am the WWE Champion.

Winning the title is so good, I get to receive it twice. In the ring at the Performance Center, on TV, Shawn Bennett, the referee, hands me the title belt. I hold it high in the time-honored way of brandishing the spoils of victory. At home, we took it out of the cupboard and stashed it under the sofa before settling down to our *Mania* viewing. In my moment of triumph, Kaitlyn picks up the belt and ceremoniously presents it to me, which is very special because, without her, there is no Drew McIntyre, World Champion.

By now all the family from Scotland have tuned in on Zoom. We had a little chat beforehand. My dad; his wife, Jane; my brother, John; his wife, Felicity; my aunt Beverley, uncle Neil, cousin Michelle, and her boyfriend, Gordon, were going to watch it together on a group Zoom call to keep each other awake. In Scotland, given the time difference, *WrestleMania* runs from midnight to just after 3 a.m.

We rejoin the family Zoom call. Everybody is celebrating, looking emotional. Dad and Jane are wearing their special edition Drew McIntyre T-shirts. Dad, of course, is in tears.

I hold the title up to the computer screen and say, "What do you think of that?"

"Absolutely brilliant, son," Dad says. "Absolutely brilliant."

I am still trying to take it all in. My brother, my original training partner when we were kids, who I had woken up in the small hours for the important stuff on the many *Mania*s we had watched in our shared bedroom, who has my name tattooed over his heart, rarely shows emotion. His wife, Felicity, secretly recorded his reaction on video, with me as Drew McIntyre WWE Champion in the background on TV, and his face was a picture. He looked so shocked and so very, very happy. He was convinced Brock Lesnar was going to win.

I am crying now . . . this is my dad's side coming out . . . My family's reaction means more to me than I can say.

Because that's where it all started.

I'M FROM AYR, SCOTLAND

I am from Ayr, a coastal town in the southwest of Scotland, in the historic county of Ayrshire, where we all drink whisky for water and run around in kilts—well, only on weekends. Scotland is a small country with only five million people, and I'm glad to be from a place where the people, including myself, are proud of our heritage and history, and unafraid to make fun of each other or make a fool of ourselves—traits that are very useful in my job.

I came into this world on June 6, 1985, just fifteen miles down the road from the two-roomed clay-and-thatched-roof cottage where Robert Burns, the national bard, was born in 1759. Robbie Burns is, of course, famous for "Auld Lang Syne," the verses sung worldwide on New Year's Eve, and also for "A Red, Red Rose," a poem that Bob Dylan claims as the biggest influence on his life. In a contest held by a Scottish television company in 2009 to determine "the Greatest Scot of All Time," Burns narrowly beat Sir William Wallace, the thirteenth-century knight whose feats in leading the Scots in the First War of Scottish Independence against King Edward II of England inspired *Braveheart*. Thanks to Burns (whose words were prized for their sincerity and forth-rightness) and to Wallace, I like to think my Scottish DNA plays well into my WWE mic skills and intelligent warrior instincts. You could add "drive" and "going places" to local influences—because John Loudon McAdam (1756–1836), the inventor of tarmacadam road surfacing, is another notable export from my small hometown.

In truth, I never needed a local hero for inspiration because I grew up with a superhero of a mother. My mum, Angela, was the kindest, happiest, yet toughest, most selfless person I have ever known. Her sole motivation in life was to do anything for her family. She loved us all to bits, as we did her. One of three children, she grew up in Ayr as a perfectly normal girl. Her father, John Robertson, stood six feet, four inches tall and served in the police force. Her mother, Doreen, worked at the General Post Office as a switchboard telephonist. My aunt Beverley, her older sister, says Mum was always a happy child who wanted to be a schoolteacher. In her late teens, she started to notice her balance was not always reliable—she would occasionally stumble and experience dizziness. She did not dwell on it, though she did confide in her sister that she was having these strange spells. One day when she was eighteen and on her way home from her job in Templetons supermarket, she fell when stepping off the bus. She just couldn't stand up and keep her balance. She would have had to crawl home on all fours had an elderly couple not stopped and helped her get back to my nana's house. From then on, she became more and more unstable, and her eyes started to dance. It was a sudden onset of something, but the local doctors didn't seem to know what.

My mum laughed it off—she hated being the center of attention—but my nana used her connections as a switchboard operator to speak to as many doctors in Glasgow and London as possible and gather opinions about what could be wrong. One doctor in London gave an ominous diagnosis: that her brain would slowly but steadily deteriorate, and she would be in a wheelchair for the rest of her life. Nana was not going to take this for an answer. She contacted doctor after doctor and finally took Mum to Harley Street to see a brain specialist, a leader in the field of multiple sclerosis, who thought he could at least stabilize her condition. She was put on thyroxine, which slightly improved her stability. The diagnosis was cerebellar ataxia, a neurological disorder that typically is progressive. It just attacks you and attacks you, essentially until a part of your brain dies. So my nana retired from her job to look after her. From this stage onward, Mum was never steady on her feet; she had to hold on to walls and surfaces to move around home, but that did not stop her leading a normal life. She spent a lot of time with her best friend, Linda, across the road in the cul-de-sac where they lived. She just got on with life; she never saw her condition as an obstacle. Like other young women, the two of them would go out to local bars with a group of friends, and she would have to be careful not to be thrown out because her balance "issues" made her look drunk, even when stone-cold sober. She'd laugh it off. Ironically, she'd say her balance always improved after a few drinks. Aunt Bev always found that amusing.

Before she started to experience the symptoms associated with ataxia, she had met my dad, Andy Galloway, at the Red Lion Angling Club disco in Prestwick—my dad and his brothers liked to fish at a local reservoir—and they fell in love. This was the early 1980s, and Dad, as his brothers enjoyed telling us later, used to wear big, tinted aviator glasses and drive around in a car fitted with shag carpet and fluffy dice, nicknamed the Pimp Wagon. My parents used to reminisce about their life before their kids came

along—little facts stuck with me, like how their first dance was
to—and it subsequently became "their song"—"The Birdie Song"
(Yep, the one that goes *With a little bit of this, with a little bit of
that, now wiggle your bum!*). Dad came from a humble background,
and was the youngest of four boys, all with good Scottish names:
his brothers were Campbell, Stuart, and Ian. He was christened
Andrew McLean Galloway III—his papa being the first, his father
the second. When I came along, I was named Andrew McLean
Galloway IV and I have always loved that. Occasionally, if I am in
one of those formal meetings where everyone introduces themselves with their full name and role, I announce myself as "Andrew
McLean Galloway the Fourth" . . . It sounds like such a dastardly
aristocratic villain!

Dad's maternal family came from the Girvan area, south of Ayr,
and toiled on the farms, staying in tied cottages, which were rent-
free accommodation offered by whichever landowner they were
working for. His paternal family name, Galloway, suggests that that
side of the family's history is rooted in the area, too. The county
below Ayrshire is called Dumfries and Galloway, at the heart of
which lies Galloway Forest Park—famous today for its beautiful
loch and mountain views and as the best place in Europe for star-
gazing. The county has ruined castles and battle sites from the turbulent era when William Wallace chased the English army south
and his compatriot Robert the Bruce, before becoming king, reclaimed Dumfries Castle, which had been held by the English.
Nine years after Wallace's death, Bruce led his warriors to triumph
at the Battle of Bannockburn in 1314, defeating Edward II of
England. All that local history would contribute to various aspects
of my wrestling career—not least in that I started off in WWE
wearing a knee-length tartan kilt. (Which I hated—it was so hot!)

From my dad I also inherited genes for height. When you consider that the average Scottish male is five feet, eight inches, Dad is extraordinarily tall at six-foot-three. He has always been a chilled-out kind of guy, and I think he was aware that he and Mum probably shouldn't have kids, because some forms of ataxia can be hereditary. But there was no way my mum was not going to have a family of her own. Soon she was pregnant with me. My nana was beside herself. No one knew how pregnancy and labor would affect her health. Mum didn't care. She was going to have me, no matter what. "I'll die before I don't have this baby," she said. When she went into what turned out to be a very long labor, the medical staff were unable to give her any form of pain relief because of the unknown side effects. My nana was a nervous wreck at the hospital. At one stage, Aunt Bev went to check on her. When she walked into the room, she couldn't see my nana for the smoke; Nana was chain-smoking through her worry.

Temperamentally, I was an easy baby, not as big at birth as you might imagine (a healthy eight and a half to nine pounds). My body was so long I had to be placed diagonally across the Perspex (acrylic) cot in the maternity ward. Four or five months after I was born, Mum was pregnant again. My nana couldn't believe that my mum was going to go through it all a second time; she couldn't believe that *she* would have to go through it all a second time too. Mum said, "Absolutely I am," and my brother, John, was born. To give birth to me and my brother, Mum endured twenty-three hours of labor with no pain relief, and she never seemed to get over the euphoric feeling that she and Dad were lucky to have us boys. We would go along to Mum's annual checks at a neurology clinic in Edinburgh, with a specialist who was a protégé of George Jelinek, the world-renowned pioneering professor of neuroepidemiology. A conclusion of "no change" was always the best possible news for her. She made sure John and I were tested every year until we were six or seven to be sure we had not inherited the disorder. Fortunately, we had not.

As far as we were concerned, growing up on Annpit Road, Ayr, there was nothing wrong with Mum; and as far as Mum was concerned, nothing was wrong with her either. She made her condition perfectly normal. Because of her stability issues, our extra-small apartment was the perfect environment for her to fly around the place safely. She was always busy, always on the move. She used the walls and furniture to balance and get from room to room. The tight configuration of our tiny kitchen was perfect for her to manage alone. It was her safe place. I remember her vacuuming and using the Hoover to balance. She'd bring my brother and me food while we played video games in our bedroom. It wasn't far from the kitchen, but she'd carry one plate at a time, with one hand on the wall. She'd give one plate to my brother, go back, holding on to the wall, get another, and bring it to me. She would whizz around making sure everything was running like clockwork, always with a smile, always happy. She was like a magician in that place. She was born to be a mum. She loved her kids, and we grew up knowing she would do anything for us.

That we let her operate like this sounds awful, but this is how normal she made it. She would not have it any other way. When it came to the washing, she'd devised a way of shuffling down the concrete steps to the garden, kicking the laundry basket along with her feet and hanging out the laundry while holding on to the line for balance. She was so happy taking care of us, not to mention all the waifs and strays we'd bring home. When our friends were there, they would be rushing to her aid, saying "What's the matter with you guys? Why aren't you helping your mum?" And we'd just shake our heads. "What do you mean? This is normal." It was the same with every household task: never a complaint. I was definitely a mummy's boy, but it wasn't until I was older that I realized I had to help her out here. And she'd make it fun, make it a way to bring us closer together. Food shopping, for example, was our "thing." We worked together getting the groceries like a well-drilled tag team who knew each other's movements by heart. She would get her balance on me, I would get a balance on the shopping cart, and we'd whizz around the supermarket, having the time of our lives.

Dad worked for a local family-owned furniture company, JRG Group Ltd. As the boss's right-hand man, he worked in the showroom and warehouse, or would be out delivering. It was a routine Monday-to-Friday, nine-to-five job, but hard work, and he would have to travel away from home sometimes. Mum was a stay-at-home mum and brought us up. My nana, who had given up her job to support Mum, took us to school. Sometimes my aunt would drive us. Aunt Bev's daughter Michelle was born a year after my brother, John, so we three cousins were what our respective mums and nana called a "wee family."

When my brother and I were about ten and eleven, Mum had a fall and suffered a clean snap of her ankle. John and I were there at the time. She must have been in agony, but she never cried out in pain or shed a tear. She was tough through and through. I remember Dad rushing home from work and carrying her out to the car to take her to hospital. It was a serious fracture that needed an operation to pin the joint, followed by months of physiotherapy to get her foot back to working order. I still find it hard to imagine how she did the rehab exercises and recovery work with her stability issues, but she did. Of course she did. That was Mum.

Later, she spent time in a wheelchair, just because it made common sense to help her motor about. She never let it slow her down. No one ever heard her complain or bemoan her lot. "There's always somebody worse off," she'd say briskly. Setbacks have littered my journey in wrestling. Whenever I have felt exhausted or frustrated, disappointed or dejected, angry or humiliated, I'd look at myself in the mirror and think, What would Mum do? The answer is always Pick yourself up and forge on. When people ask where I find the mental and physical toughness to overcome adversity, I always say, "I had an unfair advantage in life—I had a superhero for a mother and I carry her with me wherever I go."

CHAPTER 2

STOP RUNNING AROUND IN YOUR UNDERPANTS

Typically, Mum did not demur when I precociously started climbing out of my cot. Her solution was to jam a bed up against my cot so that I could land soft—clearly a precursor of my signature high-flying moves onto the apron outside a wrestling ring. Nor was she as appalled as she might have been when my destructive tendencies started emerging with dramatic, and often costly, consequences. I was less than two when I inflicted more than £400 ($500) worth of damage on my dad's new stereo system. The first stage was to destroy the needle arm of the turntable—not so bad. The next round was far more satisfying. I completely dismantled the sponges from the expensive bass and treble loudspeaker system, with its woofers and tweeters. I was extremely proud of the mess. On another occasion, Dad got a call at work because John and I had attempted to mountaineer up a glass display cabinet and pulled the whole lot down on top of us, complete with our parents' best crystal and most valuable ornaments. We were submerged in shards of glass after tying a belt around the cabinet in some *Indiana Jones*–inspired climbing stunt. In terms of rough-and-tumble mayhem, John and I were double trouble. I had a lot of strength; he had absolutely no fear.

I did not have too many interests beyond kicking a ball around with my buddies until I was introduced to wrestling. John and I, aged about five and six, were hiding behind the sofa at my cousins' house when we first saw a wrestling show on TV. They were older than us, and we'd do this thing of sneaking behind the curtains or furniture to try to watch whatever they were gripped by. At some point, wrestling came on . . . Instantly, I was obsessed. I can still remember feeling like I'd crash-landed on a new planet. There was Hulk Hogan . . . and Macho Man . . . Undertaker and The Ultimate Warrior. They were larger-than-life figures, but real human beings—so much more appealing than the characters we knew from the Cartoon Network. Their words seemed to be directed at me through the TV screen, and they put on these incredible matches. I was spellbound.

A few more trips to our cousins' house sealed it. I called my parents, my nana, and my brother together and announced my news.

"I'm going to become a professional wrestler."

Thereafter my uncle Ian, who had cable television and a Betamax video recorder, would tape shows and send the cassettes to Dad for my brother and me to watch at home. Saving up pocket money, and counting on birthdays and Christmases, I gradually built up a collection of WWE action figures that I would move around the replica ring for hours on end, marveling at their lifelike detail. I would spend hours hunched over them, consumed by this imaginary world, much as other boys move trains around a track or slot cars around a Scalextric set. My collection grew to more than 150 action fighters, and to this day Dad is under strict instructions not to throw the bag of them away.

John and I would pester our parents to rent wrestling tapes from Blockbuster Video. We had *WrestleMania VII* and *British Wrestling Tag Team* and *Tearaways*. We watched them over and over until they wore out. A *SummerSlam 1990* video met the same fate. We thought the British wrestlers looked like my dad and his friends in their underpants and were far more frightening than the oiled-up, American, larger-than-life big-storyline characters. I was more enamored of the exciting US presentation than the darker British scene. My brother and I would wrestle around the house, in our bedroom, down the park. Our parents never told us to stop fighting, because we were not fighting each other, we were working a crowd that was not there. We would put on our own little wrestling shows based on stories that we had written out on paper— playing the WWE wrestlers of the time, copying their moves, with teddy bears lined up as our audience. A pattern soon emerged. We would happily cooperate to get the moves to work. John would cry. I would get told off. We would start again the next day. We would often break into a wrestling match to try and entertain everyone around us.

Dad would say in mild exasperation, "Why not play football? Stop running around in your underpants!"

As a kid, I was shy in the classroom and quiet whenever I was around authority. The only time I came out of my shell was when I played sports. Like all kids in Scotland, I started off playing soccer with my buddies every day from morning to night, but I would get

too aggressive on the field. I wasn't interested in performing hero-
ics with a soccer ball. When everyone else was saying they were
going to be a football star or an astronaut, I told everyone I was
going to be a WWE wrestler.

It was about this time that my interest in UFOs, conspiracy
theories, and the paranormal kicked off. I had a subscription to
the *X Factor* magazine, which had cover headlines such as "UFO
Cover-Up," "Alien Encounter?," "Holy Wounds," "Crop Circles,"
"Voodoo Sorcery," and "NASA's Secret Photos." The issues covered random topics from spontaneous combustion to dangerous
diseases, and I was fascinated by the possibilities of other worlds,
immeasurable powers, and hazardous bugs. I was aware of Ebola
when I was about eleven. Inside one issue was a template letter that readers could personalize and send to the FBI requesting
access to sensitive documents on these sorts of topics under the
Freedom of Information Act. I sent mine off, asking for a list of
UFO-based documents. I came home from school one day to find
my dad, furious, waiting for me to explain why the FBI in America had sent a parcel of papers to me about asteroids and extra-
terrestrial activity!

The papers were disappointing, to be honest, but it was interesting to see how they formatted their official documents and to
note the language they used. I was curious to work out what lay behind the words and phrases that had been blacked out to obscure
confidential information in the redacting process. I tried using a
magnifying glass and then wrote down possible words on a notepad
to see if any made sense. I wanted to unravel the secrets.

How weird a kid was I? People do ask . . . and my stock response
is to be thankful for my height because I would no doubt have otherwise been bullied at school. In fact, both my grandmothers had

unwittingly fueled my conspiracy theory mindset. From an early age, they instilled in me a strong sense of a mysterious dimension beyond everyday life, with their respect for messages transmitted by their tarot cards and tea leaves. I once made a glass zip around Nana's Ouija board, and it really disturbed her. Another time, she showed me how it worked, and I witnessed the glass moving by itself across the board. She reinforced the message that the spirits were real and warned me not to mess about with them. I absorbed the notion that our futures are to some extent predestined and that there are out-of-the-ordinary powers at large. Now I come to think about it, the names of their tarot cards were not unlike a wrestling roster, with The Magician, The High Priestess, The Hanged Man, The Emperor, The Fool, et cetera, each representing an individual realm of power, with suits comprising swords, wands, cups, and coins. On a school trip to England when I was nine or ten, my buddy and I recognized the name on a board outside the shop of a palm reader we were familiar with from TV. Inside, she was offering palm readings at £10 (about $13) a shot. It was a lot of money, but I went ahead. Her reading was detailed, but all paled after I heard her conclusive prediction.

"One day," she intoned, "you will be very famous in entertainment."

As we grew older and my buddies got more realistic about their futures, imagining an office job with a regular income or working with their dads, my ambition remained resolute: I was going to be a wrestler. The strong conviction that I was born to be in the ring has never left me. I became an obsessed fan, a frighteningly over-the-top fan. I daydreamed about wrestling all day. I dreamt about becoming world champion under my "Stone Cold" Steve Austin duvet. To this day, I walk around with these montages of images in my head. My mind is so used to conjuring up imaginary scenarios.

We didn't have a lot of money growing up, but whatever new VHS tape I could get, I'd watch it a hundred times until it was worn out and the tape wouldn't work anymore. If I was playing a Sunday football match, the way I prepared—even as a young kid—was to warm up in the bedroom with wrestling playing in the background, and that's what would motivate me to play another sport. *WrestleMania* was like my second Christmas each year. The time difference meant that, in the UK, it was on at 2 a.m. on a Monday. Throughout my education, it was always on the night before school—primary school, secondary school, university—and I always wanted to stay up to watch it live. My parents recorded the early ones, but my most vivid memories are of the editions I watched in the night with my brother. At least we'd start watching it together. He'd fall asleep. I'd wake him up for the important matches. He'd get annoyed. That became the routine. Later, it became more of a ritual. We had our midnight snacks handy, and—weird, I guess—I would do push-ups and arm curls throughout the entire duration of *WrestleMania*. I wanted to be as big as those guys on my TV. I would do a thousand arm curls. If I tried that now, my arms would fall off!

At school, John was known as "the brother of the guy who thinks he's going to be a wrestler." Those same people who were so sarcastic would later text John asking for tickets! My reputation had its uses. Once, standing at a bus stop with some buddies, we were approached by some guys who started having a go at us. Any altercation was prevented when one of them recognized me as "the wrestler." John and I continued to watch wrestling relentlessly, rarely normal TV or cartoons. Otherwise, we had little in common;

wrestling was the one activity that we did together. We shared a bedroom, so when we needed something that we could get along with, it was always wrestling. In our later teens, we never had the same friends, or hung out together; we were like ships in the night, apart from the wrestling.

There was no lightbulb moment to pinpoint exactly when I transitioned from a fan into a wrestler-in-training, because I was always certain that wrestling was what I was going to do. It was more a question of *how* I was going to do it. I was intent on learning everything I possibly could about the business. I was by no means a bookworm, but I read the autobiography of The Rock as soon as it came out in hardback—Dad couldn't get over that. The book promised to share "The Journey, the Teachable Moments and 10 Rules for Success Cultivated from the Life and Wisdom of Dwayne The Rock Johnson."

Inspired, I took action to officially initiate my wrestling career. I sent to America for two books called *Inside Secrets on How You Can Enter the Exciting World of Pro Wrestling!* by Dennis Brent and Percy Pringle (known on WWE as Paul Bearer, the creepy mortician who managed Undertaker). I learned *everything* from these books: how things worked backstage, how storylines were created, the way matches were structured. It tapped into the psychology of a live crowd and explained the secret words used by wrestlers among themselves. Best of all—the bit that made me feel like an outsider being inducted into the secrets of the profession—it reinforced the biggest lesson of all. That you have to keep *kayfabe*—or *kay-far-bey*, as I pronounced it with my thick Ayrshire accent because I'd never heard anyone say the word.

"Wrestling is a business of secrets—so you've gotta keep the secrets. You've got to keep 'kayfabe.'"

I would follow the letter of this book, and in learning it almost by heart, I thought I knew *everything*. I'd let my brother in on some secrets so that we could work the best match. We would create the story, as we were already in the habit of doing, and proceed to stage it, whispering in each other's ear what moves were coming. Not that anybody was watching, but the action was always controlled. We had one incident where I broke John's foot, but we agreed that was our fault together. I would keep my private cache of wrestling books and magazines, my secret insider info, in a briefcase with combination locks that Dad gave me. Every morning I climbed up on a chair and hid it at the back of the top of the wardrobe where nobody could get to it. Then, I could go to school with a clear conscience. My buddies would talk about the TV wrestling storylines, and I played along with them, because I was diligently keeping *kayfabe*. I could not have felt more superior. I was like, Oh, wow—I've got to keep the secrets from these guys. They do not know the secrets of the inner sanctum like I do. That is how obsessed I was. Years later, I met Percy Pringle and told him I had plagiarized his *Inside Secrets* book for an English talk I had to give back at school in Scotland, and that I'd got an A grade. He was very amused.

My hero was Bret "Hit Man" Hart. I was really into him. All my friends preferred the larger-than-life characters—Hulk Hogan, The Ultimate Warrior, and so on—but I was always drawn to Bret. He had been a tag team specialist but was evolving into this cool solo star in the pink sunglasses. There was something so authentic about Bret that made me want to be like him. He was just so *real*; it was like his character was himself. I soon learned that he was part of a famous wrestling family in Canada, who lived in a mansion with a basement training school known as the Hart Dungeon.

I can still recite every twist and turn of the *WrestleMania 13* match I watched when I was eleven, when Bret defeated "Stone Cold" Steve Austin in a violent struggle that took both Superstars outside the barricade and into the crowd. Back in the ring, their brawl ended in a brilliant move: a bloodied Steve Austin passed out after one hundred agonizing seconds, rather than submit to Bret's Sharpshooter hold—and in the course of the match, so cleverly told, a shocking double turn occurred. For weeks afterward, I marveled at the shift in allegiance achieved in just twenty minutes: how Steve Austin, always the brash, vulgar antagonist, became the guy deserving sympathy, and Bret Hart, who had long been a revered gutsy hero, was now the villain.

It was the highest level of wrestling storytelling because the character development was so realistic. "Stone Cold" Steve Austin was always the rebellious character, flipping everyone off, using colorful language, telling Bret Hart to put an "S" in front of "Hit Man" to understand his opinion of him. He represented the anti-authoritarian youth of the late 1990s, and his performance was so gripping that fans started to root for him even though it was kind of taboo to cheer the heel, the bad guy. The lead-up to this match had been complex and subtle. Bret Hart, four times the World Champion at that stage, always the biggest hero, had started to display a gripey, savage side, which culminated in this match, with the relentless multiple leg-breaker moves and then this brutal Sharpshooter hold on his weakened adversary . . . leaving "Stone Cold" Steve Austin the most unlikely underdog. They told the story perfectly; the psychology behind the narrative arc was utterly convincing. In doing so, Bret put "Stone Cold" Steve Austin in a position to succeed as the huge star he went on to become.

As a kid you really enjoy your stories, be it your TV shows, books, movies—and I found the bigger guys, the larger-than-life character stories, a bit simple. I was so lucky this match coincided with the period when I was most receptive to formative influences. Bret always told these captivating stories through his actions in the ring—and I went on to recognize that "Stone Cold" Steve Austin's subsequent reign as the biggest star in WWE history would never have happened without Bret putting him in that position in this shrewdly thought-through match. He brought such realism to the ring that his was my favorite story to watch, and to try and imitate. Through appreciating his style, I started to focus on storytelling in my own wrestling. (I also loved Shawn Michaels, so it hurt that they had such a personal rivalry, but it is cool now because both became mentors to me in the end.)

I was learning that the importance of the storytelling aspect of wrestling could not be underestimated. As a combat sport, wrestling pits antagonists against each other in a ring. Each Superstar employs various techniques—strikes, throws, takedowns, joint locks, pins, aerial moves, kicks—with the aim of defeating the other. But interest in watching a demonstration of grappling holds and clinches palls quickly, however technically superb the execution, unless the action is aligned to an emotionally resonant story. So it is "soap opera in spandex"—as the line in the film *Fighting with My Family* goes—with episodes that unfold both in the ring and on the microphone, told with verbal wit and signature flourishes, from wrestlers' punned or alliterative names right down to their taunts and challenges.

Following the antics of Bret Hart and Steve Austin, I could see a wrestler has to win over the crowd; he has to have a spark that transforms the skills in the ring into a mesmerizing alternative reality. Really, wrestling is physical theater performed with top-level athleticism; wrestlers are sportsmen, improv actors, stuntmen, and entertainers wrapped up in one charismatic package. The WWE Universe is peopled with characters fans *love* or *hate*, all contributing to an ever-growing web of storylines. It is human nature to nail your allegiance to either the likely victor or the underdog. The company can put a wrestler on the main roster, but only the fans can keep him there. Hence the buildup of rivalries, the prevalence of disappearances and comebacks, the surprise alliances and dastardly acts of deceit played out in ever-evolving scenarios by a cast of heroes and villains, turncoats and snakes, hilarious egos, ringleaders, cheats, and blue-eyed good guys. I loved every aspect of the WWE Universe, from its characters and brutal match formats down to the lingo.

At the academy, which is high school in Scotland, I met Craig Ogston and soon recognized that he was a guy with a wrestling obsession to match mine. He arrived from another school. I remember noticing him because he was wearing a "Stone Cold" Steve Austin bomber jacket. I had also heard about this quiet, modest-mannered guy who had been in the vending machine area with his friends when some assholes came in and started giving them a hard time. When they went for one of his buddies, Craig intervened, launching them all around the place singlehandedly. I thought that was impressive. We got talking and quickly became close. We were on the same wavelength in our passion for wrestling. My parents had recently got Sky TV, which itself was a dream come true; I had always assumed it was beyond our means. That meant Craig and I could talk about the action from the night before on *Raw* or *SmackDown*, and we would go off fantasizing about our own walk into the ring and act out our own entrances. We had a lot of fun.

That summer we took our obsession one step further and started our own organization called XSBW, or Xtreme Scottish

Backyard Wrestling. Our first ever wrestling ring was an old double mattress that my brother, Craig, and I carried on our heads for three miles across Ayr to Nana's house. We set it up in her back garden against a wall and staged our own little wrestling matches. As a stereo system blasted out our entrance music, we would come out of the neighbor's backyard and prance down the steps as if making our way to the ring, posing to an imaginary crowd. All the action was filmed using Craig's dad's camcorder; one of us would commentate on the match, the others re-creating a raucous crowd's sound effects. As a group, our favorite wrestlers were Big Show, Undertaker, The Rock, "Stone Cold" Steve Austin—we just loved those guys. There were the high flyers like Shawn Michaels, and the technical guys like my hero Bret Hart, and we had the best time imaginable trying to imitate the big stunts and master the technical moves that we saw on TV, jumping off the wall onto the big, soft mattress.

Sometimes other friends joined in, and we would have five gimmicks each so the matches weren't always the same. We would take turns being the cameraman and commentator, but we'd each have our own scenario or agenda. We would spend time trying to piece together an engaging storyline, with the emphasis on putting on an entertaining performance for anybody watching rather than just beating each other up until someone won. I would remind the others that it is kind of boring to see people just grappling, rattling around with limbs locked together, looking like they are hugging.

"We're not just fighting this fight until someone wins, because of course I'd beat you all up," I'd say. "We're going to work together; we're going to let each other do certain moves on us so that we can provide an entertaining match for the camera and the millions of people who are going to see it." Looking back, I can see I liked to micromanage our fun according to my insider knowledge! Afterward we'd review the film to see what we could have done better. And Nana had food ready for us.

We did this three times a week and every weekend for the whole summer, rain or shine. It was awesome. Our shows were spectacular, though Dad found them terrifying to watch. It was long before the social media "Don't Try This at Home" era, and we were fortunate to end up with just a lot of bruises and the odd black eye. On one occasion I performed a front flip out of a tree and winded myself landing hard on the grass. I was copying a front flip that Ric Flair would take all the time on the floor, and I executed it well but didn't anticipate the lack of give from the grass when I slammed down from the tree onto my back. So that hurt. We tried to keep it on the mattress, but there were some spills. My brother was the daredevil among us; he has never had a sense of fear! He liked not just to climb onto the wall but to scramble up on top of the fence that was affixed on top of the wall, then stand up straight and launch himself off, flipping in midair to land on his back. It was Jeff Hardy's finishing move, "the Swanton Bomb." John and I modeled ourselves on Matt and Jeff, the Hardy Boyz. Matt was the power-based one and Jeff the high-flier, and John would scare the wits out of Dad by moon-saulting off the wall onto me.

Many years later, I beat Matt Hardy for the Total Nonstop Action World Heavyweight title and made my first defense against Jeff Hardy. I became friends with both, which was just surreal, when I had been imitating their moves with my own brother when we were thirteen or fourteen.

CHAPTER 3

THIS KID'S THE ONE

I continued to tell people I was going to become a professional wrestler, and even those who said they'd like to think people can do anything they set their mind to said I was nuts and that WWE was an unattainable goal. That wasn't going to stop me. I had started looking for wrestling schools when I was ten or eleven and discovered they didn't exist in Scotland. This was before the era when information became instantly attainable via a Google search.

I would get the magazines that existed outside the basic storyline mags, the "dirt sheets" that circulated backstage stories and rumors as if with insider knowledge. I'd scour them to find articles or advertisements for wrestling schools. Occasionally, one would pop up, and looking back, it's clear they didn't have a clue what they were doing, but they saw the opportunity to make money by attracting a bunch of dumb kids eager to learn. I got in contact with a couple and went to my mother and asked if I could go. She said, "Absolutely not." She wasn't comfortable with me traveling so young, and she didn't trust the trainers.

I approached her again every year, when I was twelve, thirteen, and fourteen, and each time she said she wasn't confident in the individuals who would be doing the training or me traveling so far from home. Perhaps my parents hoped I would grow out of wrestling, but if anything, my determination grew more resolute. I was impatient; I'd read every book I could get my hands on, every magazine. I'd studied the Superstars on TV. Mentally, I couldn't have been more prepared. Now I really needed to make it happen, to get on with putting my obsession into the process of acquiring skills, developing ring presence, working on my physical strength.

My ambition was boosted when Yokozuna, the American pro wrestler who worked a gimmick as a sumo wrestler from Japan, starred in a show that came to Ayr. In the wrestling universe, my hometown felt like the center of the Shire in the *Lord of the Rings* movies—and Yokozuna was coming to the Shire! My brother and I were beyond excited to go along and see him. He'd won the *Royal Rumble* and earned a world title shot at *WrestleMania* off the back of that. He was a two-time WWE Champion. Not a tribute act: the real deal.

The venue operated on a first come, first seated basis, so we went along early to make sure we were front of the line. As we stood there, someone walked past and we caught the phrase "We have to get fifty eggs for him." Was *him* Yokozuna? I was just amazed that somebody was going to eat fifty eggs. When Yokozuna appeared, it was clear he was *gargantuan*, the biggest person I'd ever seen in my life. He absolutely could eat fifty eggs at one sitting. Thanks to my insider knowledge, I remember thinking, He's in Ayr, he's probably just going to "phone it in." But in the ring, he worked surprisingly hard. He didn't have to go to great lengths to impress this crowd, but he put 110 percent into his match, throwing one of his side-kicks out of the ring. He didn't finish on his brutal Banzai Drop, but I was just blown away, not just by his titanic size, but by the effort that he put in for a small town in Scotland. He even let me have a picture taken with him.

Inspired, I started to focus on building up my body. I was a tall, skinny kid with long straggly arms like linguini. Physically, I felt like a freak. I had already hit six feet, three inches and was still growing. Everyone referred to me as lanky, and to this day I hate that word with a passion. My posture was appalling, and it still is; I stand tall only when I'm working and use my full height for a professionally intimidating aura. One of my buddies, Cameron, and I started to go running on Ayr Beach. Our typical routine was to run down the sand for a couple of miles to the dunes, where we'd sprint up and down the slopes until we were exhausted. I could never do that now—my knees would explode!

Before I was old enough to join a gym, my nana showed me how I could fill empty two-liter bottles of Coke or Pepsi with water and use those as my dumbbells. When I needed to step up a gear, she filled them with stones. It was like something out of *Braveheart*. "We can't train with weapons, so we train with stones." Bicep curls were basically the only exercise I did, so I was as lean as hell, with pipe-cleaner arms that had these big round bumps for biceps.

Craig, who had undiagnosed dyslexia, had a tough time at school and left as early as he could, taking up a full-time job in a gym. We'd spend hours hanging out there. He got a certificate for training, and we followed all sorts of amateur fitness courses and the Arnold Schwarzenegger bodybuilding workouts. We got into insane shape for kids. Every Friday I would make excuses and leave the Boys' Brigade (an international youth organization that started in Glasgow) thirty minutes early to hop on the train to Craig's place so that we'd have time for a drink at Ross Bar before we'd watch the wrestling through until midnight; then we'd hop on a train and go to a club in the harbor. We were fifteen, but looked like twelve, clearly under the age for drinking, and we'd get as nervous as hell standing in line waiting to get in, making stupid conversation to sound older than we were. The first time we went, I said something very loudly like "Well, man, college was hard this week!" At the bar, the next panic was what the hell to order. I tried to imagine I was at the bar in *Coronation Street* or *EastEnders*, but resorted to ordering my dad's drink at home—McEwan's Export. So these were our wild, wild teenage Friday night escapades. If we drank alcohol the night before, we forced ourselves to go to the gym first thing the next day. We made ourselves suffer for going out, but at that age, of course, you bounce back pretty quickly.

When I was fifteen, I finally found a wrestling school that Mum allowed me to attend. Just after Christmas I sent an email to Mark Sloan at Frontier Wrestling Alliance in Portsmouth, on the south coast of England, to inquire about signing up for a training camp. He recently sent my original email to me as a cool memento of how my journey started (literally a journey—it involved an epic twenty-four-hour return rail trip just to see if wrestling really was for me).

To wannabe@fwatraining.co.uk, dated Thursday 28 December 2000, I wrote:

During the summer I was thinking about going to wrestling school. I searched most and the FWA seems to be the best. I live in Scotland and so it would be a quite costly and long journey, so I was wondering if there are any camps that last a week or two. If there was not, would there be any way to have

personal training for a week or so and are there any places
recommended to stay or if allowed the gym floor? I am 16
[I wasn't], stand at 6ft 3 1/2in and weigh about 200lbs and
hope to pursue a career in wrestling and going to school is ob-
viously the best start to see what I've got and have any chance

Cheers Drew

PS: If yes, what would the costs be including staying if
permitted.

Mum spoke on the phone to Mark, the head trainer, and was
reassured this was a safe place to learn, even though it involved me
traveling the length of the country to Portsmouth and back again.
That was a heck of a journey for a fifteen-year-old—the journey
involved four changes of train. Craig and I planned to go together.
We had a map. We had a list of instructions from the parents about
how to manage the changes of train. We had basic cell phones to
keep them informed of our progress, and we had signed permission
slips from our parents because we were under sixteen.

This was it: the start of a big adventure . . .

And it was not what I'd expected. Craig and I worked out reg-
ularly in the gym in Ayr, and I was by any standards a good athlete
for my age. I thought I was going to walk in and the trainers would
point at me and say, "Oh my god, you're the next Steve Austin."
My potential and my ambition would surely be glaringly obvious.
Unfortunately, it didn't turn out like that. Training to wrestle was
so much tougher than it looked on television. And it hurt. As I
tell people to this day, you can't fake gravity. After so many years
of wrestling in my head, this was my longed-for introduction to

being inside a physical ring, my twenty-foot-by-twenty-foot canvas of dreams. We were taught how to fall safely, how to hit the ropes, how to jump off the turnbuckle, how to roll about on the mats. We went through the basics: the holds, the counter-holds, joint manipulation and footwork. I was like Bambi on ice. My last growth spurt had taken me to six feet, five inches, so I was shy and skinny and hunched over from bending to talk to people. Physically, I was still at an awkward stage, uncomfortable with my height. I felt like a freak child, and it sucked.

One of the first training drills we did was to learn how to kick the chest. We would take turns being down on our knees, and the other guy would jump and kick across the chest of the guy who was down. We were shown how to do this and were putting the move into practice when the trainer had to step out and take a phone call. Twenty minutes later, he came back and we were still booting each other across the chest, taking ten shots per leg and then swapping over. "Whoa, whoa, slow down," he said. "I think you've nailed that, let's try something else."

It was a bit disheartening that the technical aspect of wrestling didn't come naturally to me right away. If it had been anything other than wrestling, I would have quit there and then, saying it's not me. But I lay in my sleeping bag in the middle of the wrestling ring at night thinking, You've got to push through this, Drew, this is something you've always wanted to do, something you love. Hitting the ropes hurt so much. Hitting the corners, where the tension is tighter, was agony . . . I had bruises all down my ribs and my back, and a permanent headache from taking the falls without remembering to tuck in my chin, constantly whiplashing my neck. I was dejected that I wasn't instantly going to be the next "Stone Cold" Steve Austin. But I'd saved up for a long time to get this taste of the business for real—it was costing me £100 ($133) for the ten-day camp—and I kept at it.

Craig found it tough too. His sixteenth birthday fell during the camp. Instead of getting birthday pats on the back, all the guys in the camp gave him birthday chops across the chest. He was hooked into the corner turnbuckle with his shirt over his head, and everyone took a turn giving him two or three knife-edge chops until his torso was beetroot red and spattered with impressions of handprints. No wonder this turned out to be his first and last wrestling training camp.

I, however, came back totally hooked. I stuck with it, traveling back and forth to Portsmouth as often as I could, which was as often as my mother or my nana found the money. These trips tended to be three-day or week-long camps. I didn't mind the journey. If I was going to be a wrestler, I was going to go to a wrestling school and get proper training. What I learned about myself at FWA was that I had the ability to focus 100 percent on whatever I wanted to achieve from training or weightlifting; I hated stopping before I'd accomplished something. I thrived on setting myself a goal and putting 100 percent into achieving it. I really couldn't look at myself in the mirror unless I felt satisfied I'd done the best I could to improve. I surprised myself by realizing I had this endless capacity to go back and do something again and again and again until I'd mastered it. I was a very quiet teenager, but my family and buddies, like Craig, soon realized that I was extremely driven and that there was a hard man underneath my shy exterior. I thrived on the fact that wrestling training was physically and mentally so demanding, and utterly exhausting. The dropout rate was high. I was amazed to see how many people fell by the wayside each camp.

By this stage, I'd met Mark Dallas online through a wrestling forum. He went on to establish the legendary Insane Championship Wrestling (ICW). We met the first time at Glasgow Central station and caught a train to Falkirk, to check out a place billed as a wrestling school, which turned out to be run by someone who probably had no training at all. We soon found another club offering wrestling in East Kilbride, housed in a post office recreation room with a load of thin judo mats we'd arrange in a giant square to represent a ring on the floor. It was supervised by a guy who we later found out likely only ever had a few wrestling training sessions himself. For eight hours every Sunday, a group of us in T-shirts and tracksuit bottoms would reenact moves we'd seen in our old VHS collections, or on TV, trying to blindly feel our way through what we should do to learn to wrestle. I tried to pass on things I'd learned in Portsmouth.

On one occasion Jake "The Snake" Roberts visited. The former WWE Superstar, who used to bring a live python into the ring for his matches, was in the midst of his well-documented battle with drug and alcohol addiction. Living in the UK, he would turn out occasionally for small independent shows around the country. I guess he'd been offered the gig of giving a few seminars and he turned up at our little training club. He was the real thing, all right. I had studied him on countless videos. On TV, he had always seemed one of the smaller guys, but I realized that his sly and snakelike stage persona was achieved by consciously shrinking his posture. It was stagecraft. As with Yokozuna, the only other WWE Superstar I'd seen in the flesh, Jake "The Snake" Roberts was a forbidding physical specimen. He was taller than me, bulkier, just this huge, boulder-shouldered man. He looked around, assessing us all one by one. I was amazed when he singled me out.

"This kid's the one, yeah," he said, walking up to me. "You might make it."

I had so much respect for his wrestling mind. He was so smart about the psychology of performance in the ring. For a lot of people in the room, wrestling was a weekend hobby, but I took Jake Roberts's comment that he saw something in me as affirmation that I was on track to be Scotland's first WWE star.

Barry Young, or Wolfgang, as he is known in the ring, had now started turning up to Sunday training—having been alerted to the post office school by a newspaper report about Jake "The Snake" Roberts's visit—and we'd all be suplexing and power-bombing each other, doing things we shouldn't have been doing because we didn't have a proper coach. It was absolute torture. Everything hurt like hell and we loved it. Eventually we left the post office and moved to Rutherglen. We'd been able to get our own wrestling ring, and that was a game-changer. Once you get in the ring, you start learning about the importance of positioning and running off the ropes. Training increased to two days a week; we'd do four hours on a Tuesday night and eight hours on Sunday. Soon there was a gang of us—Mark Dallas, Wolfgang, Red Lightning, Jack Jester, and Lionheart, who's sadly no longer with us—and we built bonds of friendships that have endured through our passion for wrestling. Sometimes we'd get together and watch pay-per-views. Those started at 1 a.m. for us in Scotland and went on for three hours, so of course it was a party.

CHAPTER 4

VINCE McMAHON WILL COVER IT

The next stage was to appear in some shows. I made my debut match in Linwood on the western outskirts of Glasgow when I turned sixteen, up against a much older guy whose ring name was Conscience. I was so nervous: the thought of being in the middle of the ring, all eyes on me. I talked to the coach, to the guy I was going to be wrestling, and went through the storyline of the match, the moves, the sequence of events, just to make sure I had everything down. I was blown away that I was going to get to wrestle in front of a crowd of people. I wore the most horrible outfit—skintight, electric-blue PVC trousers and a black string vest. Someone said, "Drew, this is going to get you *so over . . .*" meaning I'd be a sure hit. I was sixteen years old, fifteen stone, and my opponent weighed in at twenty-one stone. I came out to Guns N' Roses "You Could Be Mine." There was a particular bit of the song that I wanted to walk out to, and I had not taken into account how long the drum intro would last. Like hours! I was making the crowd wait forever, cranking up the anticipation as if it was Undertaker coming up, and when the music finally reached my cue, out walked this skinny kid in PVC trousers and a fishnet top!

So I made an impressive entrance, but after thirty seconds in the ring, I was knocked out. Ten seconds later I was on my feet and straight back into it, with another fifteen minutes to go. The buzz I felt after the match was unreal. Craig came along with his dad's trusty camcorder. He filmed the lead-up: me traveling on the train to the event, talking behind the curtain to the trainer and my opponent. The camera was whirring right up until my entrance music hit; he captured about two seconds of that and then the battery died. Later he managed to shake a little bit more juice out of the camera battery and filmed me on the train on the way home, talking nonsense. I looked a little out of it, a bit concussed, but you could see I was happy with the match. The next morning Dad took a couple of snaps of the bootprint bruises all over my body.

There was no Scottish wrestling scene at the time, so we consciously started to develop a wrestling company, and British Championship Wrestling (BCW) was formed. We were just a bunch of kids, but the adult who oversaw our training in East Kilbride bought a ring, drove the truck to and from the venues, and used his connections to bring in foreign talent such as The Barbarian and Marty Jannetty. We were able to walk out in front of a genuine paying audience for our first show with this little Scottish company, with the headliners drawing in a crowd of about four hundred people. It was my second match and I was in a tag team with Wolfgang, who had never wrestled in front of fans before. That match was incredible, a blur of nerves and adrenaline and probably another dose of concussion. More often, we would put on shows in front of ten men and a sheepdog in a drafty village hall.

Sometimes there'd be just five people on random chairs saying, Go on, entertain us!

One event featured Japan's most famous wrestler, Mitsuharu Misawa, who was on a UK tour. He was a genuine legend who had earned worldwide acclaim in the 1990s for his crazy, high-impact, dangerous moves. In England, he was performing for audiences of a thousand or more, which were paltry compared to Japan, where he was a star who mesmerized tens of thousands of fervent fans. Next up on his UK schedule was our local show in Carluke, where the main match was . . . myself versus Wolfgang. Misawa arrived with his entourage of twenty, plus several cameramen, and they all looked absolutely horrified. For a start, his entourage almost outnumbered the thirty or so people who had turned up to support us. I remember being embarrassed to have this Japanese legend in our tiny community center. He looked at the facilities and said, "Oh no, bad ring, bad ring." The boards were uneven, the ropes disparate. We had to redo the ring until he felt safe. His crew kept pointing at me, using the international wrestling lingo for a good guy, saying, "Good babyface!" I took great pride in being a bad guy at the time, so I was saying, "No, no, *heel*! I am a heel!" And Misawa replied, "No, no, you babyface." We had this back-and-forth banter in basic English. I still look back and think how hilarious the situation was that Japan's biggest, most committed star ever— who later literally died in the ring—came to our local company in Carluke and there was nobody there.

I was, and remain to this day, quiet and introverted, but I discovered that when I got up in front of a crowd, doing what I loved, I came alive like never before. Performing as a wrestler in public was the first time I came out of my shell, and I think it was shocking for my parents to see their shy little kid become this alpha male in the ring. Whether I was a good guy or a bad guy, a babyface or a heel, I was in my opponent's face, shouting, putting myself over to tell a story. They'd never seen that side of me before.

In these early days, I'd come home after shows, and my parents would see the imprint of boots on my back. There was no messing about in the ring. Somebody had been jumping on me. Black and blue all over, I told them it didn't matter. Bruises go away. For the next two or three years, they'd come and support me in local shows in village halls or small community centers, often videotaping my matches so I could review them later. When I was seventeen, they came to a benefit in Hull. I had a pretty spectacular match, which included a full flying somersault over the top rope. They were horrified. "Don't ever do it again," they implored, but of course I did. Many, many times. Dad likes to remember the occasion when Wolfgang jumped off the top rope in one village hall and brought the ceiling lights down with him. It was a glorious learning curve.

When I wasn't traveling to do shows for British Championship Wrestling, I was training, training, and doing more training. By this stage, I had met Blair Caddis in the Duncan Bannatyne gym where Craig worked, and the three of us became the three amigos who would work out and go out together. We had a similar sense of humor and gravitated to each other, becoming tight buddies with our own nicknames bestowed in tribute to our strongest body part. Craig, or Oggie, was "The Lat Man." Blair was known as "Traps" or "Trapman," courtesy of his back muscles. I was "Bi Man," thanks to my biceps. Mum's shopping bill increased by £100 (about $130) a week with all the chicken and steak required to satisfy my protein intake, and I'd go to the shops with her, filling the trolley with my bodybuilding fuel. I was still in high school, but now that I had started working in shows, I felt I was on the right path. As much as I was disheartened by how difficult it was to master some of the moves, it felt completely natural to walk out in front of the crowds. I could visualize myself going to WWE. I loved the camaraderie, the community of wrestlers, the fun we had traveling for eight to twelve hours all over Scotland and England, packed into one car to get to a show. We'd walk up and down handing out flyers for our show, then we'd build the ring, assemble the boards and ropes. We all pitched in. Wolfgang's dad was a builder, and he had taught us how to align the scaffolding planks we used under the canvas (not much shock-absorbing give in those!). The whole crew became very experienced at being on the road. I was a student, but most of the others had to be at work the next day, so we would always jam ourselves back in the car after a show and drive through the night to get home. We had no money; what little we had we spent on junk food at service stations.

Part of the agreement with my parents was that I should stick at education. Plan A was WWE, but they wanted me to have a Plan B, encouraging me to apply to university. My teachers recommended I study Business, but there was a new course at Glasgow Caledonian University in Criminology, which piqued my interest. I was a big fan of *The X-Files* and I watched a lot of documentaries about serial killers. A four-year BA degree course in Criminology would keep my parents happy and entitle me to a student loan so I could pay for my gym membership and my protein powders and supplements in order to develop my physique so that I was big enough for WWE. Dad wanted a university diploma to put on the wall and say it was his son's, but my wrestling ambitions only grew stronger.

Mum helped me move into my student accommodations, making my bed for me, putting away my clothes in the cupboards, and lining up my books on the shelves. She expected me to bring my laundry home on the weekends. I lasted less than eight months in that apartment. I was going out too much, spending all my money on wrestling and too much time hungover or missing classes. The girls on my course were very kind in always making sure I caught up with the work. It was not a difficult decision to move back out of my university apartment to live at home, which was an easy journey into Glasgow city center.

The Criminology course taught us the language of the courtroom, crime psychology, sociology, and so on. I'm sure it was interesting, but I was so freaking obsessed with wrestling, nothing about my academic studies could capture my attention. On one occasion, I sat at a homicide trial, with the murder weapon ten feet away from me—a bloodstained Samurai sword no less—and just fell asleep. The night before I'd been a passenger on a long drive back from a show, and I may have had a few adult beverages in the car, but I'd raced back because the murder trial was a key part of my course. Sadly, I just could not stay awake during the proceedings. My priority was to proactively find a way to take my wrestling to the next level while navigating my way through life and university. One of my buddies, Lee, still to this day tells stories about how I spent my student loan on wrestling paraphernalia and supplements.

"Drew, what are you doing?" he'd say. "You should be buying more books."

I'd always say—and it became my catchphrase from the age of seventeen—"Vince McMahon will cover it!"

So, Vince, thanks for covering it!

All the while our little coterie of wrestlers was traveling to shows wherever we could get one put on, wrestling in front of twenty, maybe thirty people, mostly the families of the wrestlers, not bona fide fans. We had to put in the legwork and create a scene because Scottish wrestling was not a thing until we came along, and it became a thing. The shows that billed themselves as American Wrestling were essentially tribute acts. There might be a poster advertising DX, the collective group of wrestlers, but it would turn out to be one guy who was all of them combined. Guys would pretend to be Undertaker or Kane or "Stone Cold" Steve Austin, or dress like The Rock with a drawn-on eyebrow. You had maybe two companies that brought in some US imports for an occasional super show, like an AJ Styles of the time or a Samoa Joe, top indie stars. These were astronomical shows, and they'd attract a thousand patrons.

In my bid to gain experience and develop, I would take matches and wrestle for free, or for barely enough to cover Craig's gas, because he would often drive me to gigs. I had never had time to take driving lessons. My brother came to a show in Renfrew and asked me if it wasn't all a waste of time and effort for an empty hall. He thought I'd lost my mind (it didn't help that I was still rocking the electric-blue pants and black string vest—my character was a narcissist called "Thee" Drew Galloway). I had to work my way up from making five pounds a show to maybe getting fifty pounds. The more experienced opponents I went up against, the better I got, and I earned a commensurate fee. I had to build myself up from nowhere. I resented anything that got in the way of my ambition. In the one non-wrestling job I ever had, I worked in what we'd call an old man's pub, where the clientele nursed their pints while reading the *Racing Post*. I'd be reading an autobiography of a wrestler behind the bar and used to get unreasonably annoyed when I had to put my book down to pour a patron a drink.

It was difficult to get better when everyone I was wrestling was around the same skill level. My next goal was to get into All Star Wrestling, Brian Dixon's promotion, and work in the Butlin's summer holiday camps. It was the best place to learn how to manipulate a crowd. Butlin's scheduled entertainment every night, but the customers were not wrestling fans, so you really had to figure out how to entertain, to improvise, to engage these crowds of up to two thousand people. My summer holiday job was working at Butlin's six days a week, all over the UK, at Bognor, Minehead, Selsey . . . Occasionally, they'd bring in veterans to headline our show—Americans, Canadians, stars of World Championship Wrestling. Working with these more experienced superstars around the UK taught me so much. Robbie Brookside, who is now a trainer at WWE's developmental system NXT in Orlando, used to wrestle in a tag team with William Regal, one of the most successful British wrestlers in history. A big personality (he came from Liverpool, supports Everton, Liverpool's soccer club, and got his stage name from the Channel 4 soap set on Merseyside), Robbie taught me a lot about ring craft.

At the time I really was not at all comfortable holding the stage with a microphone. I had a manager figure who did the talking for me. With every summer camp, I started to feel more confident; I learned subtle points, such as posture, how to stand over an opponent to make myself look bigger, and how to give the audience time to react at key points of a match. The veterans emphasized that the most important thing to learn was how to *feel* the crowd. And this is the cool thing about coming from the UK. Whether there are twenty fans or fifteen thousand at a show, British crowds are always LOUD. The fans are wild. Even on the smaller wrestling shows, I never minded if there were not many people there, because as awesome as it is to have a full arena, you can't hear the individual insults. You need to be sharp on your feet, and with every show I was getting sharper. I was a bad guy at the time. It was imperative to establish a good back-and-forth banter because if a fan eats you alive, you are dead in the water.

CHAPTER 5

A POSSE OF BAD GUYS

I liked bringing back the snippets of the things I'd learned in the summer to the guys in Scotland. I wanted to better myself, but also to bring along everyone on the wrestling scene so that we were all pushing toward one target. With BCW and ICW, we had created a notable little cult scene in Scotland, and it was gaining momentum and attracting bigger crowds. With one BCW Heavyweight title already to my name, and in the mix to reclaim it (which I did in December 2006), I was invited over to Ireland to work for Irish Whip Wrestling, which had a talent-switch affiliation program with BCW—and a slot on Sky TV. It was here that I first met Sheamus, and we hit it off right away. He was seven years older than me, but we were equally obsessed with forging a path to WWE. My first impression was, Wow, he looks like how a wrestler is supposed to look. As muscled as a human anatomy chart. He was glad to see me too. Up until that point he had been wrestling smaller guys and, at six-foot-five (and a very important half an inch), I matched him for height, though not for that insane musculature.

Our first match was a lot of fun—I must have hit at least sixteen leg drops on him. One incident bonded us. I had gone to Ireland for some matches, and we all went out on the last night. Sheamus was a bouncer on the door of a place called Spirit Night Club, and we were all having a good time hanging out, meeting other people. Sheamus had to get to work the following morning by nine, so he eventually said he was heading for home. I had a dawn flight back to Glasgow with another wrestler and "Charles Boddington," the stage name of my manager Graham McKay, the owner of BCW. Somehow, I got carried away partying, went off with a gang I met, lost all track of time, and missed my Monday morning flight. I had ended up having a great time partying in Dublin. My phone battery died, and no one around me had the right charger for my phone, so I was out of contact for a couple of days. Unbeknownst to me, there were all these phone calls ricocheting across the Irish Sea— Sheamus to my parents, Charles to my parents, everyone trying my dead phone—and then I turned up three days later on Sheamus's doorstep, pretty chill, asking him how he's doing.

"Oh, you're alive? That's good," he says. "Happy days. But *where the fuck have you been?*"

I couldn't get a flight back until the Friday and that's how we became great mates. We hung out for two days, away from wrestling, away from the wrestling crowd, caught a movie, went for some pints, and really bonded. From then on, I would travel to and from Ireland, often paying my own airfare, to get the exposure on TV through IWW, and Sheamus would come to Scotland, and stay on the sofa in our front room. Mum and Dad treated him like one of the family.

It was a really cool moment when, in August 2006, I became Irish Whip Wrestling Champion at the IWW International Intermingle. I now had three belts to swing about the house. Like a big brother to a younger sibling, Sheamus was generous in passing on his tips. This might embarrass him to recall, but we would work out together in his bedroom. He would teach me the correct way to use weights, with specific techniques he had learned as a bodybuilder, such as the benefits gained from using mind-to-muscle connections. Craig and I used to throw weights around as much as we could for hours, but Sheamus taught me to focus on the muscle I was working, that kind of stuff. I started learning a lot from him too, about nutrition and fitness. He was this lunatic who always had sandwich bags on him stuffed with plain chicken breasts he had cooked on his portable George Foreman electric grill. Wherever he was out and about, he would pull shredded chicken out and munch away like a savage. He was ahead of the game in understanding you needed a massive and regular protein intake to build and maintain muscle in order to train harder. He coaxed me into a routine of eating more rice, more chicken, more vegetables to fuel my metabolism. I was happy to take it on board—plain boiled chicken in tinfoil and any other knowledge he could share that would make me look better and be better in the ring. Mum's shopping bill took another massive hike, and back in Scotland Craig looked aghast when I'd get out a tub of cottage cheese mixed with yogurt at a nightclub.

Despite the age gap, Sheamus and I were on a similar level. He had originally gone to the US, got hurt, and it didn't work out, so he came back to Ireland and took a break from wrestling, which meant I had technically been wrestling longer than him even though I was younger. He restarted in Ireland, but he had to fit wrestling around his full-time job in IT. I was a student getting away with pursuing wrestling full-time while he was an adult with a real job. We had the same ambition, the same mindset about wrestling, and we would communicate on the phone a lot. In IWW we got to dictate what we did, so we would plan to put on a submission match as a specialty match, or we would try a two-out-of-three-falls match. We would try these different matches, we would film them, watch them back. He was a Bret Hart fan as well, and we would try to replicate certain sequences. It was an important growth period for both of us. I was pushing him to look at the wrestling moves and the mechanics of it all, and he was pushing me to get my body bigger and better. We were pushing each other to improve. We had more time in Ireland to develop the way we talked on the microphone because we had the one television show, *Irish Whip Wrestling*, that was on the Wrestling Channel in Europe.

Sheamus ended up having a falling out with the promoter. I was the champion at the time, and the promoter called me and started bad-mouthing Sheamus, and said he was out. I just said, "Okay, I'm not back, then. If he's done, I'm done." I refused to go back, and just handed the title to someone else. I don't think the promoter realized how close we were, but I felt that Sheamus had done such a lot for the company and they weren't fair to him, so I refused to go back.

Sheamus had also started working the Butlin's circuit, although he nearly bombed on his first experience. He was so excited to get a trial at All Star Wrestling and join me on the road, learning from the veteran performers and having the litmus test of trying to entertain non-wrestling fans. He turned up for his first interview at Butlin's forgetting it was a public show packed with families and kids, and not the alcohol-fueled adults-only crowd he was used to. "You're all a bunch of twats!" he announced. Everybody was mortified. The promoter was freaking out. Backstage I was saying to anyone who would listen that I was sure it meant something completely different in Ireland, and that in the particular place he came from it was just slang for "You are all rubbish!" Sheamus panicked, thinking he'd never get the opportunity again, but thankfully he did, and he came back to the summer shows many times. We would film every one of the Butlin's matches, and when we'd all finished, we'd hook up the television and, guided by Robbie Brookside, give each other completely honest appraisals: that's terrible, that's cool, that looks good, why the hell did you do that?! We'd watch how the crowd had reacted, and be completely blunt to each other even though we didn't always like to hear it. We knew what we had to do to get to the next level.

I met Wade Barrett, aka Stu Sanders, during the IWW period. I was a bad guy, but still not as muscular as I'd like, and Sheamus was much more of a hulk, so to make our storyline more credible I thought it would be helpful if I had a little posse in the ring to help me surround and attack the big Irish hero. Sheamus had met Stu somewhere, and it was obvious he was eager to learn. We went to a pub to meet up with him and discuss our plans. My Ayr accent was a thousand times thicker then, and I naturally talk very quickly. Add in a tendency to mumble, and Stu couldn't understand a word I was saying. He'd brought along a power-lifter mate, who ended up flash translating every other sentence for Stu. But Stu was getting so frustrated, so infuriated—angry!—and I thought, Perfect, this is the guy for my posse of bad guys!

The first time I announced him at an event, I was on the microphone in the ring and said—dramatic pause—"I'd like to introduce my good friend Big *Steeevve* Sanders." He entered the ring, turned around to acknowledge the crowd, and I saw emblazoned on the back of his tights, "STU SANDERS." We did a little interview to proclaim ourselves, plus a French guy, as the Foreign Legion, and eventually I defeated Sheamus for the title. Stu went on to become one of the best talkers, but he wasn't as competent in the ring then. He had been taught an old-fashioned grappling style of wrestling, which was ground-based and on mats and didn't have a ring, so he had a lot of catching up to do to get up to our skill level, but he was a great guy and we soon became close. He joined a few of the All Star Wrestling shows, which he juggled with a full-time job. That was hilarious. His nine-to-five role was as a manager of an office in Slough, and his colleagues were a cast of characters with funny nicknames. He was basically David Brent from *The Office* (Michael Scott in the American version).

By this stage, I was the top wrestler for the companies I was working for, especially in Scotland. I was in every main event, every match against an imported star. My name was associated with the marquee matches. During this period, Mark Dallas founded Insane Championship Wrestling in Glasgow. Even as a teenager, he'd always wanted to be a promoter. After attending all those training sessions to learn the business from the inside—or, as he puts it, "getting the shit kicked out of me even though I was never going to be a wrestler, in order to create our own brand of wrestling"— he started running his first shows. The aim was to take elements from the things we respected in WWE with the Attitude Era, like ECW (Extreme Championship Wrestling), and amalgamate them with traditional aspects of British wrestling and create a unique Scottish wrestling scene. The early shows in the Maryhill Community Centre were a shambles to be honest, with many a kid being taken away screaming at the apparent violence of our show, so we moved to nightclubs and became a sort of underground, over 18s cult promotion that tapped into a zeitgeist—a bit anarchic, more than a bit crazy. It was more like being in a band than a wrestling promotion.

On October 15, 2006, I was crowned the company's inaugural heavyweight champion after defeating Darkside and Allan Grogan in a three-way Iron Man Match billed as ICW: Fear & Loathing. My character was still "Thee" Drew Galloway, a full-of-myself ladies' man who oozed arrogance. I entered the ring to Chesney Hawkes's "I Am the One and Only," which seems ridiculous now, but worked fantastically well at the time. Dallas, with no money to film this milestone moment properly, tried to capture it on a crappy camera he had bought secondhand. The tape has long since disintegrated. An Iron Man Match is supposed to last an hour, but by the time we came into the ring, we'd run out of time, and Dallas couldn't afford to be charged extra for the venue, so the match went twenty-three minutes, and I became the first ICW Heavyweight Champion.

Over that last year or two, the British wrestling scene transformed. We had all started from scratch, learned our craft the hard way, and raised the game. I had morphed from someone who said he was going to be a wrestler to someone who was a wrestler. Did I still have doubts that I was going to make it to WWE? To go and live and ply my trade in America? From Scotland? Totally. My ambition still sounded completely insane. Nobody had ever done that before. America seemed so far away, like somewhere only accessible via TV. There wasn't a developmental setup like NXT UK then. It seemed almost ridiculous to everyone except me and my family, who supported me and believed in me. Not many people believed I was going to do it, except this guy writing this story.

CHAPTER 6

TAKE A WALK WITH ME, KID

The next stage beckoned. Sheamus had a contact at WWE Talent Relations, and he informed me what we had to do to get a tryout. It seemed a huge leap of faith in ourselves to think we were ready to be assessed by WWE, legendary home of global Superstars. We had played out our big rivalry in IWW on TV, wrestling each other in Scotland, England, and Ireland, and we remained steadfast in our intent on getting ourselves to WWE. It was the logical next step. He told me to send an email, with pictures and video clips. He seemed sure I would get a tryout. I sent all that info and got a message back, "Drew, you're coming to Manchester!" The tryout date was in November 2006—three months down the line. In the lead-up I trained intensely, eighteen hours a week, to pack on some serious muscle. It became an obsessive quest.

On the day of the tryout, I traveled down to Manchester with Craig, excitement and nerves increasing throughout the four-hour car journey. When we arrived, we were shown to a locker room where we met up with Sheamus, his manager, Stu Sanders, and Miguel Varrish. We walked into the canteen for lunch, and it was like walking onto the set of a movie. There was Vince McMahon sitting next to Ric Flair! Right in front of us. It was incredible to see the guys we looked up to on TV each week just hanging around, chatting casually, eating lunch—Show was there, Kane too. I was way too much of a fan to see them as real people at work. I tried telling myself that one day these guys would be my colleagues, but to see not just one but a whole host of them milling around was intimidating. I turned a corner and there were Randy Orton and Edge, who were tag team champions at the time, walking down the hallway wearing their gear with an intangible Superstar aura. I introduced myself to them, and it hit me how much bigger, taller, and more impressive than me they were in every way. I was mesmerized by the muscle definition in Randy Orton's quads. He is not that much older than me, and I had always observed that we had a similar body shape, but my takeaway Message to Self was: I have got to get my legs much bigger.

It was clear the WWE machine welcomed new talent. Sheamus and Stu Sanders were pulled out to appear on *Raw* at the Manchester Evening News Arena that night, as part of a security team ejecting D-Generation X from ringside. I was asked too, but they wanted me to cut my hair in order to look less like a wrestler and more like a security guard. I grew my hair even longer then than I have it now, and I said I was not prepared to cut it just to run out for sixty seconds on live TV. My hair was what made me stand out. It used to be that all wrestlers had long hair, but around 2006 the Superstars all had short hair, so my hair was a distinctive part of my look. I remember being jealous at the time that my buddies were getting that runout on *Raw*, but I was hanging around for my tryout.

That was slated for the following day, when Sheamus and I had the opportunity to get in the ring together. Having wrestled each other a bunch of times now, we knew how to put on an impressive match. We rolled around, beat each other up for real. It was very quick, maybe a bit too quick. I remember seeing Undertaker and Chris Benoit laughing close by the ring, and I thought, Oh my goodness, they are laughing at us! How humiliating. Now—having been in that position, close by a ring, during trials—I realize that they were not watching us at all and were almost certainly laughing about something else. At the time I felt a bit disheartened: Were we so terrible it was laughable?

After we got out of the ring, Bobby Lashley paused to give us some advice. He reassured us our match was very good and told us to maybe just to slow it down, calm it down. A few minutes later, I was pulled aside by WWE agents Steve Keirn and Dean Malenko.

"Wow, Drew, you've done a great job and you would be signed today if John Laurinaitis were here, but he's not," they said.

"Oh, so who do I talk to?"

"Nobody. We'll see you in six months."

Back in our tiny locker room, we were all buzzing, just elated to have entered the WWE bubble and participated in front of the real deal. We were offered tickets to that night's show, but we thought, Forget that, let's go out and celebrate. We nipped out to a club in Manchester's city center, conned our way into the VIP area, which was empty, and ordered some drinks. A few drinks down the road, I felt a tap on my back. Turning around, I saw Bobby Lashley and The Boogeyman. Quite an incongruous situation for a bunch of WWE hopefuls having a drink on the sly.

"Hey, big man, hey, Superstars," Bobby hailed us.

Oops, we thought. We've been busted—but that wasn't the

case at all. He was absolutely fine with us being there, and we all had a great evening. It was cool.

Craig and I traveled back to Scotland, talking all of the two-hundred-odd miles about how I could use the next six months to get as big and in as good a shape as I could. What had I learned from the experience? I learned that Randy Orton and Edge were *really* big, even though they were not the biggest guys on the roster. I always compared myself to Randy because of our similar physique and because he was a young guy who got his opportunity and maximized it. Randy weighed in at about 245 pounds on the same body frame as me, so I set my goal at being at least 245 pounds in six months. Craig and I trained like crazy. He made sure I trained no matter what. If I was too tired and lying in bed, I'd hear his car pull up. And then he would become annoyed because I would insist on eating first and he would have to wait an hour for me. If it were not for him, I might never have got into the shape I got into. He was a very patient friend. I was as annoying as hell at the time. If I wanted to sleep, I'd sleep. Even if Craig had a full day of classes at the gym, he would always make sure we had our workout, driving me on toward the Randy Orton target I had set for myself. If I was hungover one day and wanting to lie in bed a bit longer, he would still make sure we fitted in the training I had to do.

The second tryout, six months later, in April 2007, was in London. I traveled down and stayed with Sheamus, who was living in Romford, Essex, while juggling wrestling with a day job working in IT for a financial company. This time John Laurinaitis was present. Also known as Johnny Ace, Laurinaitis has been around a long time. He had done well in the ring and then became known for his creative abilities backstage—coming up with great ideas for finishes and that sort of thing. Well spoken, he looked the part in a suit, and Vince had put him in charge of Talent Relations. Jim Ross, his predecessor, had signed the era's big stars. Johnny's signings were in a different mold—all fairly similar, bigger, good-looking, in-shape guys. I was told at the first tryout that I fitted the bill perfectly, and I was only twenty-one, which was good.

In London that day, I was very aware Laurinaitis was the one I had to impress; he was the one who signed people, who made or broke careers, who decided if you could come to WWE or not. Vince McMahon did not run around signing people himself. Back in 2007, he was the guy who had to see us in the ring in order to decide to hire us or not. Seeing him ringside, it was like, now or never, and I thought, Oh crap, this is where I have to turn it up even more.

I remember Arn Anderson standing outside the ring, and there was myself, Sheamus, Stu Sanders, and a few other friends. Some of the other contestants were giants—Rob Terry, who would be assigned to Florida Championship Wrestling, and a giant of another guy I have not seen since. The two gargantuan guys were invited into the ring first. "You and you. Get in." It turned out Rob had never wrestled before but had this great physical presence, and the other guy was in monstrous shape but was not supple enough to do a forward roll. Rob could do a forward roll. They were impressed enough—okay, there's a giant—one box checked—who can do a forward roll—another box checked. "Okay, you two get out."

Next, Sheamus and I became the center of attention. "You and you . . . Get in."

In this our second trial match, we remembered Bobby Lashley's advice to keep it calm, and we did pretty well together. They fed in Stu Sanders, who was not quite at our level, to wrestle me next. As we were moving around the ring, I tried to tell him to do certain moves, and he wasn't able to deliver, so I got a little frustrated.

This was my big chance! I wanted to put on a great show!

I got so infuriated—because I knew it had to be perfect—that I elbowed Stu and knocked out his tooth. There is a happy ending . . .

When the match was over, John Laurinaitis pulled me aside and said, "Take a walk with me, kid." He ushered me around the place, which was milling with familiar Superstars as we walked toward the catering facility. I felt so awkward, trying to make conversation with him, knowing the power he had over signing potential talent. But he put me at ease; he turned to face me and said, "I'm thinking about bringing you to America."

I looked him in the eye and said, "Johnny, I'm thinking about letting you."

Contract in hand, I phoned home straightaway. I was ecstatic. I had been signed by WWE. It had always been the plan since I had announced my ambition to my family back when I was five years old, but it seemed totally unreal that I had been singled out for this walkabout by John Laurinaitis. (I hadn't ever imagined that little scenario in the dream montages I conjured at night, my head resting on my "Stone Cold" Steve Austin pillowcase.)

The brilliant thing was that Stu was also pulled aside and signed. Sheamus came over, a bit panicked. He had not yet spoken to Laurinaitis. He sprinted off and found him, and Sheamus was signed as well. It was freaking incredible that all three of us, good friends, were signed by WWE at the same time. We went to a concession stand and had a couple of celebratory beers.

"They obviously see great things for you, Drew," said Sheamus, noting how I had been taken off alone for a stroll-around with John

Laurinaitis. I took that to heart from my "big brother." It is fair to say that was one pretty cool day.

I came home and waved my contract under my brother's eyes. John thought it was a joke, that I had got one of the lads to draw it up and print it off, but no. I explained it was for real, WWE had offered me terms and wanted me to move to America. My family were over the moon for me. After they had watched me going off to do shows wherever I could for four or five years, watched my childhood obsession grow into a single-minded mission, they saw I really was going to the other side of the Atlantic Ocean to chase my dream. Even better, I was going on this adventure with two mates.

I fell off cloud nine shortly after. There was horrifying news about Chris Benoit, the guy I had mistakenly assumed was laughing at us with Undertaker during our first tryout. We had seen him at the London tryout as well as the Manchester tryout. He was one of the greatest technical wrestlers in history, a hero to many. To this day, little light has been shed on what prompted the double murder-suicide incident that shocked the world far beyond the wrestling community. As I knew from my Criminology degree, people can snap for a myriad of different reasons, with tragic consequences. From the euphoric high of being signed by WWE, Sheamus and I plummeted to the pits of despair. Wrestling all over the world was under scrutiny. We assumed our dream would be put on hold, if it was going to be fulfilled at all.

Sheamus was quick to call me to discuss the ramifications. I took the phone out to my back garden so my family in our small apartment could not hear what we were talking about.

"Mate, it's over," he said. "Wrestling's going to have a hard time until they establish what happened. No company will take on any new trainees. They will probably terminate our contracts."

But they did not. However much we saw Benoit as a huge WWE figure from our fan's perspective—not least because we had mingled in the same trial room as him—the incident was also a terrible personal tragedy.

A few months later, visas sorted out, plane tickets booked, excitement off the scale, I was off to begin my life as a WWE Superstar.

CHAPTER 7

NO, DREW, THAT'S NOT NORMAL

had been so focused on making it to WWE that I forgot the part where I had to go to America! Chasing my dream meant leaving behind life as I had always known it. I would be relocating lock, stock, and protein-powder barrel from the familiar surroundings of home in Ayr to the land I knew only through television and the movies.

The next few weeks were a whirlwind of high fives, bear hugs, and expressions of good luck from my buddies; meanwhile, I had to sort out the paperwork and the visa and fit in plans to say good-bye to everyone. I remember spending one evening with Mark Dallas, the kindred spirit I had met online at fourteen whose parallel path had seen him become the promoter of Insane Championship Wrestling, the company that would prove so integral through the ups and downs of my subsequent career. Little did we imagine that night, as we sat laughing over episodes of *Nathan Barley*, a British sitcom, how Drew Galloway and ICW would come together seven years later and electrify the wrestling community. We loved the bumptious Nathan Barley and the way he parodied the cool-but-insecure world of the new internet players. How right he was in predicting a future of memes, vloggers, and social media—and how crucial would "social media buzz" prove to me down the line. Mark let me take the DVD to America in case I felt homesick. To this day, he insists he wants it back.

On the eve of my departure, I held a leaving party in a bar in Glasgow that Wolfgang's family owned. I raffled off some random wrestling gear. I may have made it to WWE, but it was on a trainee's salary, so I was keen to raise a bit of money to add to the sum my parents had given me to help me get a good start in America. On September 7, 2007, I officially left home. We'd spent the night at my papa's girlfriend's house close to Glasgow Airport, and then the next morning Mum, Dad, John, and my buddy Adrian, who wrestled as Lionheart, waved me off through the security barrier.

If I had taken time to dwell on the ramifications of that long journey from Glasgow, I might have felt a big wrench. I was heading to Louisville, Kentucky, where Ohio Valley Wrestling, the established WWE developmental center, was based. Not seeing my family and friends would suck, but even the anxiety of managing two transit changes at London's Heathrow Airport and Chicago's O'Hare could not dull my excitement at heading off to live in the WWE Universe. Always in the back of my mind was a scene in one of the *Tough Enough* VHS tapes I'd worn to shreds. In it, Triple H addresses a group of young wrestlers in a training session, and says, "It's not an easy life. It's two-hundred-plus days a year on the road. You either want this. Or you don't."

I wanted this. No question.

Home would always be Annpit Road with Mum, Dad, and my

brother at the center of our close extended family, along with my local buddies and wrestling friends, my life down at the gym and in downtown Glasgow. I could navigate my way around our small town with my eyes closed—past my primary school, Newton Park, where I'd kicked a football around with my school buddies, the harbor pubs and clubs I'd frequented with Craig, the church hall where I'd attended Boys' Brigade meetings, the academy, and the station where I'd hopped on and off countless trains to Glasgow in the cold and rain. Just up the road from our apartment, the Carlton Hotel was a place where everyone knew everyone else and where my parents and their friends were often to be found enjoying a drink together. I would be swapping the seventies' domestic architecture of our neighborhood, tucked behind the long stretch of Ayr Beach and its adjacent golf courses for, well . . . I had no idea. Sunshine and palm trees!

America was a sort of immense, unmarked field of dreams in which I was going to fulfill my wrestling ambition. I was good at envisioning details of storylines and stunts and crowd dynamics set in and around a twenty-foot-by-twenty-foot ring. Beyond the ring, my imaginative capabilities quickly faded; I had no inkling of what to expect and was unable to conjure anything in my mind. Technically, when I signed with WWE, I was in the last year of my Criminology degree studies. I had a few final assignments to deliver and the flurry of preparing to leave meant I lost track of whether I had even handed them all in. I assumed I would not now graduate, since Plan A was on track. (Later I made inquiries, and it turned out that I had done enough to earn my diploma, although I have yet to collect it. Dad's wall space awaits.)

Having traveled all over Scotland, England, and Ireland—each country with a distinct identity—I wasn't expecting America to be a massive culture shock.

But it was. On so many levels.

Louisville was something else. I still do not know why I was sent to OVW—the established training facility where you would expect to be fast-tracked into regular work. Like a beacon to young, driven wrestlers like me, the huge letters on the front of the building spelled out the slogan "Tomorrow's Superstars Today." Sheamus, meanwhile, had been channeled into Florida Championship Wrestling in Tampa, which was a basic setup still largely under construction. It had seemed ideal to be jetting off on this life-changing venture with two great buddies, but pretty crap to learn we would actually be based three times farther apart in America than we had been in Ayr and Dublin. What's more, Sheamus, the man with the world's fairest Celtic skin, was living it up in the Sunshine State while I had been assigned to a region where everyone spoke in a slow drawl that, to me, sounded like someone kept pressing the pause button on their speech. More disturbingly, there were stores where you could pick up a gun with your Coke and chips. I saw guns in every shop.

After checking into the lodge recommended by WWE, I went straight out for food. The Longhorn Steakhouse was the first restaurant I came across. A legendary big, juicy American steak seemed just the thing. The place was done up ranch style. The walls were studded with huge taxidermied heads of cattle, with their big doleful eyes giving diners the black-eyed stare as they, the diners, tucked into prime cuts of their cousins. I'd never seen anything like it. I disliked the idea of eating what I was looking at on the wall. Who would do that? Only a psycho, right? As if on cue, a guy with intense eyes approached and directed me to a table. I tried to order from the menu, but he struggled to understand my accent.

"Where're y'all from?" he asked, *y'all* being just me.

"Scotland," I said.

His staring eyes widened. "I'm from Scotland too," he said. "I'm related to Robert Burns, a poet who writes songs—'Auld Lang Syne,' that's one of his," he added, as if referring to a recent single release. "I'm planning on visiting him one day."

Okay, I thought . . . And Robert Burns has been dead since the 1700s. This was too much. Nor was he able to grasp what I was trying to order after I had repeated my choice several times.

"You know, buddy, there's nothing Scottish on this menu. Maybe I'll come back later," I said, and fled.

Back in the hotel, I called home. "These people are crazy," I said. "The first person I've met is saving up to visit his close family member Robert Burns, who has been dead for hundreds of years!"

During the call, I had the TV in my room on in the background. As I was regaling Mum with the story about the psycho waiter, I saw a series of low-budget corny ads for local businesses. On came this commercial with an over-the-top businessman and a cheap, animated dog, shaking like it had rabies. The business boss turned to the dog. "How are the competitors' prices, Rex?" "Www-rough!" barked the dog. The commercials were insane too.

"I think I want to come home!"

I was twenty-two, unworldly in many senses, and finding it difficult as an introvert with an indecipherable accent just to talk my way around those first couple of days in Louisville. On the few occasions I'd been beyond the United Kingdom before, it was on a family holiday to Spain or Greece. I had never had to fend for myself in acclimating to an alien cultural environment, never had to establish my own routine or think about rent, grocery shopping, and laundry. After that brief spell in university accommodation just up the road in Glasgow, I had been living at home and had never had to deal with real-life management and bills. Mum, always on top of domestic arrangements, kept a spick-and-span home. My pile of laundry would mount and then magically disappear as regular as clockwork. When I got to America, the pile towered up, but it refused to disappear. I needed to grow up, and fast.

After that call home, I walked to the gas station and bought some beef jerky—which reminded me of Johnny Bravo, the character on the Cartoon Network who eats jerky and tries (and fails) to get girls. After further exploration, I discovered the lodge had a kitchen, and I soon got into the habit of stocking up on supplies at the local supermarket. In this settling-in phase, I did not want to lose condition. This was OVW, and on all the DVDs, everybody at OVW looked huge. Would I match up? OVW had helped forge many wrestling legends. A roll call of greats—John Cena, Batista, Randy Orton, Brock Lesnar, and many others—had passed through its doors. Arriving three weeks before Wade Barrett was due to fly in, I had the chance to spend time with some of the roster. With my wrestling license pending, I traveled to a couple of shows to take it all in. I saw two in the first two days, and watching those shows calmed my nerves. I couldn't wait to get into the ring. Thanks to the All Star Wrestling experience, I was confident about acclimating to this new world in the ring.

Meanwhile, vignettes of local Louisville life made me feel like I had stumbled onto the set of *Deliverance* (no offense, Louisville). One day, I walked into the gas station, and in the line to pay was a gentleman, four hundred pounds, wearing overalls with nothing underneath, bald but with a lot of body hair. The guy behind him wore a flannel jacket and dirty baseball cap with a straggly ponytail sticking out of the back. From his lips dangled a lit cigarette—in a gas station!

On Day 3, the WWE writers hit town. I took this as normal, but in fact my first week at OVW had coincided with one of the biannual visits of the creative team. The majority were seasoned writers, responsible for developing the characters and amazing storylines I had grown up following; some were former wrestlers, others had never been in the ring but understood the crazy world of WWE. Putting on great shows, week in, week out, is a huge team effort. All the wrestlers were fine-tuning their interviews, preparing their matches, getting their tans just so. You could feel the buzz. In the days before NXT gave developing stars a platform, wrestlers training at OVW worked hard to put on a bravura act for the writers to get their chance of being plucked from obscurity and planted on the path to stardom. Everyone wanted to make a big impact to get "on the road," a status that elevated you from being paid the basic wage to earning extra money per show, per appearance on TV. I could see it was key to show the writers who you were and what you could bring to the ring. What better way to study the selection process and identify what the WWE creative team were after than to observe from the sidelines in my first few days?

I was sitting to one side, quietly taking it all in—imagining this would be me, six months down the line—when the cry went up that they were a body short.

"Kid?" Someone called my attention. "Will you just get in the ring and be a good guy for this bad guy that we're going to take a look at?"

Kid? I guessed that was me.

I did as asked and went off to change into my wrestling gear. (Number one rule in wrestling: always have your gear.) I rolled around in the ring and was a creditable foil to the heel, and did the requisite interview afterward. I had no fear. I was swearing and being as crude as hell. I thought nothing of it; I was the new guy and rent-a-fodder for the wrestler they were scrutinizing.

The following week, I got a call and immediately recognized the distinctive booming deep voice of Howard Finkel, the famous WWE ring announcer. This was pretty freaking cool in itself. Before I had time to wonder why he was calling, he informed me that I was going on the road for television. Wow, I felt pretty pleased, but assumed this must be normal. Immediately, some of the guys who had been friendly and welcoming seemed to have cooled off. A couple cut me dead. Why? I wondered. What was the matter? I asked Paul Burchill, the first guy signed from the UK, and a big OVW star who looked out for me when I first arrived. Straight up he said: "It's because you've not even been here two weeks, and you're going on the road."

"Isn't that normal?" I asked

"No, Drew, it's not normal. Some guys have been here eight or nine years, waiting for their chance."

I had signed for WWE Developmental to see if I could make the transition, and for the creative team to figure out where I'd go, and already I was up and running as a name on the WWE roster. A few weeks earlier, I had been wrestling in front of a hundred people maximum for an adult-only audience in grungy local halls in the back of beyond around the UK. Now five years of hard work had paid off: barely two weeks after touching down in the States, that new young guy who had been floating around OVW asking for advice had unwittingly leapfrogged the queue of other aspiring wrestlers and was all set to walk out on a prime-time show in front of millions of viewers. It was like a young actor going for an audition among more experienced performers being plucked out for a blockbuster Hollywood film. Great for me, but maybe a bit galling for others.

I tried to process everything in my new normal as "normal"; I tried to go with the flow and get on with whatever I was asked. Luckily for my sanity I failed to register just how out of depth I was in terms of televisual technique. The ring has always been my comfort zone. What difference would a few more lights and cameras make? Even if I had stopped to consider that I might not be ready, I was hardly going to say, Er, thank you but no, I need a few more months to train.

I rang home. "You may want to watch *SmackDown* on Friday," I coolly suggested.

CHAPTER 8

YOU'VE GOT TO BE TOUGH TO WEAR A SKIRT

Come the day of the show in Detroit, Michigan—October 12, 2007—I did start fretting about my debut. This was it: my initiation into the real-life business of working for WWE. I have always been able to hide my nerves well. People often assume that people my size don't suffer stage anxiety; we do—and I was sweating bucketloads in the lead-up.

Standing in the gorilla position—the backstage area from which wrestlers emerge to walk to the ring, named after the spot behind the curtain that the legendary commentator Gorilla Monsoon made his own—Vince McMahon's daughter, Stephanie, an integral member of the family business, whispered:

"Is Drew Galloway your real name?"

I nodded.

Before I knew it, Stephanie and Michael Hayes, who was on duty as agent for that show, escorted me swiftly upstairs to Talent Relations. Twenty minutes before my live WWE debut on *Smack-*

Down, we were in the office that deals with training info and travel sheets, frantically Googling Scottish names. I needed a ring name, fast.

I knew Stephanie from TV, of course, where she is so convincing as an evil character. In real life I found she was incredibly nice and helpful. I was adamant that my ring name needed three syllables so that it would be chantable, and she agreed. Michael suggested McDonald, but there was already a professional wrestler Drew McDonald (who had memorably teamed up with Big Daddy to defeat Giant Haystacks and Fit Finlay as part of ITV's 1984 FA Cup Final coverage). We continued scrolling until we hit McIntyre. *Mac-In-Tyre*—three good, strong, hard syllables. That would do. We dashed back to the gorilla position.

Michael got word to the ring announcer that my name was now Drew McIntyre, but it was too late to change the letters up on the Titantron, the giant screen that projects our walk-ons to the ring while our entrance music blares out. If you look at footage of my debut against Brett Major that night, you can glimpse "Drew Galloway" in bright lights up on the screen while Drew McIntyre walks in (an early example of my existence as two selves!).

Brett sprinted down to the ring with his brother Brian, balls of pent-up energy, waiting for me and Dave Taylor to come and take them on.

Introducing next . . . From Ayr, Scotland, weighing two hundred and fifty-three pounds, Drreeeeewww Maaaac. Iiiin. Tyyyyrre!

Wearing an electric-blue tartan kilt that reached below my knees and black-trimmed white boots, I walked out to my first live match on network television with Dave as my corner man, a sort of veteran and prodigy pairing. Dave was a British legend who was hired by WWE as a mentor to incomers. He not only added gravitas to my debut but also gave me reassurance. Trying as I was to look confident, I was pretty terrified walking out for the first time on this grand stage, with a huge crowd discernible behind a neon-blue haze of laser light, and the noise of the crowd's roars competing with the ominous entrance music. I had rarely wrestled in front of more than a few hundred people, often in a church hall complete with pews and organ pipes. With more than twenty thousand in Detroit's Joe Louis Arena, this was like walking out into a sporting cathedral dedicated to wrestling. My music was William Regal's music—presumably to induce a Pavlovian response and signal *British wrestler!*

I was concerned about how I would come across in the ring and how I would manage the dynamics of the match. Thank goodness I could not hear the commentary, which was building up my debut with lines like "It's going to be sink or swim if this kid doesn't make it." Never in a million years had I anticipated that television would require a further, sophisticated skill set.

When the bell rang, I tore off my kilt and threw it aggressively toward Dave. I was ready to wrestle. The referee leaned toward me and said, "Work the hard cam, okay?"

"Work the *what*?"

The referee's face fell into a pantomime-stunned expression.

"The hard camera!" he yelled. "The main one!"

Lesson number two: the hard cam is the fixed lens you look down, you play up to, you use to enhance the drama of your moves. It is the eye of the world that you engage in order to channel your story to millions of viewers in a live *SmackDown* match. There is nothing more important in winning over your audience than the ability to work the hard cam.

And I had no idea what or where the hell it was.

Those *Inside Secrets* of Dennis Brent and Percy Pringle, which I had considered the A to Z on all pro wrestling matters, had not delved into the technical aspects of broadcasting in-ring action!

Earlier, on the mic, I had set out to win crowd allegiance. "I know how much you Americans love to cheer for your own," I said, enunciating painfully slowly, as I had been instructed. "That is why I have applied for dual citizenship. And, tonight, it would be great to hear you say *U! S! A!*"

The match was over in a five-minute blur. Gratifyingly, the crowd did chant in my support, and even more gratifyingly, I won. I was thrilled. As the commentators said, "You have to be tough to wear a skirt!"

Jerry, one of the Briscoe Brothers who was a legendary wrestler and part of Vince's inner circle, was quick to come up and congratulate me afterward. "Great fucking job," he said. "When you made the referee grab your arm and raise it? That's a heel!"

It was my first compliment. It has always stuck with me, and the referee-grabbing-my-arm gesture became my thing. I use that to this day even as a good guy. It would not be the last time Jerry looked out for me. He once invited me over for Thanksgiving dinner because he knew I lived close by and would otherwise be alone. It was just a kind, thoughtful gesture that still sticks with me.

The impact of being on TV was immediate. I got a shock when I looked at MySpace, the big fan social network at the time, and spent two hours accepting new friend requests. My buddies in Scotland were giving me a hard time about my dual citizenship line. And My. Slow. Speech. Everyone seemed pleased, but the *SmackDown* crew realized this kid needed to catch up.

CHAPTER 9

RIDDLES FROM THE DEADMAN

Life on the road with *SmackDown* was six months of go, go, go. Wade Barrett arrived in Louisville shortly after my debut. It was great to hang out with an old buddy. We stayed in the same apartment complex and tried to establish a good eat-gym-sleep routine on our rare rest days. First week he was there, we had to find a local gym to join. Without a car, we went out walking one evening in search of a gym and were puzzled to find the streets deserted. A crazy siren was sounding, which we dismissed as some kind of building alarm. We entered the nearest gym, which was open with lights on and equipment out on mats. Not a soul was there. A guy who must have heard us wandering around emerged from the back and asked us what we were doing. "Come to inquire about joining," we said. Frantically, he ushered us into a back office, where we found a group sitting in a huddle.

"Didn't you hear the tornado sirens?" one of them said.

They clearly thought we were bonkers. Some crazy weather

system was about to hit Louisville, and here were these two British maniacs strolling leisurely along of an evening, hoping to sign up for some light training.

We hurried back to our apartments just in time. When the twister struck, wind howled all night like a damaged turbo jet engine. Heavy, almost horizontal rain swirled around and lashed the windows. I awoke to find the McDonald's just around the corner crushed to smithereens. Only the giant arches remained standing.

The weekly schedule was tough. We'd fly into another city in another state on a Friday or Saturday, hire a car, look for food. For a 7 p.m. Saturday show, I liked to get to the locker room by 5 p.m. The show would be over by 10:30 p.m., when we might hit the road and drive sometimes up to five hours to reach the next destination. I would wake up in a hotel in a place I had yet to see in daylight, and it would be gym, eat, and then travel into the locker room to watch VHS cassettes of the previous night. I loved these critiques led by Undertaker. Everyone participated, and the comments were never about the execution of moves; they were about how to best project the drama of the story: where we should pause and let the crowd react to what they'd just witnessed. "You've got to let the fans digest," Undertaker would emphasize. Primed in this way, we'd then prepare for the Sunday show. Monday was the day we taped shows. Tuesday was the day we taped shows that would air later in the week on television, an entirely more grandiose production than our weekend shows, which were seen only by the live audience in the arena. Wednesday, we'd travel back to Louisville.

In my first six months, I learned so much from hanging out backstage with the more experienced wrestlers. They had wrestled around the world and in different territories in America before WWE had sprinkled its stardust on them and turned them into big names. Their stories were entertaining: often colorful and lewd, but also peppered with takeaway nuggets of information or warnings about hazards that stuck in my subconscious. I learned that the first and last matches of a show are the most important. The opener sets the tone and shows the crowd the moves and gets them into foot-stomping mode; the last is high drama, which leaves the fans marveling and discussing the action all the way home. I could also see that backstage respect is earned by hard work, and being humble and appreciative of other people's contributions. I saw someone like Undertaker, the headline act who wants to share his passion and contribute to the collective performance without any ego. In contrast to today, where sadly there is a sense of entitlement that I would like to weed out of the sport, all the guys stuck around after their matches and there was a lot of congratulatory banter after the show.

It was a tough culture built on respect you had to earn by showing you were a team player. As a new guy, I had a harsh welcome. There was a little bit of good-natured hazing. I remember I couldn't grow a beard at the time, and I'd get comments like "I have more hair on my ass than you have on your face." I felt small, even physically, especially after watching all seven feet, one inch, and 347 pounds of The Great Khali pick up my maximum bench press weights in a hotel gym one morning and just flick them up and down on the shoulder press with his huge hands. And, of course, it was always amusing to get the kid totally drunk!

The irony of going all the way to WWE in America was that the first dates on the *SmackDown* schedule took me straight back to Europe for a series of shows in Luxembourg, Belgium, and the UK—in Butlin's Minehead, Newcastle, Birmingham, Manchester,

Nottingham, Glasgow, and Aberdeen. Evidence of my adrenaline-fueled survival of these early days is that I can hardly remember any of it. Brain fog contributed to the strangely disorientating routine of airport, hired car, hotel, venue, gym, repeat. (There have been some cities in my career where I've made a point of seeing an iconic site—the Colosseum in Rome, the pyramids in Mexico—but that was just a case of asking the taxi to stop on the way to the bar.) I know I didn't see my family on that return to the UK because it was eighteen months before I saw them face-to-face after the wave-off at the airport, and then only because they traveled to the twice-yearly WWE show in Glasgow, where we met up after the show, in the hotel where all the wrestlers were staying. As Triple H warned in that *Tough Enough* video, the schedule was nonstop.

Getting on a plane with the whole crew for the first time was another lesson learned. I sat in the seat in the exit row that the crew member pointed me toward as we all filed on board. Some of the older guys made a big deal out of the fact that "the kid" had taken a seat in the sought-after row. I was embarrassed when I realized that it's part of the unwritten etiquette for the senior guys to have the seats with extra leg room. I was mortified and tried to give up my seat, but I was talked out of it.

We were close to touchdown at one airport in turbulent weather when there was a huge jolt and kick-in of jet power and the pilot accelerated back up to a higher altitude. The plane was shaking under the surge of power, and everyone—huge wrestlers included—was screaming, crying out, and making frantic signs of the cross. It turned out another plane was on the runway and the pilot had taken quick evasive action to prevent a collision.

Early on, maybe in my second or third week on the road, we

were in Las Vegas for a show. I walked into the hotel room that the company had booked for me, to find myself stepping into the biggest suite of rooms I had ever seen: a vast living room, a couple of bedrooms with a palatial en-suite bathroom, a dining room, full-size kitchen . . . I thought, *Oh my goodness, someone's messed up and given me Vince's room or Undertaker's.* I was trying to figure out how this mix-up might have arisen and thought I'd nailed it . . . My name is Galloway; Undertaker's real name is Calaway. Instead of enjoying this giant, luxurious suite, I sat in a panic waiting for Undertaker to beat at the door, having come from some broom closet he had been misallocated and demanding to know why I was in his room. I spent the whole night worrying that I was in the wrong room. I hardly dared unpack. In retrospect, I wonder if it was a case of Johnny Laurinaitis saying "Give him a cool room so he gets a taste of how it could be . . ."

My original crew was an interesting group—Dave Taylor, Luke Gallows (who wrestled as Festus at the time), Mike Knox, and John "Bradshaw" Layfield or JBL, as he was known—all notorious for being able to put away alcohol. Straight from university, and Scottish, I had no problem keeping up—which may have surprised them. The minimum legal drinking age in the States is twenty-one years old, so they may have assumed I had not had time to develop a tolerance. I remember JBL and Festus squaring up face-to-face, talking back and forth—JBL to Festus: "I like you because you're a barrel-chested *heel!*" At the time, Festus was the very opposite of a barrel-chested heel, but JBL was so far gone, he hadn't a clue what he was saying. I listened to the banter thinking, I can't believe this is WWE, and I'm having these crazy times with the guys I used to worship on the TV screen.

Carmel, my girlfriend from Scotland, flew out and came on the road with me. I was hiding a big secret from the more experienced wrestlers: I could not drive. I worried that if they found out, they would not keep me on the road. The tradition—another custom I was gradually taking on board—was that the young kids would drive the older wrestlers around so that the older guys could have a drink. I thought I was being clever. Carmel liked to drive and had an international license, so she could rent a car, and she would drive me from town to town, wherever the WWE schedule took me, and no one would know I couldn't drive. I paid for her to fly back and forth, which meant I was spending most of the money I made on keeping my secret.

Ultimately, I was too focused on wrestling for the relationship with Carmel to work. And it would probably have been better for my relationship with the senior wrestlers had I ridden in the car with them more often. Some would ask if I wanted a ride with them and I always said no, and they probably thought, Who is this young kid who won't drive with anybody?

Those six months on the road represented a huge learning curve, both inside and outside the ring. I learned how lucky I was to get that early break on *SmackDown*. I was more of a stopgap measure than a performer they wanted to launch with a fanfare and my own storyline. Apparently, the creative team had been planning to bring on another young talent, who had pulled out late in the day. Mr. McMahon asked the OVW setup whether there were any younger stars they could put on. My name came up. The plan was just to see how it would go. It seemed to me that my role was a hired hit man. I just rolled with the punches and had a lot of fun. Along the way I took out Brett and Brian Major (Zack Ryder and Curt Hawkins, who went on to become The Edgeheads). I got to wrestle JBL on his comeback. And I got to wrestle William

Regal, one of the most successful Brits ever, with years of incredible storylines under his belt.

Working with Dave Taylor was fun. He is phenomenal in the ring, if a bit salty at times! He and Fit Finlay sold out venues across Europe—they were two hard British wrestlers. Having Dave in my corner kind of protected me. He would tell me straight up if something was rubbish or if it worked well. He told me always to be wary. The in-ring veteran-prodigy dynamic was not without its awkwardness. Before I arrived, Dave and Paul Burchill were creating a lot of buzz as a British tag team, and there was talk about them getting a TV slot, so they were not exactly thrilled when I turned up at OVW and two weeks later made my debut in a one-on-one match. When I was brought in, their act went out. They understood it wasn't my call, and they were as nice as could be, but I remember one meeting with them and Johnny Laurinaitis when Dave stood, upset, and in front of Batista and Undertaker and a lot of other top guys, he said he and Paul had been getting a great reaction on the road and he couldn't understand why they were being dropped.

I had grown up wrestling with my tight circle of buddies in the UK, where we'd basically taught ourselves and pushed each other hard to improve in a sort of musketeer spirit of brotherhood. At that age, the goal was to get to a level where we could enter the professional circuit. And all those wrestlers from BCW—Jack Jester, Lionheart, Wolfgang, Carmel Jacob, and Red Lightning—would go on to become big players in the British scene, with ICW in particular. Now I was signed to WWE, I found myself in a competitive, professional environment with people whose motivation was to use their wrestling skill and passion to earn serious money. There were politics to navigate. To see the raw, new kid get a break on TV was maddening for some. Television puts you on a different pay level: you get a fee per appearance, per show. I realized there were a few older guys, a bit jaded and bitter perhaps, who believed I had not paid my dues.

I felt under a lot of pressure through the winter of 2007–08 with OVW, but I made the most of being in the ring with so many experienced stars. Undertaker was "the man," the locker room leader who commanded so much respect for the shrewd way he evolved with the times. He had disappeared and reappeared in the 1990s; he was good and he was bad. He reinvented his dark Deadman character as a badass US biker version of Undertaker— feeding the appetite around the turn of the century for more realism—and then morphed back into his zombie mode, bringing layers of intrigue with him and a new arsenal of moves. I could see straightaway that for ring and life advice, he was the guy to listen to and learn from.

Taker would speak in enigmas and give me a hard time, but not in a malicious way. I was told to listen to nobody except him, so I would harass him all the time for advice. He was generous with opinions in the after-show video critiques. There is a basic ring psychology that you can be taught, but his wrestling IQ was off the scale, acquired through experience and just so much natural intuition. Sometimes it sounded like he was talking in riddles because he spoke at such an advanced level. We would all gather in a room with a monitor and rows of chairs, and I would squat near him, not wanting to miss any of his pearls of wisdom. He would talk about how to present your character in the right manner, how to let the crowd breathe and absorb a particular moment so that our storytelling had dramatic cadences. After these sessions, I would try and apply every tip and observation he shared.

"You need to stop playing a wrestler and just *be* a wrestler," he told me frankly. I was so tense, trying so hard to act the part that I came across as hammy. Instead of begging for a reaction from the crowd, he said, I should just feed off the natural energy. He was so right.

CHAPTER 10

I LIKE TO SAY
WRESTLING IS
MODERN SHAKESPEARE

Exhilarated, exhausted, but still eating, sleeping, living, and breathing wrestling, I learned the hard way on *SmackDown*. Being on the road was the school of hard knocks, all right. Ever since the hard-cam incident on my debut, I had clocked the setup of the state-of-the-art cameras and sound systems and had worked hard to improve the technical aspect of performing inside a sophisticated television bubble, where the production quality was unbelievable. Typically, there are more than seven cameras on *SmackDown*: stationary cameras, mobile cameras, some fixed for the wide shot, others for the tight frame. There is a real art in telling a story in the ring, to know where the cameras are and maximize their potential to showcase your telling tics and gestures. Guys like Undertaker conjure a dramatic nuance just from a simple smirk or grimace.

It takes a while before the technical aspect becomes instinctive. When we walk out for a match, we go out with a blank canvas. I like to say it is modern Shakespeare. We adapt and improvise as we respond to the feedback of the fans. Sometimes storylines change twenty minutes before you are going on live. Imagine an actor who had learned a script for a movie arriving on set and being told to forget the lines they'd learned, the plot had been rewritten! As a wrestler, I learned you have to be comfortable working as an improv actor, *while* doing your own often risky physical stunts, *while* keeping the crowd invested, *while* visually and vocally projecting to the correct cameras and microphones. There is a lot of pressure and responsibility. At the age of twenty-two, I found it hard to keep a cap on stress levels.

It takes time to learn all the tricks of the trade; trying and testing is the best method. When you first start, you tend to put together a match from A to Z with little room for improvisation, but that can mean you're so busy effectively remembering the choreography that there's little scope to just *be* your character. With a little more experience, your time in the ring is all about the story, not the moves. Most storylines—rivalries, vendettas, disappearances, comebacks—start with the creative team. Vince will almost certainly have an opinion. The wrestlers get a final version of the narrative arc, and we use our own repertoire of skill to build the drama with the microphone followed up by what we do in the ring, all of which is reinforced by the commentators. You learn to factor all sorts of things into your match, like the importance of producing an interesting twist or stunt just before the commercial break. You and your opponent will discuss the finish, and talk through how you might get there—what he wants to do, what you might do—and then we make it up as we go along.

A lesson I soon learned was that it was smart to get to know the camera guys. If you have a crux point in your story, a moment the match pivots on, I learned to go to them, and we'd work together to ensure they framed it well for the television audience. You can tell them to look out for a particular moment, and then focus on your face. I remember the No Holds Barred Match in July 2019, which pitted Roman Reigns and Undertaker against me and Shane McMahon at the *WWE Extreme Rules* pay-per-view from Philadelphia. I had pitched this scenario to Taker where he does his trademark hand across the throat gesture and prepares for the Tombstone move and I just rise up behind him, unseen by him, but Roman sees me and stops my kick. That's the sort of moment I would alert the camera guys to, so they could enhance the drama with their camera craft.

I knew I needed to acquire that sort of finesse. Through texts and the odd email, Sheamus, now immersed in FCW, was telling me great stories about how much he was learning from the rigorous training schedule in Tampa. It was basically like being at a wrestling college: a week timetabled with ring time, strength and conditioning sessions, promo classes, critique meetings, and the opportunity to talk to different coaches, writers, and show agents. I had been quietly pushing for a move there, and one day, while we were on the road, Johnny Laurinaitis told me that WWE was closing down the OVW facility and relocating most of the wrestlers to Florida. I was one of the lucky ones who would be transferred to FCW.

On one level, I was a tiny bit disappointed. Being taken off the network television schedules made me feel like a bit of a failure to the outside world, like I'd messed up. Shortly after I moved to Florida, it was *WrestleMania XXIV*, and some of us trainees from FCW had to take down the ring after the event, which was staged at the Citrus Bowl in Orlando. Because I had been featured so recently on TV, some fans that were still hanging around were shouting my name as I did ring crew work. It was definitely a humbling experience. To add to the crushed ego, a huge light fell from a rig above the ring and almost crushed me and Sheamus.

Realistically, however, I knew I was just too raw to continue winging it show after show on the road. I realized deep down that I needed to step back in order to step forward. I needed to be able to relax and concentrate on learning and take stock of all the incredible experiences I had just had, working alongside masters of their craft like Batista, Undertaker, JBL, Fit Finlay, and Rey Mysterio. If I had stayed in the mix with *SmackDown*, I think my career would have had an earlier ending than it did.

In the UK, I had always looked to Sheamus for advice. I trusted his assessment implicitly. Hearing all the positive things he was learning at FCW, I knew that Tampa was where I needed to be. As I had learned firsthand, there is a huge difference between wrestling on a blockbuster TV production with a live family-friendly audience, and wrestling to a crowd of beer-soaked patrons in a local community center. At FCW, the technical guidance was superb. Cameramen gave classes showing examples of the different ways Randy, John, Edge, Undertaker, all these Superstars, worked the range of cameras. Looking back to my arrival in Louisville, I realized I had gone straight on to live TV with none of that knowledge. We were signed at the same time, but OVW and FCW had offered me and Sheamus very different introductions to the business.

Going from Louisville, Kentucky, to FCW in Tampa, Florida, was like flicking from an old black-and-white movie to Technicolor. I had grown used to life in Louisville, and there was nothing I actively disliked about the place, but Florida was how I thought America was supposed to be: sunshine and palms. The place more than lived up to my expectations—perhaps a little too warm for someone from the windy west coast of Scotland, where summers are cool and winters are long, cold, and wet! Wade Barrett and I lived together in an apartment in the same sprawling South Tampa complex as Sheamus, called Camden Bayside, which had landscaped gardens, swimming pools, and holiday resort–style facilities as well as beautiful views across the bay. Reasonably priced—I was back on basic pay after coming off the TV schedule—Camden Bayside had a good atmosphere, as a couple of other aspiring WWE wrestlers lived there too.

I loved the high-tempo camaraderie as each day we went into the FCW facility, sat in classes, and learned the tools of the trade from the best trainers. With three hours of ring time three days a week, we kicked lumps out of each other and loved it. After the stress of trying to figure it out as I went along on *SmackDown*, I relished every minute of my time at FCW. It was a lively, energetic place.

Wrestling is a business where you are only as good as your last showing, and that sense of Big Brother–scale assessment started here. Every day we were judged by coaches, writers, our own peers, and, of course, key members of Vince McMahon's inner circle. I was aware of the high attrition at the WWE Developmental Centers. When I saw the caliber of the new intake at FCW, I realized that training is just the counting-sheep stage of dreaming about WWE superstardom. The ideal wrestling talent has world-class athletic abilities based on strength, flexibility, and agility, a great physique, telegenic charisma, a coachable temperament, an immense work ethic, and a strong sense of professionalism. We had all been signed because we checked some boxes and had *potential*. Some might be gargantuan in strength but weak in in-ring versatility. Others were great at projecting their personality, and loved the spotlight, but struggled with physical stamina. There could be impressive athletes with no sense of subtlety in storytelling and little wrestling IQ—the sort of intuitive know-how that tends to come from growing up as a fan from childhood. We came from all walks of life, from the independent wrestling scene, mixed martial arts, college sports programs, the military, bodybuilding, gymnastics, and the NFL—and from all over the world. Who among us would fit the criteria for global appeal by the time we were ready to graduate to the official WWE roster?

We had a great lineup of coaches to teach us the physical art of wrestling. It was interesting going through the broad-spectrum basics as taught by the WWE experts. You might be a gifted athlete, but how do you translate your abilities into a twenty-foot-by-twenty-foot ring? And how do you do that with an opponent in the ring? We went through basic footwork, how to move with another person, how to lock up and move around the ring, and how to do everything with safety in mind so that you never hurt your opponent. We'd go through the application of holds at a rudimentary level and then finesse that knowledge by considering what reactions we might add to inflicting a hold or being held in one. The emphasis was on making everything look legit and believable. The next stage was to tie your character to the physical drama we were creating in the ring, boosted by learning to speak on the mic, and to always stay "in character." At the advanced end came live events followed by skull sessions, which comprised video reviews of our matches followed by constructive critiques and an open discussion to bounce around ideas.

Tom Prichard—aka "Dr. Tom" from his stint as "Doctor of Desire" Tom Prichard of The Heavenly Bodies in Smoky Mountain Wrestling—was the consummate trainer. With his laconic Texan drawl, he had a great way of explaining the narrative aspect of wrestling and was easy to talk to. He had trained a host of Superstars, including The Rock, Edge, Shane McMahon, Kurt Angle, Dolph Ziggler, and Christian, and it was clear that if you matched him in passion for wrestling, you earned his respect. From him, I learned so much about putting a match together and the psychology behind projecting a story.

Steve Keirn, who was at the trials in Manchester and London, has been training wrestlers ever since the 1980s. There is nothing his eagle eye has not seen. He has an uncanny ability to determine what trait makes each individual different. If you have a gift, he can enhance it. He was quick to home in on my "aggression." Sheamus's too. "You've got something here and I'm going to help you bring it out," he said. A lot of people got beat up pretty badly by Drew McIntyre when I was in FCW, because Steve was trying to dial me up as high as he possibly could on the principle that it is easier to dial somebody down. We got to the point in our weekly shows where I was beating everybody up every time I was in the ring. That was the intention. Steve saw that my calling card could be being the biggest brand of badass. When it was time to dial me down, they put me with Fit Finlay, who'd been a real bruiser in his career, and if I didn't dial it down a bit, Finlay was sure to beat me up.

Under the guidance of Norman Smiley, one of the nicest guys in the business, I worked hard to improve my technical game, finessing specific holds and counter-holds and bringing out the individuality of particular moves to enhance my wrestling style. When

I pinned an opponent, for example, I naturally popped my hips and went up on my heels. My opponent would be on his back, and I'd be on mine holding his leg aloft to pin him. I'd lift my hips up, driving my shoulders and heels into the canvas with the effort, and Norman liked that. "Credible body language," he'd say. Those were the sort of compliments I collected to boost my wrestling repertoire.

Billy Kidman, who was just coming to the end of his own career in the ring and really spoke the wrestlers' language, was enormously influential in his grasp of the New Age style, a fast-paced hybrid of the more innovative independent style and classic WWE traditions. Building on Undertaker's advice to *be* a wrestler, rather than play a wrestler, I was becoming more attuned to acting naturally in front of the cameras and using them correctly. I could breathe easier in the ring, processing lessons without the immense pressure of having to apply them right away.

Every Tuesday we would stage a show in a smoky bar called Bourbon Street in New Port Richey, about an hour's drive away. We would carry our equipment in and set up our ring, which was small, sixteen feet by sixteen feet, compared to the twenty-foot-by-twenty-foot rings at the training center. The changing room was cramped and the setting far from glamorous. This was when smoking indoors was still allowed, and the crowd consisted of a mass of people drinking, smoking, and being rowdy. The aim was to give us crowd experience. Steve Keirn would film the shows and let the camera rest on any interesting characters in the audience to show us reactions. On Wednesday, we would review the shows. It would amuse us to see some of the wild personalities who had been watching us. One regular wore a mask and was hooked up to an oxygen tank. Every so often the camera would cut over and he would have removed his mask and be puffing away on a cigarette. He could have blown us all up in an instant.

John Laurinaitis turned up once to check out one of our shows, took one look at the Bourbon Street environment we were training in, and said, "No more." He shut it down immediately. I guess it didn't fit in with the shiny, family-friendly audience WWE aimed to please. Shortly afterward the training center live ring opened up for our use and we started hosting regular shows. One day each week, we'd have promo classes: we'd each have to prepare an interview and stand up and perform it in front of the other wrestlers. My verbal skills—or lack thereof—still worried me. It was definitely a box that hadn't been checked with ink yet.

As if on cue, in came Dusty Rhodes, one of the top-money acts of all time. Vince McMahon once remarked that no wrestler "personified the essence of charisma" like Dusty, who had made his wobbly physique part of his common man act. His reputation went before him as the tough white guy who could relate to fans of all races and backgrounds. He sure had the gift of gab and was adept at conveying his lovable personality in popular promos. Once Dusty started working with me, I could feel myself improving week by week. Everyone was terrified of his feedback in our weekly promo class because his approval was like gold dust. Wade Barrett and I would always try to go first and second, so we didn't have to sit with nerves bubbling up inside as we waited our turn. I would then sit and eat my chicken and rice while watching everyone else. Some gave good interviews; others gave really, really bad ones. It was always a laugh.

On Beginners' Friday, the less experienced talent got the chance to take part in matches while the more experienced among us took a day off. There are only so many falls you can take in your career, so it was good to have a day off to let my body recover. I was used to the physicality. Like rugby players taking tackles, you get used to pain early on, but I remembered my first wrestling lessons, hitting the ropes for the first time and getting sores and welts all over my back, and hitting the corners and getting even more wounds. The tightest part of the ropes is next to the corner pad, so if your timing is off, you will collect bruises in your armpits and down your ribs. Taking falls on the mat, you keep your chin tucked to prevent whiplash. I used to get headaches every day when I was training; I referred to them as "brain pain." Many years later, during the COVID-19 pandemic, I would wrestle maybe once every three weeks instead of once a week, and I felt the pain again. I was black and blue all over. I had cuts on my legs and back. Chairs didn't feel good to sit on; it absolutely freaking hurt.

All that year I had my eye on the big whiteboard in the main training room, which showed our current rankings. All the coaches would contribute to assessing us each week and then our names would move up or down the list accordingly and everyone could see who was in the Top 10. I would drop by in order to make sure I was still Number One, or, if not, see who was. I was vying for the ultimate accolade of emerging from FCW as one of the top guys with Sheamus, Eric Pérez, Joe Hennig, and TJ Wilson—all five or six years older than me.

That level still seemed a long way off.

CHAPTER 11

YOU'RE ONLY TWENTY-THREE? WHAT THE HELL!

Early in our time at FCW, Stu Sanders (soon to become known in the ring as Wade Barrett) and I tagged together. We were a big bad British team called The Empire. We entered the ring wearing duster coats emblazoned on the back with the geographical outline of the United States filled in with the Union Jack. We were a play on The Road Warriors, a tag team from the eighties also known as the Legion of Doom: Michael "Hawk" Hegstrand and Joseph "Animal" Laurinaitis (John's brother), who were essentially two tough guys in face paint who just beat people up and didn't really take much offense. The crowd loved them. In 2008, Stu and I defeated the Puerto Rican Nightmares, aka Eddie Colón and Eric Pérez, and reigned as the FCW Tag Team Champions for three months or so.

Tag team wrestling demands very different tactics to singles.

In a tag team, two wrestlers are teamed up to wrestle two other guys. Only one wrestler from each team is allowed in the ring at one time. You switch wrestlers by the outgoing wrestler touching or "tagging" the incoming wrestler. If you are a member of a tag team, the idea is to keep the fresher guy on your team on the offensive, while keeping the weaker, more worn-down guy of the opposing team in the ring by preventing him tagging his teammate. By adroit tagging on your team, and by preventing the like tagging on the opposing team, you maximize your chances of winning. A standard scenario will see the action build to the point where the tired good guy tags in the fresh good guy, who attacks the worn-down bad guy. However, truly bad guys—like Stu and me—might do something dastardly and cheat. We were masters of evil. We ground and pounded our opponents into submission. If they were lucky enough to make a tag and admit the fresher guy, they might get a little bit on us, but we'd usually still crush them.

Dusty Rhodes had other ideas for me. He told me Vince Mc-Mahon saw something in me as a singles guy. "We want to work on you to the point where you're an FCW champion," he said. "We start now." I didn't believe him. Why would Mr. McMahon know what I was doing at FCW? Surely he had more important things to worry about. Anyway, we lost the tag title in the very first show we did when they had finished building the nice new arena, and I turned to singles action.

On October 7, 2008, I entered the FCW Florida Heavyweight Championship and defeated Gabe Tuft, who competed as Tyler Reks, to make the four-way final with Sheamus, Joe Hennig, and Eric Pérez (who shortly afterward became Eric Escobar), which I lost. On March 19, 2009, I got another crack at the title against Escobar, and this time I won it. Winning the title was a pretty cool moment—it meant I was a top guy, I had checked all the boxes—and I successfully managed to defend it until June 11 of that year, when Tyler Reks wrested it from me.

I was still wearing my Glasgow Rangers–colored kilt into the ring and I hated it. The material got in the way and was too hot. But it was my visual identifier as a Scottish character in the ring, and I could lose it only if I moved back to one of the big shows like *SmackDown* or *Raw* with a new storyline. So it was a good thing for me to lose the title, a good sign. It was time to step up another rung in the business and be a leader, a wrestler entrusted with being part of the last match of the event.

When I moved to Florida, it was a big deal to me that no one knew my age. My peers among the developmental talent at FCW were all in their late twenties, or even thirty, and I didn't want anyone to know that I was just twenty-two. I didn't want to be dismissed as "the kid." I wanted to show them that I was a top guy, that I was going to be both a valuable team member and a credible leader. By the time I had turned twenty-three, I had proved my-self and it was okay to hear the astonishment. Everyone was like, "You're only twenty-three? What the hell!"

A few of us had been given the heads-up that we would probably be getting the call to appear on TV soon. So when Vince Mc-Mahon showed up one day at FCW with his right-hand men, Bruce Prichard and Kevin Dunn, WWE's head of television production who controls the technical trucks and directs the cool visuals, we figured this was effectively an audition in front of the big cheese. There was a distinctive buzz in the air as they took three seats in a row by our training ring.

Some people refer to him as Vince. Others as Mr. McMahon. I have only ever called him "sir" to his face. The first time I met him was when I had gone on the road with *SmackDown*, having had the call from Howard Finkel. I was sitting in catering, the self-service setup we have on the road, eating a mountain of chicken and rice, and knew before I saw him that he had walked in. He has such an imposing presence. Still a bodybuilder at the age of seventy-five, he's a big guy with a personality to match his frame. I remember he came over to my table and asked me how I was doing. He probably didn't understand a word I said in my thick Scottish accent, but I thanked him for having me as part of the team and told him I was excited, all the stuff I felt I should say, I guess. The whole time I was thinking he was freaking huge. *Oh my God, I am a wrestler and the company boss is so much bigger than me!*

Throughout my first year in America, I had no conversation with him other than that courteous little exchange, though I had seen him zipping all over the place. He was very hands-on with every aspect of the company back then, and he would sometimes pop into the FCW Training Center if WWE had had a TV show in Florida the night before. His studied presence by our training ring, though, was pretty intimidating. I had known since I was that young boy who first became enchanted by WWE back in the early 1990s that Vince McMahon was the man responsible for creating wrestling as we know it today. He took it out of the high school gyms and the smoky bars, and by bringing it into people's homes via cable TV and pay-per-view, he transformed it into mainstream sports entertainment and a global phenomenon.

Here he was, assessing the latest recruits, match by match. It wasn't a glamorous setting. FCW, housed in a warehouse, wasn't exactly NXT. It was just our training ring and a row of seats in the middle of the big hall. Everyone, it seemed, had matches assigned to them, *except me*.

It was just an oversight, but . . . it was a freaking worrying one.

At the last minute, Steve Keirn said, "Oh shit, I need to get Drew a match," and scrambled to get me set up with a match that would close out the session. He ended up pairing me with Alex Riley, who was maybe four years older than me. He was a nice guy, a big personality with star presence whose father was a famous sportscaster. Out of the ring, I noted he wore the strongest prescription glasses. We didn't have time to put a match together; we had to make it up as we went along. I told Alex to stick to the basics and be aggressive. This was my moment to impress Mr. McMahon. I walked out and stared the big boss down, glaring and glaring at him before I got in the ring. Mr. McMahon *was* the crowd, and I was the "bad guy." Alex and I rolled around and reached that point in the match when the bad guy—i.e., me—has had his moment and the good guy comes running back, knocking the bad guy down, and the crowd goes crazy. It was time for my opponent's comeback . . . I had worked my butt off to build up to this switch in dynamic, super-conscious of Mr. McMahon sitting right there a few feet away from me, his granite features fixed in a poker face.

Here you go, buddy, time for your comeback.

I threw Alex behind me, turned around, and braced myself for him to go crazy on me. All I saw was him lying on the floor, in a heap, out of breath.

Oh my God! Get up! Get up! Do your thing! This is your time!

"I can't breathe," he whispered. I picked him up one more time and tried to give him one more chance to catch a quick pin on me. He fell down in a heap again. Alex was clearly too exhausted to continue as planned. So I did the only logical thing I could do in that situation. I gave him a brutal kick. I picked him up, gave him my finish, and beat him. I was extremely annoyed and over-the-top in my aggression. It was not only my match that he had messed up—it was his opportunity too! I stared down Mr. McMahon and left.

I was convinced my chance had been torpedoed, but not long after Mr. McMahon's visit, five or six of us were called into one of the coach's rooms. Everyone except me was told they were going to be part of an ECW "new Superstar initiative," established specifically to introduce new talent to WWE programming.

"And Drew . . . You are going to go to *SmackDown*."

Afterward I asked Dusty privately whether this was a good thing.

"Yes," he shot back, "it is a very good thing!"

CHAPTER 12

KILLING OFF RUNWAY MAN

All the others—Sheamus, Eric Escobar, Joe Hennig, TJ Wilson—started making their live debuts through the ECW new Superstars initiative right away. A couple of months flew by and I still wasn't on *SmackDown*. One by one, I watched my buddies make their big entrances and, man, I was jealous. Everyone was starting on TV, starting on ECW, and they had got this buzz going on the internet. Fans were getting to know who they were. But I was still sitting there, twiddling my thumbs, working out in the gym, waiting to get on the show. I was mad with frustration.

Ten years or so ago, individual wrestlers that ranked as emerging talent didn't have much say in formulating their ring characters. Someone in the creative department had this idea that I was going to be Runway Man, a male model off the catwalk. I thought this idea was terrible. I had no connection to that persona! I have never cared about fashion or trends; never been obsessed with wearing a particular brand. I'll get a nice pair of sneakers, sure, but then I'll wear them until they fall off my feet. But I did not want to lose my opportunity, so I did what I needed to do in order to be ready to go and get out there under the neon lights and whirring cameras.

In The Empire tag team with Stu Sanders, I was a 265-pound brute. To play Runway Man, I had to lose forty pounds of bulk and lean up considerably. I hated the effect on my body. I became sickeningly ripped, like a human (non-blue) avatar with a sleek ponytail. For as long as I could remember I had been obsessive about building myself up; it felt so unnatural to be aiming for a more svelte silhouette. In the peak of my newly acquired male-model condition I was called in to discuss the plan with Mr. McMahon. I kept a straight face throughout, but inwardly I was thinking, This is the worst idea of all time. A successful wrestling persona is said to be your essential character amplified by ten, but there wasn't an iota of Drew Galloway in the proposed Runway Man.

Mr. McMahon asked me for my view.

"Sir, if you like it, I can make it work," I said.

I don't know if he could see that my heart wasn't in it—my poker face was really unconvincing in those days—or whether he saw something else in me, but he made the instant decision to drop the 225-pound Runway Man and let me be more . . . *myself*. From all he had seen and heard of me at FCW, I was this big, imposing, Scottish brute. That was the birth of my new character: essentially Drew Galloway with the volume turned up full.

The wait continued. I worked hard to replace the forty pounds. I have a fast metabolism, so it was easy to lose that weight but so much harder to build it back up again. For me, that process was a steep uphill battle. If I don't eat enough on an ordinary day, I drop weight fast. I have to be fastidious about eating to maintain my weight and look. So much so that I can get quite agitated if my schedule prevents me from taking food on board at regular intervals. You think I'm a mean monster in the ring? You should see me when I'm *hangry*!

And in the meantime, what was in store for me now?

Was my big break ever going to happen? Did they have plans for me?

Sure enough, it finally happened.

On August 28, 2009, I was back on *SmackDown*.

Shawn Michaels as The Heartbreak Kid was a favorite of mine when I first started following WWE. He was part of the *Smack-Down* brand setup and very hands-on with my debut. If only my teenage self in Xtreme Scottish Backyard Wrestling could have seen me then (or indeed later, when Shawn became a key mentor).

"Why don't we have Drew in the ring already?" he suggested.

Sometimes, the WWE brands would bring in "enhancement talent," a mix of developmental or local talent, to add a flash of interest to the standard roster. A typical scenario would be for a new talent to get beaten up by one of the regular Superstars. They would take up position in their ring. The Superstar would strut out doing their big TV entrance. The commentator would be announcing, "This is such-and-such, and in the ring already is Jimmy McGee from Parts Unknown." The new talent's job was to make the Superstar look good and build some momentum before the Superstar took on fellow Superstars.

Instead for my debut, Shawn's plan was to reverse this dynamic and use an established Superstar as the enhancement talent. I would be waiting in the ring when R-Truth, my opponent, showed up and did his walk-on. R-Truth is one of the most electric, charismatic personalities. He did his hip-hop and rap thing, and the crowd has always loved R-Truth—he brings a lot of energy into the ring. They would sing along to his music. He'd yell, "What's up?" They'd chant back, "What's up?" His matches were *so interactive*.

I stood there while he approached the ring in his spray-painted jeans and did his breakdance thing. People would expect to see him beat me, but as soon as he climbed through the ropes, I kicked him in the head, beat the crap out of him, and got out of there. That was the plan.

Wuh? What the hell just happened?

No one had seen that scenario before. Usually the "nobody" in the ring—i.e., me—was just there to lose. And I had beaten the stuffing out of R-Truth in a matter of seconds and walked off.

The reaction was: Who is this guy?

The following week, and for weeks afterward, I was just attacking R-Truth in every situation. Wherever he was, backstage, in the ring, I was there ready to assault "the dancing fool." I was going to ruin all the little parties he had with the crowd, because they loved him. I continued to attack Truth over the following weeks, claiming to be around to be recognized for the Superstar I was and not a party animal like R-Truth. Having the chance to work with R-Truth in such a unique way was a pretty cool reintroduction to *SmackDown*. On one show, while Charlie Haas was waiting to face R-Truth, I came to the ring to explain that R-Truth had "suffered an accident" in the backstage area, and I fooled Haas into thinking he had won the match on forfeit. Then I attacked Haas and left the ring to resounding boos. I was that arrogant young badass that people were beginning to love to hate. I was on a vicious rampage against R-Truth for no reason . . . and the commentators were helping build up the drama. *Who. Is. This. Guy?*

So I was back on the road, establishing myself as a villain with a cool new move, an underhook DDT, which became known as the Future Shock. It was a big lifestyle shift again after the settled routine at FCW. Sheamus was on *Raw*, so we crossed over on our day off to catch up. The storyline with R-Truth flared and seemed to be leading up to a good singles opportunity. Confirmation of that inkling came on September 25, 2009, in Oklahoma.

CHAPTER 13

HE REMINDS ME A LOT OF ME

BOK CENTER, TULSA, OKLAHOMA, SEPTEMBER 25, 2009

I was standing in the gorilla position, behind the curtain. I was hovering nervously, excitedly, in a dark suit and bright blue shirt, steeling myself for the moment when I would hear my cue and walk out to the ring like a badass, take the microphone, and tell the crowd how good I was, how no one had yet clocked my unlimited potential. I had been told that before I cut my promo and delivered a monologue, Mr. McMahon was going to address the crowd and say a few words. My instructions were to wait until he had said his bit, then go out and shake hands with the boss. Okey-dokey. This did not seem particularly unusual. Vince was very involved in every aspect of our shows: he would handle the rehearsals, and during the performances he would sit—as he does to this day—in the gorilla position with his headset on, directing the show.

I was behind the curtain, poised to make my entrance, watching Mr. McMahon on the monitor and marveling at the way he masterfully engages the crowd, building up a sense of anticipation, from his very first line.

"I'd like to introduce you now to a gentleman that I personally signed here on *SmackDown*."

I saw him like everyone else, the avuncular big cheese in a soft brown suit, blue shirt, and striped tie. And then I heard his words.

"He reminds me a lot of, uh . . .

"Well, he reminds me a lot of me, quite frankly.

"High intellect, a man who is extraordinarily aggressive. Handsome son of a gun as well.

"This man, ladies and gentlemen, is going to be a future World Heavyweight Champion.

"This man's attitude can be summed up with one phrase. He is simply 'badass.'

"I would imagine he doesn't appreciate Oklahoma any more than I do . . ."

Cue boos from around the stadium.

"With that in mind, let me introduce you to . . .

"From SCOTLAND, here is Drew McIntyre!"

Wow. That was pretty cool. My music hit and I was trying not to freak out. I had to remain in character, stern and scowling like this almighty badass when all I wanted to do was grin from ear to ear. What an incredible introduction! I was dazed, thinking this was totally crazy. And I have got to climb into the ring now and live up to that billing with the straight face of the newest heel in town.

I shook his hand and composed myself. It was wild. I could not hear a thing beyond my own turbulent thoughts. If the crowd had reacted with the loudest boo of all time or cheers off the decibel register, I would not have noticed. My mind was like a cartoon character bouncing around on the top of a burst hydrant of emotions.

I don't want to downplay that moment. It was amazing. The way it happened was surreal. Such a pronouncement was never made in WWE before or since.

Up to that point in my career, I had always been fortunate to get top billing, to be put in a top position. In the UK, I was always the number one guy in the independent companies. Without a formal structure to learn my craft in the UK, I managed to maneuver myself into the best work going, like the Butlin's summer camps where I could perform alongside the most savvy people in the business and learn every step in the ring on the way. It did not always feel like it at the time, but my progress was consistent. I had been signed by WWE at twenty-one, gone to the fast-track developmental center at OVW, and, within weeks, been plucked out and put on television. I came to FCW, I was an FCW Tag Champion, then FCW Heavyweight Champion. And now, back on *SmackDown*, I had been singled out by the legend that is Vince McMahon as The Chosen One. It was crazy. I registered it as a fantastic moment, but at the same time it was my "normal." Stage by stage, the sketch of my childhood dream was being colored in. Mr McMahon's Chosen One statement, as it later became known, simply moved me further up the ladder toward my goal of being WWE Champion. On the Snakes and Ladders board, this big public endorsement zoomed me up within reach of the winning position. In retrospect, I probably should have had a deeper respect for the significance of that scenario. But I had never *not* been in a prominent position, at the top of the board. So this was great, but it felt normal, on the continuum of my career to date. The speech was unexpected, but the spotlight was totally in tune with my wrestling dream.

Which is an insane thing to say, because it was not normal.

One thing I learned growing up watching WWE is that Mr. McMahon does not lie. If he had publicly announced that one day I would be the WWE Heavyweight Champion, then that's what I would be. He had written the first few sentences of my WWE story. I certainly did not project forward and think how long I would have to wait until I could fulfill Mr. McMahon's prophecy. I just thought, Okay, I am The Chosen One. *That* is my storyline.

My buddies back home flipped out.

"They're strapping the rocket on you!" said Craig.

"No pressure, then!" a few of them joked.

One or two privately thought it put a massive target on my head, but that is what being a wrestler is all about, isn't it? I took their comments literally: I was now the guy to beat. Looking at it from the mindset of the young wrestling fan I used to be, I had made it. I was marked for glory. I was on the roster of Superstars performing live on *SmackDown*; I was a character in the WWE video game, even an action figure I could add to my childhood collection. And I was soon enjoying a pretty good run. I continued putting on matches with R-Truth. The momentum built and built, culminating in my first pay-per-view event, in Newark, New Jersey, on October 4, 2009.

To feature on a pay-per-view is a huge deal. My entire wrestling life from the age of five onward had been structured around antic-ipating these festive showcase events—originally just the Big Four of *WrestleMania, Royal Rumble, SummerSlam*, and *Survivor Series*. Staging the culmination of every rivalry that had been simmering and erupting on *Raw* and *SmackDown*, they are akin to the finale of a dramatic TV show or a playoff game in sports. *WrestleMania* is obviously the biggest PPV, WWE's Super Bowl, but getting a match on the PPV stage meant my storyline with R-Truth was a big enough deal to earn top billing. There is a whole roster of talent getting matches on the weekly shows, but only a select few get that marquee PPV spot.

My own milestone moment coincided with the inaugural *Hell in a Cell* event, which was set to provide an annual stage on which the most entrenched rivalries would reach a resolution. The "cell" is a twenty-foot-high square compound constructed from steel-mesh, chain-link fencing that descends from the rafters to enclose the ring and ringside area for the headline match. Its confines induced a no-escape brutality that ratcheted up the tension between epic rivalries—and I would not fully comprehend its challenges until my own first *Hell in a Cell* match eleven years later. This event was a big deal to be part of, a super-card show filmed in front of a crowd of 12,356, with four main event matches featuring talent from *Raw*, *SmackDown*, and ECW.

R-Truth and I were the second main event match, due on right after Randy Orton vs. John Cena. Talk about tough acts to follow . . . Randy and John were such established stars, at the height of a bitter rivalry vying for the WWE Championship, and theirs was a huge match full of spectacular gimmicks. The fans went wild. Randy and John did a bunch of crazy stuff using the cell walls as they each dominated at different points of the match. It was a frenzy of body slams, DDTs, pin attempts, stepover toehold face locks, and violent brawling until Orton executed a punt kick to win the title. When they left the arena, you could sense the satisfaction and emotional exhaustion of the crowd. How the hell (in a cell) could R-Truth and I walk out into that vacuum and live up to that intensity?

To be honest, R-Truth could make a party out of nothing and

nowhere, and he danced his way into the ring and re-engaged the audience with his "What's up?" gimmick. Once he'd done his stuff, my music hit and I'm strolling out like, "Hey, everybody, yo, I'm the new guy!" The match lasted all of six minutes, during which you could have dropped a pin and heard it hit the ground. People had no idea who I was, and probably did not care; they had given their all, cheering to the insane climax of the latest twist in the tale of Randy Orton vs. John Cena.

But I cared. R-Truth twice countered my new Future Shock move, but, third-time lucky, I threw him from the top rope and followed up with the Future Shock to score the pinfall. It was my first pay-per-view. And I won.

This time I was very aware of the hard camera and everyone at home. I had a long way to go. I was still as raw as hell. I had always had confidence about my ability in the ring, but now I felt better about interviews, thanks to working with Dusty. The wrestling ring was my comfort zone. I was no longer playing a wrestler; I *was* a wrestler.

CHAPTER 14

THIS IS STEP ONE, BELIEVE ME

The Intercontinental Title, or IC, is traditionally a springboard for WWE's brightest talents, and it reached a point when the only guy standing between me and the leather and gold-plated metal belt was John Morrison. Days before the event, Morrison, a great all-round talent, had mocked my Scottishness by dressing up as a *Braveheart*-inspired William Wallace. But at the *TLC: Tables, Ladders & Chairs* event, I avenged the insult and managed to pin Morrison after a thumb to the eye to win the title, my first championship in WWE.

There it is in the record books: December 13, 2009, Drew McIntyre became the first ever Scottish Intercontinental Champion. That gave me unbelievable satisfaction. Previous IC title holders included The Ultimate Warrior, "Macho Man" Randy Savage, "Stone Cold" Steve Austin, The Rock, Triple H, Ric Flair, and plenty of others who went on to have a significant impact. To my buddies at home, it seemed an indisputable fact: with my first major singles title, I was on the cusp of greatness.

Backstage, the chairman of the company shook my hand. "I'm not going to let you down, Mr. McMahon," I said. "This is Step One. Believe me. This is just the beginning."

I was so proud to have wrestled and gotten a bona fide WWE title under my belt (so to speak). So much so, I remember the night I won it, Randy Orton told me there was a plan for us all to go to an Applebee's restaurant. He said, "You've got to wear the title belt down to Applebee's. It's tradition." I was, like, Okay Randy. I mean, it seemed I had to do it. I put on this great belt with the huge main plate showing the globe and the WWE logo and marched into Applebee's to eat out with the guys. Everyone found it hysterical. He got me good! Thank you for that, Randy! I was so embarrassed. I am Intercontinental Champion of the world and I am sitting here wearing it in public. It was wild, but I was so proud to show it off wherever I could.

What made that night extra special was that my old buddy Sheamus defeated the legendary John Cena to win the WWE Championship, making him the first Irish-born WWE Champion. I remember the two of us sitting in a hotel room together before the event, recalling how it all started for us and thinking, *Wow, this is pretty crazy—we've only just got to the US!* That's enshrined in history because Sheamus's title victory, just 166 days after his WWE debut, stands as one of the shortest times ever taken by a debutant to capture the WWE Title.

Everyone wants to be WWE Champion, but if you win the Intercontinental Championship, then you know you're the workhorse. You're good enough to carry anyone through any match, and you can go ten, fifteen minutes, half an hour, putting on a spectacular performance. It means you have checked all the boxes: athletic prowess, ring skills, storytelling, ability on the microphone, and character charisma. I know I keep using the word, but everything really was *surreal* because even as a kid I had always had a very specific image in my head of how my career would go, and it was panning out exactly as I'd daydreamed. I was following in the boot prints of Shawn Michaels and Bret Hart, who had won the WWE Intercontinental Title before winning the WWE Title.

I loved every aspect of life on Planet WWE and working with everyone, especially John Morrison, who I think was underrated, and Kofi Kingston, who had just stopped being billed "from Jamaica" and was reintroduced as from his home country of Ghana. Kofi and I had some great matches—some televised, others not—but I especially loved the non-televised matches. It was a fun period, particularly antagonizing Teddy Long, general manager of *SmackDown*. That was one of my all-time favorite storylines.

As the GM, Teddy was the show's authority figure; he put on the matches and performed as a prop in many storylines. In ours, I would use my status of being Vince's special kid to get away with everything. In real life, my visa had expired (I never did apply for dual citizenship). I had to go back to the UK to renew it, missing a week of live TV; in the ring, the storyline was that I was getting deported because of visa issues. Teddy fired me, stripped me of the title, and held a four-man tournament for the title in my absence, which Kofi Kingston won. A week later, I showed up in the ring, all swanky in a white suit, bringing a letter from Vince, which I handed to the referee, who read it out. The contents declared the title was still rightfully mine. So Kofi had gone through this whole tournament and heroically won the title by defeating Dolph Ziggler and Christian along the way—only for me, cool as a cucumber, to walk in with a letter from the boss and take the title back.

It was a crazy real life/ring life whirl because I did have to make the round-trip to the UK to sort out my visa and get back, ready to play my part. I arrived backstage and got some grief for not having a suit, which was a key part of my look for that role. No one had told me to bring one. I was just expected to have one. With the clock ticking down, I raced out to a store, hoping no one would notice I had disappeared from the building, and bought the first suit that fit, with the shirt, the shoes . . . I had to buy everything. I ended up purchasing a $1,000 white suit that I only ever wore once, that time on TV. Kaitlyn eventually turned it into a *Nightmare Before Christmas* Halloween costume, painting it black and white to transform it into a Jack "King of the Pumpkins" Skellington outfit.

That incident started my rivalry with Kofi. Meanwhile Teddy Long and I were locked in another long-term program of our own. Everything Teddy said, Mr. McMahon would overrule. On one occasion I made him go down on his knees and beg for his job. "Think about your kids, your beautiful wife . . ."

I was this brat of twenty-four, Vince's guy, just being a prick; it was really cool to be such a badass! Back then, my character had no redeeming qualities. I was just an obnoxious brat who got his own way the whole time, a 100 percent bad guy who physique-wise looked like a genetically engineered avatar.

While I was Intercontinental Champion, *SmackDown* toured Europe, and I got to hang out with my childhood hero, Bret Hart. A huge champion admired all around the word, especially in Europe—and particularly in Germany—Bret had been a super-hero for as long as I could remember. The tour schedule included several dates in Germany, and Bret was added to it and given stellar billing. His presence made the whole tour circus an incredible experience for me. I sat up every night with Bret, listening to his stories, hanging on every word of his anecdotes, the sort that stay backstage and you certainly would never hear aired in interviews. I kept thinking, If only my thirteen-year-old self could see me now! We took a picture: Bret, me, and the Intercontinental Title belt, the title he was synonymous with when I was a kid. It remains one of my favorite pictures. It was cool to get to know him and hear about the wacky stuff they got up to back in the day.

On one of these late-night occasions, I had the honor of helping his niece Natalya Neidhart carry him up to bed after he had drunk too much. Natalya's father, Jim, was Bret's brother-in-law and longtime tag team partner. That was awesome. Many years after I had spent hours wielding the tiny Bret "Hit Man" Hart action figure around my toy wrestling ring on my bedroom floor in Ayr, here I was picking up his limbs for real to get him to bed!

The feeling that life had come full circle was overwhelming. In Germany, I had no one from Scotland to share that with. I used to call home a lot and use Skype. I used Facebook to message my old buddies. I wanted to know what they were doing, what they were getting up to. I wanted to hear about the pub, about what they were watching on TV. I wanted to hear normal stuff, because my life was so abnormal, traveling all over the country, all over the world, performing everywhere, living it up like a WWE Superstar. It was just absolutely insane. Often during this period, I'd get a ride in William Regal's car (he hated my driving) and we'd reminisce about great British comedies: he was a huge fan of *Fawlty Towers*, *Blackadder*, *Still Game*, and *Are You Being Served?* I loved those journeys. That's how you learn in wrestling, traveling alongside the legends and listening to their stories. I started to look upon him as a mentor—and in 2017, it was William Regal who asked me to take that call from Triple H . . .

But I'm getting ahead of myself.

In 2010, I genuinely felt I was going to be the first British WWE World Champion. Everything seemed to be falling into place. I was undefeated. And, more importantly, I felt unstoppable. How was this happening? Could life get any better? I'd always pictured this kind of scenario, but how had it actually become reality?

CHAPTER 15

SNAKES IN THE GRASS

Little did I register during this euphoric time—although it soon became apparent—that being dubbed The Chosen One by Vince McMahon had ruffled feathers. There were a few older Superstars nearing the end of their careers in the ring who felt that they deserved any big opportunities going. Why was this young kid coming in and not only getting a lion's share of the limelight, but also being endorsed as a future World Heavyweight Champion?

When I first gleaned an undercurrent of resentment, I took it as motivation. I quietly soaked up the pressure; Mr. McMahon's speech was affirmation that I was on the right track to winning the most prestigious prize of all. His words amounted to a challenge, which was cool. That's the public face of pro wrestling, right? A world wrought with challenges, antagonisms, and rivalries. Among the wrestlers on the roster, there's a blurred line between ring names and real names. Outside the ring, too, rivalries and antagonisms exist, just as they do in any workplace. The sort of smoldering resentment that might fuel theatrics in the ring was, I later learned, aimed at me by a few in the locker room.

Those of my buddies who had expressed concern proved to be correct to some extent. As The Chosen One—a moniker the wrestling media took up and ran with—I was a target. I was too naïve to see that it made me vulnerable to envy and bitterness; but I understand that now. Imagine a typical office, where the owner of the company comes in and singles out a young employee in front of the rest of the staff and announces, "This is the future right here, this guy, not any of you. And just so as you are in no doubt, I am going live on the news tonight so everyone in the world knows." Vince McMahon never did that before, or since. Some of the guys in the locker room must have been thinking, Hey, I have been working hard for a while, paying my dues, waiting for my shot. Why is this kid getting all the attention? It never occurred to me that in the world of WWE the storyline bestowed on me from the top as The Chosen One would cause ill feeling. I hardly saw or heard any of it myself. The people who were causing trouble for me were doing so behind my back, whispering untruths or bad-mouthing me to friends in prominent positions in the company. If I did sense an element of it, I just thought, Their problem, not mine. I am not going to name names. I am long over it, and I don't let the past bother me. And I did not really care too much at the time because I had gained a lot of confidence in my ability at FCW. Of course, I didn't realize how far I still had to evolve and develop in order to become a genuine champion contender, because it requires so much more than what goes into the ring.

As far as I knew, Vince McMahon had put Undertaker in charge as my mentor and in the same conversation said the goal was to build up to a big match. I found out later that this was mooted for *WrestleMania XXVI*, which would have been amazing. (Not as good then as it would be now, with where I'm at as a performer, but it would still have been a great story.) Technically, it wouldn't have been a main event, because those are for the WWE title matches, but any match with Taker is considered a major event. At the time I was just happy to hear I would be in the Money in the Bank Ladder Match, as this was my first *WrestleMania*, and I didn't actually know that a possible match-up with Taker was the original plan. Better still, I was told in advance I would be winning the Money in the Bank match. To beat nine fellow Superstars for the coveted contract would have been a massive deal and the next logical stage for my spoiled character.

What was disappointing was that it became clear that I wasn't winning the Money in the Bank match after all—because it was "too obvious." The change of plan wasn't communicated to me or explained. It just happened, and I felt elbowed aside. In the event, Jack "The All-American American" Swagger took the honors, defeating Christian, Dolph Ziggler, Evan Bourne, Kane, Kofi Kingston, Matt Hardy, MVP, Shelton Benjamin, and me. As I've said, I'm good at blocking out negative thoughts, but in retrospect I see that episode as a bit of a double whammy for a young guy just concentrating on trying to figure out himself, his character, and his responsibility to make the most of this new high-profile position he found himself in.

Years later, I heard about the negative things that had been brought up in meetings about me, of which I was completely unaware at the time. I was twenty-four, and no paragon of virtue. I did things that did not help my case, but a few individuals were not looking out for my best interests. If I gave them a reason to disrespect me, that story might be exaggerated ten times over. I was seeing somebody at the time, and if we had a disagreement, for example, my detractors would take that and exaggerate it to ridiculous levels, which created a huge drama with no basis in truth.

Word reached the top that I was difficult when it came to putting matches together; certain people made it sound like I was insisting on getting in stuff to make me, and only me, look good, which was never true because I have always been about putting on the best match to entertain the crowd. Another accusation was that I hit people too hard in matches—which might be true—although I never injured anyone. The way I looked at it: in the ring, we are two grown men and you can take a hit. People tune in to the televised shows with a preconception about wrestling. You do not want to throw it in their face by doing stunts that look fake (a non-televised show is a different thing). I have always believed you have to make it look as real as possible. That is how I was taught. That is the British style.

At the time, it was hard to know there were a few snakes in the grass. Everyone was nice to my face. Some gave advice, but not the best. Or went to management and embellished on half-truths or things that were not true at all, that did not make me look good. I was blind to it because plenty of the older wrestlers looked out for me.

Fit Finlay, for sure. He became a valued mentor. I even lived with him and his family for a few months. That is how close we were. He helped me find myself in the ring. Fit worked for WWE in the offices behind the scenes, but he was still wrestling in the ring too. We wrestled across the world together. I learned a lot from him and he tempered my views. For example, when I envisioned the story I wanted to tell and play out in the ring, I wanted to do things in the ring that were not familiar in WWE. I wanted to introduce a freshness that would be associated with my character.

The style is different now, but back in 2009–10, I had a repertoire of indie-style moves, many of which involved using the ring itself and the ring apron as a weapon, which others in WWE weren't doing at the time. Watching WWE now, it's hard to believe that, but in 2009 you would be hard-pressed to see a lot of moves on the apron. I was trying to make that style of combat my "thing." I used to say I was using the structure of the ring as a tag team partner. I'd use the apron as a weapon to slam my opponent down as I jumped off the steps and went underneath the ring to glue him into the metal framework . . . just coming up with creative ways to use the ring and give the crowd something new.

I was getting criticized for these antics being "too much." Fit Finlay was all about helping me adapt that style and rethink actions that were unacceptable to WWE. So I compromised and tried to do unique things, but not as over-the-top as I wanted; just things that WWE had never seen before. I got a lot of push-back against that. Now it is standard stuff, everyone does it. NXT, the third WWE brand after *Raw* and *SmackDown*, helped usher in more of that independent style that put the crazier moves at the forefront. Along with a few of the other younger guys, I was certainly trying to popularize that style before it became accepted practice.

I had heeded Undertaker's word to stop playing the wrestler and just be one, but I was still tense in many areas. In the ring, I felt happy with the way I could get the job done, but come the microphone stuff, I was trying too hard to remember the words to be relaxed while delivering them. I may have looked confident, like I knew what I was doing, but I could see when watching recordings of myself that I wasn't fully invested in the meaning of what I was saying. I was too busy trying to learn the words. To the average viewer, I may have looked comfortable, but I wasn't, and that was causing a disconnect between me and the crowd. It takes a while for the crowd to accept somebody—and to put somebody straight in on top is a big ask. It demanded a lot of the crowd to accept this person who had parachuted in as if from nowhere, and it demanded a lot from the people backstage to accept me as The Chosen One. Today, the NXT format gives instant opportunities to young wrestlers, but that was not the climate back then.

Right up to mid-2010, I was happy pursuing my dream. I was a young guy on the other side of the world from my family, and my job came with all the intensity, adrenaline, and pressure of wrestling live on TV in front of huge audiences. I had always found it difficult to unwind after a show. I was not going to slip back to the hotel to sip cocoa and get a lot of sleep, because I could never switch off my brain. I enjoyed the locker-room banter, going out with the boys, having a few drinks. That is all well and good when everything is going well, but those habits take a darker turn when life does not go to plan. I had been living the dream in my WWE Superstar bubble. The bubble was about to burst.

CHAPTER 16

FROM THE CHOSEN ONE, TO ONE THAT DOESN'T GET ON TV ANYMORE

Upheaval became the theme of my life. In May 2010, I lost the Intercontinental title to Kofi Kingston at the *Over the Limit* event . . . and then my storylines dried up. I was suggesting ideas and potential angles, but no one seemed interested. I used to get regular calls and updates from management, but then I noticed they stopped too. People who had been super-nice were no longer super-nice. I learned that when you are doing well, everyone wants to talk to you; when you are not doing so well, no one wants to know you. I had no idea how to turn that situation around. From a professional standpoint, I wanted to try harder. I had been in a great position; I did not want it to turn to nothing. At the same time, outside the ring, I was going out after most shows and making bad decisions, drinking too much. I never abandoned my routine at the gym, but I was not underpinning it with good sleep and nutrition.

In the ring, I was well schooled in surviving changes in dynamic. As a heel, I could pummel someone to smithereens and dodge attacks, waiting to sense the moment when I would give the good guy his cue, and then happily let his blows rain over me if that was what the crowd desired. I could stick to a game plan but let the crowd dynamic dictate the timing. Bruises, cuts, physical blows . . . I had no problem soaking them up. But emotional knocks? They were something else altogether. In my personal life, I had little experience of heartache or of processing a trauma like serious illness or bereavement. A lot of negative things were going on, and each one built up in my mind until I started to come undone. I am good at blocking out negative things in life, but this was a time when I found it impossible to do that. Every avenue I wandered down in my mind ended up in an emotionally raw situation.

I found out that my mum, the most important person in my life, was sick. I was at Disney or some other theme-park setting with friends when we had the phone conversation. I had to sit down amid the faux-jolly noise of the amusement attractions and take in the news that she had recently had a hysterectomy and that the operation was cancer-related. We had lost her mum, my nana, to cancer when I was seventeen, so instantly my stomach plummeted faster than any theme-park roller coaster. I had to sit down. Typically, Mum, in her selfless way, insisted she was fine. She was receiving good treatment. She looked set to recover. My first instinct was to drop everything, jump on a plane, and come home to be with her. She knew that, of course, and she was adamant that she did not want me to jeopardize my job, my wrestling dream, my exciting new life in America. At her behest, my dad and brother had not told me about her initial diagnosis. That was her call, and I think they felt bad about keeping me in the dark. I could see on our regular Skype calls that she did not look well, but I had to play dumb until she was ready to tell me the full extent of it herself. And when I found out the nature of her illness, I was devastated—overwhelmed with unbearable sadness thinking of my mum going through the round of hospital visits and painful radiation treatment, while I was thousands of miles away.

That is when things started going sour.

Wrestling was the perfect escape. It must have been agony for my family in Scotland to see Mum suffer during treatment. It was hard for me too, to be several time zones away. When I woke up in Florida, she was already halfway through her day, and what did that entail? By the time it was my evening, she had already gone to bed. When I wanted to feel close to her, the five-hour time difference exacerbated the sense that I was far removed from home in Ayr. In the ring, I could block out the real world and direct my anger into my character's aggression. It was tough, even then, to try to push reality to the furthermost recess of my mind while going out to be front and center of a live TV entertainment. Reality would hit me after the show. I would always go out for a couple of drinks with the boys, but now I relied on either going out and drinking with the boys to numb the pain or drinking at home to keep reality at bay.

Meanwhile, I was going through a divorce. In July 2009, a couple of months before The Chosen One night in Oklahoma, I had become engaged to Taryn Terrell, who performed in WWE under the ring name of Tiffany. A year later we married, and a year after that we divorced. We were both young kids. It did not work out. I moved back to Tampa. The end.

It was pretty excruciating going through a divorce and all the ramifications of that on top of the anguish of worrying about Mum. Increasingly, I looked to the ring as my escape. When the bell rang, I gave it my all, and felt comfortable and assured in my performance. Outside the ring, everything continued to go wrong. Struggling as I was in my personal life, I was not in a position to be a great representative of WWE. There was no chance of management trusting me with a prominent position. Even in my hungover dazes, I could acknowledge that, and it was de-motivating. I knew I was going out way too much, and that wasn't exactly the way to deal with things, but I was still a young guy a long way from home, ill-equipped to handle these kinds of emotions.

The troubles of Drew Galloway, rather than of Drew McIntyre, were the reason that WWE couldn't keep me on an upward trajectory to being the Number One guy. No chance. Looking back, I would not have trusted myself. But living in the moment, I was incredibly frustrated, angry, and emotional. There are all these clips from the time that I see occasionally on social media and I remember my face then—hostile, vacant, fed up, at war with the world—and that is how I felt. It was obvious to everyone, not just the people back home, but backstage sometimes, and that is not a mood you want to be giving off. On one level, I was a liability; I didn't have my life together out of the ring, and I was not a person who could be trusted to represent the company all the way to the top. On another level, it gave those few who resented the opportunities I'd been given, and who might want to mess with me, license to do so, because the state I was in was written all over my face.

Workwise, I was sliding fast down a spiral of despair. I was cutting promos in the ring, and the responses from the creative team sounded like they were sending me and the viewing public a message. And it was not positive. Teddy Long, who had been my on-screen foil, said, "We're going to have to think of letting you go if you don't rediscover your original passion." My reply was 100 percent genuine—"Nobody is more passionate than me"—and that reply was probably the most genuine utterance I had ever made on TV up to that point. That *was* how I felt about wrestling, but it was not how I was able to operate as things came undone outside the ring.

I was wrestling under a thick blanket of emotion, but I didn't open up to anyone about it. I was not helping myself by drinking too much. The people who had been out to get me all piled in on top of each other. Inevitably, obviously, the process of getting divorced from a fellow WWE performer did not help. A few incidents along the way were exaggerated. I always say, "Don't believe everything you read on the internet, because I have firsthand intimate experience of things going online that are absolutely not true." But negatives stick, even false reports. To my dismay, I went from being "The Chosen One" to "One That Doesn't Get on TV Anymore."

And talking to my mum every day on Skype and seeing how brave she was, how sick she was despite her reassurances that she was fine . . . that really sent me overboard. She was adamant that she would be upset if I came home. She didn't want to mess up any storylines I might be involved in. She wanted me to pursue my dream and become a WWE Champion. She had such belief in me. She was so positive; she wanted me to be happy in the world I'd always set my heart on. We talked on the phone and we talked with my dad, the three of us, on Skype all the time, and I could see where she was at. It really sucked.

We had never been in the habit of saying "I love you" on the phone. During this period when she first became ill, I made a point of saying it to her. "It's a given!" she would say cheerfully. "We know that!" "That may be," I explained, "but I want to say it." After that conversation, it became the way we ended all our phone or Skype calls, and I am glad it did. We had always had a special unspoken bond, but I wanted to reinforce that from my new home thousands of miles away. She was such a strong woman. She overcame everything, and I know she maintained that toughness because she thought it would make the situation easier for us all to deal with.

Eventually Mum was given the all clear, or at least told she was in remission. After my fears for her throughout her treatment, the relief was immeasurable . . . but by then, the damage to my state of mind was too far gone. I had been spiraling down, down, down, and by this point, I had plummeted as far as it was possible to crash. I was out all the time. I was coming to work without a care for the job. I was in a shitty mood: sometimes arguing with people, sometimes acting out in a match and doing something I wasn't supposed to do. I was not actively hostile to my locker-room peers; I was simply not in a good place. And the drinking to self-medicate continued. Wrestling was no longer the most important thing in my life. I could not bear to think of my mum's ordeal; I could not imagine the prospect of losing her. I started coasting at work, just getting by, not putting my heart and soul into wrestling.

Did I care about my career? I was incredibly frustrated. I felt I should be working into a top spot, and I was aware that some of the older generation weren't going to be there for much longer. I was angry and telling anyone who would listen, "You have to put me in with these guys, who I could learn from, before they are gone, or I can't teach the next generation."

No one within WWE knew about my mum's condition. I kept that quiet. WWE is a family-friendly company; in retrospect, I realize I could have asked for time off to go home to Scotland. But Mum did not want that. And I myself did not realize that my underlying emotional turmoil was the reason why I was so out of control. It took a very long time for me to learn how to deal with the sadness and the fear of losing her. In the meantime, my world came completely undone. I drank. I made excuses. I blamed everyone else. I blamed creative. I blamed management. Like, what is everyone doing? How is it that this guy, me, is not on top of the world?

I would drink after the shows because that's what a lot of wrestlers do, but then when I was at home, I would have to drink on my days off too, because you have to see your buddies when you're home, and that can turn into four, five, six, seven days a week that you're going out. I numbed myself and tried to pretend that what was going on at work, and what was going on in my personal life at home in Scotland, were not real.

CHAPTER 17

THE BEST OF TIMES, THE WORST OF TIMES

In the spring of 2011, Mum, Dad, and John flew out for *Wrestle-Mania XXVII* in Atlanta. It was the first time they had managed to visit me in America, and the plan was to go on a leisurely family road trip. Scotland, even the entirety of the United Kingdom, is so small that you can practically drive from one end of the country to the other within a day, but we were off on a *National Lampoon's Vacation*–style adventure. Mum and Dad were keen to see what I did, where I lived, and get a feel for my WWE lifestyle. By that stage, work had just become work to me. It was what paid the money. I could never have imagined not being at WWE, but I guess I had started to look on it less as a place to fulfill my dreams and more as a place where I worked, and where I would work until I retired. I still enjoyed wrestling, but I was jaded. I lacked the passion or the depths of motivation that had once led me to leave home. To have my family come over and rent a big SUV for our trip from Atlanta, Georgia, to New Orleans, Louisiana, was so exciting, liberating.

For *WrestleMania* week in Atlanta, I put them up in the W Hotel, which was one of the nicer, trendy hotels I used to like to stay in. I wanted them to be in the cool downtown area. On the first night I even made them go to the nightclubs that all the hipsters hang out in, and we took a picture of us all sitting there with our champagne surrounded by the trendy clientele. Mum, Dad, and my brother, John, sitting in the corner, with rap music blaring, the lights low . . . They were used to the small pubs of Scotland; I wanted them to experience the very different side of life I had seen in America.

In a quiet moment at the hotel, Mum told me the devastating news that the cancer had returned. She asked my dad to give us some time alone, and we then had a conversation about it in their room. I was devastated—she seemed so happy and well in spirit—but it made me feel even more determined for us to enjoy every minute of this trip. We went out to a lot of great specialty restaurants. Wherever we went, I encouraged them to try different food. We went to a hibachi place where they cooked the food on a sizzling metal grill in front of you, with the chef doing all his tricks with fire and knives. I encouraged my dad to order some sushi—which I'd never eaten until I came to America. "Och, raw fish, that's weird," he said. "I don't want to eat that. I catch my own fish, gut my fish, cook my fish—I'm not eating that sushi crap." I turned away for a minute and heard a sudden gasp from him. When I turned to address him, his face was bright red and sweaty. In front of him was an empty bowl of wasabi!

We had so much fun together. When Mum and Dad went to bed, I would take my brother out to some cool bars. We came across wild places, just by chance. One underground bar we found had an octagon at its center with a mixed martial arts tournament in progress: men fighting, women fighting, little people fighting . . . What was the chance of stumbling over something as crazy as this anywhere else?

Then came the *WrestleMania* events. It can be quite chaotic having family at an event, because the arenas are huge. To get from backstage to the friends and family box means walking for miles from one end of a stadium to the other, around the perimeter corridors. At the very end of the televised show, my family came backstage, largely because Mum was in a wheelchair as a result of her ataxia and we could go out the back door and find the car right there. I remember Vince McMahon walked up and introduced himself. I could see Dad frantically trying to find the right words . . . He was talking to *Mr. McMahon*! He made the point that this was all I had ever wanted to do and that he and Mum were very happy to see me living my dream.

And then we were off on our road trip, driving for hours and hours in a straight line with few turns across the Deep South of America. When we finally got to New Orleans, we spent a few days visiting some of the city's historical stuff and immersed ourselves in the local culture. We went to a speakeasy and a badass dueling piano bar where you gave a tip and suggested a song and they would play it on the piano. You could ask them for literally any tune from any musical genre—country, rock, pop, rap—and the pianist could just tickle away on the ivories. On the last night we went to Bourbon Street in the French Quarter, home of the legendary hurricane cocktail. Mixed with two types of rum, fruit juice, syrup, and grenadine, and served in huge glasses shaped like old-fashioned hurricane lamps, the signature drinks are the strongest stuff ever. My limit was three; Mum got to three no problem. That was a cool end to an unforgettable trip for the four of us.

Soon after she returned home, she began chemotherapy. Her health truly started to decline. This time it was clear the long-term prognosis was not good. The next year or so was tough as hell on all of the family. I was already completely off the rails outside the ring, but not being able to be with her sent me overboard. "Don't you dare come over," she would say. "You stay there and keep chasing your dream." It seemed such a cruel blow to have cancer on top of ataxia, but she never seemed remotely upset or down when we chatted. She made it sound like it was the latest little challenge she had to get through.

The next time I had a few days off, I flew home. It was the only time I recall seeing her visibly upset. She had lost her hair, which bothered her a lot. She was aware how much of a shock it would be for me to see her, and that troubled her. I remember Craig, Traps, and Lee coming round to visit, and leaping in there to amuse Mum. Lee, being a hairdresser, messing with the spare wig, acting daft, making her laugh. It was like old times with my buddies being around, being the life and soul and entertaining Mum. It made her smile, but it hurt me to see that underneath her good humor, she was distressed in a way I had never witnessed before.

We had some great times together, thankfully, and I returned to the States.

At the end of October 2012, I came home for a long-planned visit. I couldn't wait to spend time with my family and catch up with friends. I knew Mum's health was up and down, and that she'd been through some dips, but as far as I knew when I flew home that day, she was stable, and I imagined having fun with her at home. She was always such good company. At Glasgow Airport, I was surprised to be met by my dad and brother. That was unusual. Before we left Arrivals, they took me to a café and told me we had to go straight to the hospital. Things were not looking particularly good, Dad said. The doctor wanted to talk to all the family together.

I had caught a night flight and was pretty jet-lagged, but I had imagined I'd be sleeping that off in the comfort of being home with my family. I'd had absolutely no sense of anticipation that this was the end of life as I had always known it.

We drove straight to the hospital, and I was shocked to see Mum lying in bed, heavily medicated. Mum's sister Beverley, my aunt, was there with my uncle and my cousin Michelle. A doctor came in and quietly told us he thought she had three days or so, maybe fewer. And then she would be gone. I had flown home just thinking I was visiting everybody, relaxing at home with Mum and Dad, catching up with all the family news, and within hours of arriving I was informed that in seventy-two hours' time Mum would be gone.

Shock, anger, outrage, pain. Terrible news affects everyone differently. As the medical team warned us to prepare ourselves to say our goodbyes, I was consumed with anger. I had images of myself picking up a chair and throwing it through the window. Everything I looked at in the room I was assessing in terms of how I was going to destroy it. I could not begin to process the implications of the doctor's words. All I could think of was destroying every physical object in the room. I guess it was the manifestation of a lot of emotions crashing about. I had to steel myself not to physically wreck the room and cause a scene.

There followed a couple of hazy days in the hospital by her bedside. She was obviously in pain, and that made me so angry. I would rush to speak to the nurses, who would try to tend to her, but every action they attempted to make her more comfortable looked to me like they were hurting her. She was so fragile. One night we all stayed in her room, dozing on and off. At one stage I woke up and Mum was awake. We locked eyes. She was unable to say anything. I was talking out loud about how I felt about her. I could see she was upset at not being able to respond. I just did all the talking and told her how much I loved her. I will always be glad we had that moment. Everyone else in the room was asleep, and it was just the two of us in that little bubble of time.

It was a tough couple of days.

And then she was gone. She was only fifty-one.

I had lost my mother. And it fucking sucked.

I do not remember what happened immediately after she passed. I know I was pretty messed up. I stayed awake all of the night before the cremation, sharing stories and remembering so many good times with friends, and then I lay down next to her casket and slept there to keep her close for as long as I could. For her funeral service, we did not want everyone dressed in black. She was a fun, joyful, positive person. We organized a service that would honor her spirit rather than be a mournful occasion. I wanted to do something special. I arranged for a horse and chariot to carry Mum so I could make sure her last ride was fit for a queen.

Mum's passing hit us all hard. Of course it did. She was the magical presence at home that made everything good for us. She inspired me to go out and seize my opportunity in the world. It was a struggle to pack my bag and get back to America. The home I was leaving would forever have an emptiness at its heart. Dad encouraged me to fly back to my life in WWE.

"It's what your mum would have wanted," he said. "She is always with you. What's done is done. You need to move on because you know she is always going to be with you. She's at every match, and you carry her within wherever you go."

CHAPTER 18

TOO MUCH ROCK 'N' ROLL

And so I returned. How do you process the emotions of losing someone you are incredibly close to? Someone who has not just given you unconditional love and support, without fuss, without sentiment, but someone who has always been an inspiration in how to live life. I always had so much fun with Mum. I felt so loved, so understood. I certainly did not know how I could go forward without her. I bottled up my emotions; I tried to be strong, but I felt angry about losing her, the family powerhouse of positive thinking. A lot of elements combined to fill me with fury and aggression—the pressure of having a lot put on my head at a young age in WWE, the fact that the future champion I'd been so publicly proclaimed to be had not come to pass, the fact that I'd been pushed down the show, the fact that I had been fulfilling a grueling schedule when my mum was ill thousands of miles away from me. The fact that I was no longer considered a singles guy but playing air guitar in a comedy act . . .

A couple of months before I came home for what turned out to my mother's final few days, I was told I was to be a member of a comedy "rock band," 3MB, with Jinder Mahal and Heath Slater. I was not as angry as I might have been had the idea been posited a year prior, because I had been doing nothing for so long. I was not involved in any great storylines. I had been on *Superstars*, one of WWE's secondary programs at the time, just floating, but otherwise I seemed invisible. Simply being factored into a new plan sounded exciting, especially in the way it was presented to us. Jinder and Heath were both great talents. When I'd moved back to Tampa, a group of us had had a night out. Jinder and I ended up chatting and bonding. We had a lot in common. We were pretty much the same age, we had both moved to America to wrestle; we were instantly best friends. Neither of us had had the chance to grow up because we had been at university and then gone straight into touring the world with WWE.

And our careers seemed to be dwindling.

I am told the writers drew straws about who was going to tell me about my role in 3MB because they were worried I would flip out and attack whoever broke the news. One writer walked me to the stands and sat me down far away from everyone before explaining the character, and I was fine with it. I thought, Okay, this is an opportunity to show a different side to my personality. More importantly, I had been asking to be involved in a storyline for a long time. With 3MB, I had a storyline, and that was all I cared about. We were members of a world-famous fake rock band that never played a song. It was very lighthearted, not least because none of us knew how to play an instrument. Everyone seemed invested in the gimmick, all the way to the top. In the locker room earlier that day, Jinder had heard Heath say that Vince had given him his own band. Everyone was guessing who was going to be in it—Dean Ambrose? Curt Hawkins? Fandango, who was Johnny Curtis at the time? Jinder said as a complete joke, "You watch, I'll be in the band." Bumping into Scot Armstrong, the producer, who had the card for that night's show, Jinder asked what he was down for in the show. Scot went, "Uh, Heath Slater with Drew McIntyre and Jinder Mahal versus Brodus Clay . . ."

Oh no, he thought. I'm in the band.

No one seemed to be aware that I needed wrist surgery at the time. I had landed badly a few months beforehand while wrestling Ryback and broken my left wrist. He was figuring out a character and practicing his act on non-televised shows, and I was basically helping him develop it in the ring. He pushed me up in the air, ready for me to take a belly fall, which I should have taken horizontally, but for some reason I kind of tilted down like a dart and landed with my thumb pointing backward. I felt pain at the time but not to the extent that I stopped working out or deadlifting. Eventually I decided it did not feel right, so I saw the doctor. He pushed my thumb and hand around in different directions, and it was "Ouch" or "Ow" with everything he did. An X-ray revealed a break, so I wore a cast and wrestled in it for a while. I didn't take time off or have surgery. In a house show, I accidentally punched my good buddy Ted DiBiase Jr. with the cast. I'm right-handed and I was giving him right-handed punches, and I don't know why, because I never throw left-handed punches, but I decided to throw a left-handed punch, but I had the cast on. I knocked him silly.

By the time 3MB started, the doctor said I should have an MRI scan because the break wasn't healing. I had been wrestling and working out on it, so of course it wasn't mending! The MRI revealed I needed surgery. This was after 3MB had started. I had surgery to put a screw in my wrist and was back on TV with 3MB and a big cast.

It was not like 3MB were suddenly going to be The Shield—WWE's mercenary trio of Dean Ambrose, Roman Reigns, and Seth Rollins—but whatever vision management may have had for us initially was greatly affected when I had to have that wrist surgery and could not be involved in physical combat for about six months, right at the start of the gimmick. The plan had been for me to be "the heater"—the guy who beats people up—but I was just the cheerleader until my wrist had healed and could tolerate physical work again.

But all three of us threw ourselves into it. It was the most fun I had had in a long time. I wore a headband and old leather trousers. I have always liked Guns N' Roses and Black Sabbath, and I got to portray that side of me in the ring. Working with Jinder and Heath was entertaining. For Jinder and me, it was a chance to step out of our serious foreign heel characters. Our role was to smile, play air guitar, dance. The first time we were on, no one had communicated to us that they expected us to be playing air guitar. We just did our own thing, dancing around. When we got back to the gorilla position, we got yelled at, so we actually set up formal air guitar practice in the FCW Training Center. Head trainer Bill DeMott gave us the big room and said he was there if we needed anything, and the three of us choreographed some air guitaring!

In 2012, Tout, a social networking site, had come out. WWE encouraged us to make Tout microblogs—short video clips that they would show on *Raw*. We had some crazy skits. There was one where we set out to get 3MB tattoos on our butts, but we ended up messing up, because that's what 3MB did, and I got MP3 and Jinder got 3GB. We would grab Dustin, the social media guy, to film us wherever we were—New York, New Orleans, etc. In Nashville, we crashed a genuine band on stage mid-performance. We were expecting the crowd to boo us, but being Nashville, the music fans were all like, "Give them a chance. Let's see what they got!" But the security guards showed us handcuffs and we got off the stage.

Funnily enough, people still talk about how popular 3MB were. As an act, we held our own. My buddies in Scotland like Wolfgang and Jack Jester would say that Drew in 3MB was the Drew they knew from the clubs and Glasgow!

Did we live up to that rock-star lifestyle outside of the ring? Oh yeah, and worse. In terms of living the life, I think I put a lot of bands to shame at times, which is not something I am exactly proud to admit. On the road, I acted like a legit rock star, but that was wrong: I was a WWE Superstar, and my priority should have been training, watching what I ate, and taking care of myself. Instead I would drink, sleep in, and then try to work out with a hangover. The boundaries between my ring character and myself got a little blurred, so to speak. I had come to WWE to be a major player, not a bit-part performer dressing up one week in Union Jacks, another week as a Rhinestone Cowboy. In my heart, I still wanted to be that top singles guy. But I was clearly considered now, at best, a mid-card player. I couldn't see a way out of 3MB.

Thank goodness I was with Heath and Jinder. We all kept an eye on each other. We are genuine friends, more like relatives. And they looked after me during that time. They could see I was in a tough spot with everything that had been going on. If I was set on going out and drinking a lot, Jinder and Heath would come out with me. They were happy to go out for a few beers too, but it was often more to make sure that I was okay. If I was going to go down the path of getting drunk, they would go down with me to make sure I did not go too far. Once, on tour in South America, I was up all night at the hotel in a very self-destructive mood; Jinder stayed and sat with me all night to make sure I was okay.

On TV, in 3MB, we were getting beat the whole time. We played our air guitar, we'd do a little comedy, they'd bring someone in to beat us up, the crowd would cheer . . . That was how it worked, on repeat. Each time my dream took another hit. There was no question that from a professional standpoint, I had gone from being a potential leading man, a James Bond figure, to the comedy sidekick, the butt of every joke who loses every match. I would try and position myself as best I could. Thankfully, Heath was the entertaining one. He would do the talking. Jinder would do whatever he was asked because he is such a nice guy. Even though I was in a comedy group that lost all the time and could hardly look any worse, I had not lost all self-respect. I still resisted certain suggestions I did not like. I was still conscious of presenting myself the best way I could on TV.

I still had my supporters. I remember before 3MB when I was on *WWE Superstars* against Chris Masters, my childhood hero Bret Hart put out a criticism on Twitter of how I was being used: *I honestly can't believe that the best way 2 utilize a talent like Drew McIntyre is 2 waste him on Superstars. Whose genius is that? Idiot!*

Little interventions like that meant a lot. Some of the agents, and some of my fellow wrestlers, would say they couldn't understand why they were not doing more with me. I didn't look as good as I could and should, because I wasn't eating and training the way I should. But I had always trained hard. People would say, "You're a big guy, you look good. You're so good in the ring, they should be doing more with you."

That was the general consensus I'd hear from people who were in management, but not from those in the top, top positions. Superstars like Rey Mysterio told Vince they would like to work with me. The wrestler Christian also went to Vince with well-thought-out ideas of how he wanted to put together a story with me. They could see I represented potential for some great rivalries. I used to speak to Rowdy Roddy Piper a lot on the telephone. He was always bubbling over with ideas, and it would have been such a natural story: Rowdy Roddy Piper, from Canada but with Scottish ancestry that entitles him to wear the kilt and play the bagpipes. He was a huge name when I was growing up, battling in the first *WrestleMania*s with Hulk Hogan and co. Roddy also approached Vince to pitch an idea for the two of us, but his plans were shot down. I appreciated all these people, all these legends, trying to make something happen. They still saw something in me, even though management may have had some buyer's remorse. Yet it was a demonstration of the value of their investment in me that people were still looking at trying to make something happen.

Rowdy Roddy Piper was generous in giving his advice. At *WrestleMania* in 2011, he and his son Colt came to my hotel room, where I was with my brother, so he could watch one of my matches to critique my performance. I was pitched against Rey Mysterio from *SmackDown*, the match that prompted Rey to tell Vince that he'd like to do a story with me and get shot down. Roddy was giving me advice. His son and I were watching him get animated—he was a very animated guy—as he told me what I should be doing character-wise, things to think about, how to approach things. I looked over and saw my frickin' brother had slumped asleep on the chair because he had drunk too much. I screamed at him to wake up. There was Rowdy Roddy Piper, in our hotel room, watching my match with his son, while my brother, a huge wrestling fan, had got himself too drunk to hear all this top advice and comments from a legend—stuff that money can't buy!

There were interludes of fun, but there was no denying that I was in a funk. I was on the road all the time, traveling a lot, living out of hotels. The job was, is, nonstop. And when I was home, I continued the cycle of going out too much. I remember coming into work one day, hungover but also genuinely sick with food poisoning or a nasty stomach bug. I just lay down in the training room, feeling like death, my clothes reeking of stale alcohol. I had come in to see the doctor, but Jinder—always looking out for me—saw me crashed out, stinking up the place, and said I had to leave. Lying slumped in a rancid heap like a tramp amid the bustle of the training room was not a good look for a professional wrestler. I was lost, and I did not see at the time that it was impossible for me to activate the reset button within the machine of WWE. There was no way I could have found myself within the system. I was just in this depressed haze.

What changed the course of my life?

My wife. She 100 percent changed everything. Without Kaitlyn, I would not be the man I am today. And I would not be Drew McIntyre, World Heavyweight Champion.

CHAPTER 19

ENTER KAITLYN

I met Kaitlyn about a week after my birthday in June 2013, and that was for a reason. I was out of control, a wild child, living with Sheamus, which was a recipe for disaster! I needed to find someone to help me realize that if I focused all my energy into wrestling, I could do whatever I wanted. Everyone in life looks for a soul mate, don't they? If you're on your own, you just do what you like, and you may not make the right choices. You need a yin to balance a yang. Kaitlyn is my yang. I believe the way we met was heaven sent; it was my mother bringing her into my life. I am not conventionally religious, but I do believe in the power and energy of those who have passed on. I know Mum is my guardian angel who directed me onto the right path when I was veering off kilter. And that is what happened when the beautiful woman who was to become my wife walked into my life.

Thanks to Kaitlyn, I am much, much more balanced and level-headed. She has been a calming, stabilizing influence. In many ways it was ridiculous that I had reached the age of twenty-eight and still had so much growing up to do. At the academy, I was told what to do and where to be. Ditto, at university. From the age of twenty-two, my life in WWE was rigorously scheduled by a whole department of planners and Talent Relations officials. I was a boy who had never learned to take responsibility as an adult.

The irony was that Kaitlyn was twenty-one when we met, still a second-year student in college, studying for a bachelor's degree in Biology at the University of South Florida. Working part-time to pay for schooling and for the rent on her apartment, she was practical, sensible, and clearly had her head screwed on. She hates me telling the story of our first meeting, as it's not the most romantic, but we met in a bar, like a lot of people do. MacDinton's in Tampa. Sheamus and I had been at John Cena's house to watch the Stanley Cup—the Boston Bruins against the Chicago Blackhawks—and on the way home we ended up going downtown for a few beers. Kaitlyn was with a girlfriend, Angelica, and she approached us because she thought she recognized us from Powerhouse gym, where she worked the front desk or watched kids in the kids' club while members worked out. It was a small, private, exclusive gym and many of the members were professional athletes in Tampa. And she was right—Sheamus and I had worked out at Powerhouse (and Sheamus is pretty hard to mistake!).

She had no idea we were wrestlers. In fact, she had zero awareness of the wrestling industry. The bar was very empty and so it was natural for us to settle into a chat. We were just a group of four normal, down-to-earth people hanging out. Kaitlyn remembers trying to engage me in conversation, but I was unforthcoming—shy I guess—and she thought I didn't like her. She ended up chatting away to Sheamus and to some other guys who went to her school.

For some reason I just *knew* I had to talk to her. I felt an immediate connection. I wasn't one to go up to girls and get their phone numbers, but by the end of the night, I knew I *had* to get her number. It wasn't until we were standing outside, saying goodbyes, that I saw her walk away across the parking lot. I forced myself to bite the bullet and walk after her and ask her for her number. She gave it to me, but looked completely taken aback because she thought I'd given her the brush-off earlier on.

Kaitlyn came into my life when I was spiraling down toward the inevitable end of my WWE career. I was drinking too much, having long nights out. I wasn't motivated about being in 3MB, I could no longer take my career seriously. My main strength had always been my wrestling, and the only physical thing I did in the ring was strum my air guitar. I didn't even have the chance to talk as my ridiculous, over-the-top 3MB character, so I felt mute. All that experience of working out how to best tell a compelling story in the ring and how to deliver challenges to rivals over the microphone was in cold storage.

Mostly, though, I just missed Mum being in the world. It was less than a year since we had lost her, and like the rest of the family, I was just crushed.

On our first date, we went for dinner like a normal night out. I probably should have dropped her off afterward and said thank you for the night. But then I thought I'd be cool and take her on to a bar. We went to the bar, that's fine. But then after closing time, I knew a bar that would still be open. I thought, Ooh, she will be so impressed if I take her to this after-hours place. That's what my mind was like at the time, I had a completely warped sense of reality. I was so used to drinking and drinking, it was just a habit. I took her to this grim, after-hours place, and I remember it was just . . . aargh, there were just not nice people there. The manager, a good guy, always looked after me. He let me lead Kaitlyn up on the stage, and there were these two lawn chairs set up like thrones. We sat in them, and I looked at her and said, "Sorry, babe, we're the king and the queen of the after hours"—thinking she would be so impressed.

Aaargh, such an idiot!

I don't know why Kaitlyn put up with me. But she stuck around, and you know there were a lot of things I'm not exactly proud of during that time—just the amount I was going out and drinking, etc.—but she saw something good in me, and believed in me. We had quite a bit in common. We both grew up with very influential and inspiring women to learn from (Kaitlyn and her sister were raised by their mom after her parents divorced, though she has always had a good relationship with her father). We both spent childhoods in small towns without much exposure to diversity or culture (she grew up in a country town in West Virginia before moving with her mom to Florida); and we both had to learn how to adapt and make our own path in a new place, Tampa, at an early age.

I found it refreshing that she had no interest in wrestling. She had no idea what being a wrestler even meant. Kaitlyn represented life outside the bubble. When I told her I was a wrestler, she switched on the TV a few times to see me and get the measure of what the wrestling business was all about. Once, sitting with her mom on the sofa, she pointed to me and said to her that was the guy she was seeing . . . It was 3MB, so they had a laugh.

We were kind of inseparable almost from the start, living with Sheamus for a year. Everything about the relationship was easy. Kaitlyn said it was as though she had known Sheamus and me in a past life, as if we had already known each other for a thousand years. We just clicked. When I was on the road, Sheamus and Kaitlyn easily became great friends. He had time off for an injury, and she would help with shopping and daily tasks when I was away. I wasn't recognized around town as much as Sheamus, but when I invited Kaitlyn to accompany me on the road, I would get a lot of attention from fans, and that was a shock to her. She would tell me she could feel the death glares and tension from female fans in the airport. At times, they even blatantly and loudly hurled insults at her. Being so young, that hurt, and I understood how it might make her feel insecure. She learned to brush it off, but it wasn't an easy thing to deal with. She has always been open-minded about my career. It's all she's ever known me to do, and hearing Sheamus and me talk, she was learning more about the industry the longer we were together.

There was one area of life where we clashed at first. Kaitlyn is a homebody who prefers to stay in. I was still burning the candle at both ends. She came from a family who never drank, and we met when she had only just reached the US minimum legal drinking age of twenty-one. I explained that drinking is a central part of social gatherings in Scotland. Every time we went over to visit my family, she was shocked to see people drinking until the early hours of the morning, but just assumed it was our culture. Back at home in Tampa, I was still going out with the guys. On a couple of occasions, Kaitlyn packed my bag for me, tried to pick me up out of bed and get me in the car because I was so hungover, and then she'd drive me to the airport to make sure I got on the flight for the next WWE show.

I was going through the motions, but my heart wasn't in wrestling anymore. Going out drinking had become a habit. And I was one incident away from it becoming a tipping point.

CHAPTER 20

DREW, BAD NEWS, I'M AFRAID

Ping: *Are you okay?*

Ping: *Is everything cool?*

On June 9, 2014, Kaitlyn and I moved into our first apartment together. We were both excited about embarking on the next stage of life. For the first time since I'd lost my mum, I really felt life was coming together again. I was in such a positive place. Kaitlyn and her buddy Rita had bought a couch secondhand and a table, which Kaitlyn painted. (She likes remodeling stuff.) We'd been there for three days with a nice basic setup, our first ever place together, and I woke up late to find a bunch of concerned messages on my phone and a missed call from Mark Carrano in Talent Relations. I can't remember where Kaitlyn was, maybe at work or school that day. I turned on my laptop and checked out WWE.com, prompted by what I'd seen on the text messages. Black Friday was a well-known WWE thing. There'd be a breaking news flash—"WWE Releases THREE Superstars!"—followed by a brief sentence wishing them the best in all future endeavors. The company used to do a mass re-lease of unused or unpopular performers right after *WrestleMania*, but more recently they had started simply not renewing contracts to avoid hard feelings.

I saw a headline, "The biggest pro wrestling company in the world got a little bit smaller on Thursday." In that first dozy glance about the release of ten Superstars, I saw the name of Jinder Mahal, and so I called him and said, "Oh my goodness, I'm sorry, buddy, are you okay?" The thought had not crossed my mind that my name would also be on that list; it never occurred to me that I would be fired. I'd been at WWE so long I was blind to the possibility. It was all I knew. I'd grown up there in my twenties, and 3MB were on everything; every TV show, every live event we'd appear on in some capacity. Fifteen minutes in a main event or thirty seconds on *Raw*, we made the best of it and had a lot of fun, living like rock stars out of the ring too. My WWE career wasn't where I wanted it to be, but at least 3MB was a regular gig.

I gave Jinder the talk, "Man, it really sucks. I feel really bad."

And then I had a missed call from Carrano again. The penny hadn't dropped. I assumed he was calling to tell me I'd be on more shows on the weekend. He called again. I picked up, and sure enough he said, "Drew? Bad news, I'm afraid."

I didn't get angry on the phone. It wasn't Mark's fault. His nickname's The Heater for a reason. It's his job in Talent Relations to deliver bad news, and he sounded genuinely surprised himself. The feedback on the internet amounted to a catalogue of people expressing their shock, but I was more numb than astonished. I'd been going through the motions, wearing the leather pants and strumming my air guitar, and I hadn't been all there when I was working for a while now, but the reception for 3MB was always

good. I went through a strange turmoil of emotions. I've only recently remembered these emotions. I'm so good at banishing negative thoughts! In the version of this moment in my head for so long,
I just took the call from Mark and thought, No problem, I'm going
to take over the wrestling world and show them they've made one
hell of mistake.

But that's not quite how it happened.

Revisiting my state of mind at the time, prompted by Kaitlyn,
I realize I was more than just numb. I was angry. I was disappointed. I felt shame, like I had just proved to be not good enough
in the end. Chris Jericho asked for my response on his *Talk Is Jericho* podcast. Our exchange reveals how disoriented I was, having
had zero indication that I was set to be released. "To be honest, it
was a bit of a shock, a BIG bit of a shock," I told him. "Whatever
anyone thinks about 3MB or my wrestling and my wrestling ability, we were on everything, fulfilling a role. They felt I shouldn't
be filling it, I guess, in their opinion. And we were literally on
everything, so, yeah, to say it was a surprise is a very accurate
statement."

I was also consumed with worry about how Kaitlyn and I
would survive in the immediate future. We had just moved into
this new place, and I no longer had an income. I had to steel myself to tell my dad, because I didn't want to worry him at a time
when he was a bit all over the place himself, finding it difficult to
get over the loss of Mum. I felt scared, and totally lost, because
wrestling, and WWE, was all I'd ever wanted to do. What the hell
else could I do?

I tried not to let Kaitlyn see my fear. I didn't talk about my
anxieties. I used drink to forget about being fired, I wanted that
sort of numbness to dull the pain. She would try to talk to me,

but I shut her out emotionally. I didn't want her to worry about whether we could keep the apartment next month, in case she felt she would have to stop taking classes and work full-time to take care of us. I avoided talking to her. I'd go for a drink in the evening, which turned into a few days at a time. My phone would die. She would have no idea where I was, alive or in jail. I was in the deepest funk, and I didn't have the energy or the will to get out of it.

And it terrified the hell out of me.

After a short period of wallowing, I came to a decision: It does not end here. I'm going to figure out how I'm going to make this work. I don't know how yet, but I'm going to pick myself up and come back stronger. Wrestling had always been my passion; there were no alternative options. I wasn't qualified for a more stable job in an office or something. I woke up one morning and looked at myself hard in the mirror, and asked myself, *What would Mum do?*

At many points in my career, when I was exhausted and rundown, I would think, What would Mum do or say to support me? And the answer was always: Pick yourself up, push on, never quit, and do it all with a smile on your face. She soldiered on through life's cruel health blows with a courage that remains a touchstone of inspiration for me. She did everything in her power to help me follow my dream to WWE; she always knew I could do it.

I could see now that I did need to fall on my ass. I did need a reality check. I had to get out and find myself or give up my wrestling dream completely.

With Kaitlyn's support, I picked myself up and took control of my destiny. Sitting at the table in our new apartment, I drafted a Drew McIntyre 2.0 Mission Statement.

1. *Dominate the UK wrestling scene—and help put it on the map to the extent that dominating the UK wrestling scene really starts to mean something.* [More specifically, go to ICW, Mark Dallas's indie promotion back in Scotland that was catching fire.]

2. *Let the world know who I am—*me, myself, Drew Galloway—*as a personality.* [No more cartoons, you know what I mean? I was going to be the Bret Hart of UK wrestling.]

3. *Create some buzz on the mic.* [Speak from a place that is real in order to tell a story that feels real. This would soon become my calling card.]

4. *Create some buzz on social media.* [I may have just turned twenty-nine . . . but these Twitter fingers could still go viral.]

5. *Put your working boots on.* [I remember one of my first appearances wrestling back on the indies was at an Evolve show, and they had me going on last. Before my match, I ended up watching all the guys on the undercard. The card was stacked . . . I just had no idea. Like, Ricochet was out there making jaws drop. Roderick Strong was out there blowing people's minds. I wasn't familiar with them at all—but I sure was after that. And that's when I realized that a few slick promos wouldn't be enough. I had to be able to get in the ring with guys of that caliber and bring it.]

6. *Become the busiest guy on the planet.* [I took every booking that came my way, simple as that. Basically,

I ceased to have a life. Scotland, Australia, Germany, Denmark—you name it, I was there, grinding, getting better, projecting my name and whatever indie company I was working for.]

7. *Prove yourself outside of WWE—at a level that the people inside WWE can't ignore.* [And then re-sign with WWE, make a triumphant return, headline *Wrestle-Mania*, and win the world title.]

I wrote my list of aims and mentally locked it away, like I used to padlock my secret wrestling insider info in the briefcase and hide it at the top of the cupboard in my childhood bedroom. I was tapping back into my original love of wrestling.

My phone had blown up the day I got the release call. Everybody and their uncle was trying to book me on wrestling shows. I was miffed that Mark Dallas, the ICW promoter, was the one person who didn't message me, because I was starting to get a picture in my head. I could never orchestrate a dynamite U-turn to my status while I was still a cog in the WWE machine. It was clear that to become the person Kaitlyn believed I could be, the person WWE needed me to be to represent the company—in other words, the person I am today—I had to get out and find myself. Or I should just give wrestling up completely.

If I was going to make it back to WWE, I had to start at ICW with a nuclear mission statement—that was the plan.

For too long I'd been in my own head. I needed to show people what I could do. I was going on a strict mission to surround myself with the best in wrestling, to help wrestling in any way I could and get my message out there: We had to stamp out the crap in wrestling, because there are a lot of crappy wrestling shows going on. My comeback trail would start with a rejuvenation of the British scene. It didn't matter who I was up against. I was going out there like a man who was unrestricted.

I had been kicking ass all over the world for years. Everybody in ICW had been doing a great job holding the fort. The ICW all had day jobs, but wrestling was my job, my life, all I did, all I knew.

I messaged Mark and reprimanded him for not checking in with a booking request. "My buddy lost his job, and I wanted to give him space and make sure he was okay," he said. Then he started fishing and talking about booking me in a wrestling show. He was thinking months ahead. I was thinking weeks. I had formulated a plan in my head, I wanted to go ahead and implement it. I wanted to go home, to the place and the people my wrestling dream started with. Against incredible odds, we'd created a wrestling scene in Scotland from nothing, and if I was going to make a mission statement, the only place to do that and make an impact was with ICW in Glasgow. My drive was back. I knew that every year Mark put on an ICW show called "Shug's Hoose Party," named in his dad's honor for his birthday, and it would be in three weeks' time, on July 27.

"I'm there," I said. "And we keep it a secret from everybody. No one can know, only you, me, Kaitlyn, your wife, and the person who books my travel."

That was my starting point. Then I got on the phone and sought advice from some guys I knew who were doing well in the independent scene. There seemed to be some well-trodden paths: You stick to the WWE character that you played on TV and take it around the world and get paid a lot. You take it around the world a second time and get paid less. You find companies that want to keep using you as your WWE character and you drop to a wage that you stop at. That becomes your going rate, and then hopefully one day you get back to WWE. Discussing this with Kaitlyn, I realized this made no business sense for me. I didn't want to be that guy pigeonholed into 3MB. I wanted to show everybody what I could really do. If I was going to do this, I was going to go all the way with it. I didn't see myself as one of the guys; I saw myself as The Guy. It was up to me to make something of it because I knew that one day WWE were going to want me back. It terrified me that I had not been in a match for a long time and I'd barely cut any promos, but I was going to storm it. Social media had become such a big thing, I could take everybody on this ride with me through my online presence. Starting with Insane Championship Wrestling.

I had scripted my personal mission statement. Next I was going to make a public declaration, in the ring. That was key. I was going to be Drew Galloway, myself with the volume turned up to 10. And what I said had to be extraordinary, so much so that I was scared to start writing it.

It had to be perfect, and it was a long process. I started at home in Florida, then continued at my dad's, where I stayed for three days with the curtains and blinds closed so nobody could see me. My old buddy Craig picked me up from the airport. I had my hoodie up. Only a couple of airport security guys recognized me, but thankfully they seemed a bit old to be using the internet. We snuck into Dad's house. I spent the days just playing *Guitar Hero* with my old buddies and wrote reams of stuff, a lot of which never made it to the final script. I wanted to put myself out there in a dramatic manner, say some pretty momentous things. I was going to make it clear to everybody that I was going to take over the wrestling world and be the number one guy. I was also going to tell everybody that the world was going to know the name ICW. I was going to sound insane, but where better to do that than with Insane Championship Wrestling? In order to relaunch myself, I had to believe it, and everyone else had to believe in me too. Hunkered down secretly in my dad's house, I was working myself into a frenzy to strap a rocket on my own back.

JULY 27, 2014.

I got to the building—a nightclub that has since sadly burned down—and it was brilliantly configured for sneaking in a six-foot-five-and-a-half-inch guy of 265 pounds. I could hardly turn up at the front door, or the side door, where people might have nipped out for a cigarette, if we were going to maintain this huge surprise element. I was dropped by a taxi in a neighboring street, from where a fire exit tunnel ran under several pubs and clubs. With my heart racing, I arrived backstage, where all the wrestlers were bustling around lacing up their boots, and I just said, "Hey, guys, I'm back."

It felt good to be back.

Throughout the show, I could hear the fans' noise spike as something big happened in the ring. At one point, they went completely insane. The actors who played the old Glaswegian pensioners in *Still Game*—the famous Scottish comedy show I used to chat about in the car with William Regal—were making a special appearance. *Chewin' the Fat*, the sketch that evolved into *Still Game*, was the most-quoted TV show when I was growing up, so they were kind of cult heroes. Before they went upstairs, I'd said to Greg Hemphill, one of the two actors who I'd actually met a few years beforehand while I was at WWE, "If you overshadow me, I'll kick your ass . . ." They were getting a raucous reaction. Greg was going to get that beating! I was back in that distinctly riotous, loud British crowd dynamic, and hearing that sound from downstairs, I started worrying about following that. Was my plan, forged in the anger of being dumped by WWE, misjudged? When had I last walked out for a singles match? I had to fix my confident face on to take my turn and walk up to the curtain.

I looked in the mirror and just told myself, "This is going to go fucking awesome."

And it went fucking awesome.

Mark had set up this scenario where my old friend Jack Jester from our early wrestling days was being attacked by the New Age Kliq and there was a particular line that was the cue for the lights to go out, when I would appear as if by magic. It was a cue that came from an old wrestling video that we probably watched back in the post office training days, very much an insiders' line. It came from *WrestleMania VIII*, in 1992, as Hulk Hogan was being assaulted by Sid Justice and Papa Shango, and Bobby Heenan said: "No one can help him, he doesn't have a friend left." And The Ultimate Warrior ran to his aid. So the cue I was listening out for was "You've got no friends left!"

The lights went out in the building, you could hear a rumble in the crowd. Moving in the dark, I climbed into the ring, adrenaline exploding inside me. The lights came back on, and I yanked my hood down, puffed out my chest—and the reaction was mind-blowing.

Who would have thought fifteen hundred people could make that much noise? The rafters nearly blew off the building. Pints were being thrown in the air, people screaming. It was pandemonium. As drama, we absolutely nailed it. To this day people tell me they re-watch it on YouTube just for the goose bumps!

I felt so bad for the guys who were in the ring with me that night because I kicked the crap out of them. I think BT Gunn lost a tooth during the scene where I rescued Jack . . . I really laid into the guys. Then, evil guy that I was, I turned on my old friend Jack, kicking him in the face, throwing him off the stage through two tables, leaving him in a battered heap. By now, the room was rapt. I picked up the mic and the crowd hung on my every word. When I used to speak on WWE TV, I had to Talk. Like. This. Suddenly, I was talking the way I talk now. I was just being myself, telling jokes, announcing that I was about to do some big stuff. I was about to take over the world. The world was going to know my name and not just that, I was taking ICW with me. We were going to take over.

I was thinking: *I believe in this roster; that's why I came here first. I believe in myself. So, let's do it.*

This is what I actually said:

"My name is Drew Galloway.

"I'm the former British champion, the former Irish champion, former WWE Tag Team Champion, former WWE Intercontinental Champion, and I was the first Insane Championship Wrestling Champion.

"And hell, I'm from Scotland.

"I have something to say . . . The Commonwealth Games are down the street in Glasgow, and everyone thinks that's the cool place to be. What do you think?

"APC Glasgow is the place to be tonight. Right now is the time to be watching because history is being written right now.

"Usain Bolt! Usain Bolt! That's who the media talks about . . .

"All I wanted to do is be a professional wrestler. All I wanted to do is entertain the fans and give my family and friends something to be proud of, Scotland something to be proud of.

"I think I did an all right job so far.

"I was at a crossroads in my life recently. I looked in the mirror once I stopped in WWE and I said, 'Do you still want to do this? You've been doing this for thirteen years, you've spent seven years in WWE. Maybe you should give up? You're twenty-nine. You've got plenty of years left. You could get a regular job and have a regular life for the first time in your life.'

"I really thought this, then one morning I woke up and I looked in the mirror and I drew my hand back as far as I could and I bished myself on the face. I said, 'Screw you, Drew! Not only are you going to keep going, you're going to become the biggest and best wrestler on this planet.' I don't need the machine behind me.

"And where am I going to make this announcement? I'm going to come back home to the cra-aa-ziest people, you crazy Glaswegians, and make this announcement.

"Have you heard of Bannockburn?

"In 1314, the Scots fought the English for their freedom. We were outnumbered, three to one. They were laughing at the notion that we could possibly beat them. You could say we kicked their asses and sent them back where they came. That's 1314 . . . us going against the odds to become the biggest and the best. It represents all of you who have a dream, and you're fighting the odds. People are laughing at you because you're thinking outside the box, or you're starting a business against the odds. Say 'Up yours! 1314!' It represents Drew Galloway leading ICW again on television. That's 1314.

"This is bloody incredible. I cannot believe how this is going . . . You're part of a moment right now. I have goose bumps and I'm sweating so much. This is unbelievable.

"I've just got one or two things to say.

"Let's talk about what's 'best for business.' Best for business. What makes a professional wrestler? How tall they are. How they look. Their body. Their in-ring work. Their talking ability on the microphone. Charisma. Yes, all these things make a wonderful character, and that's what you need to be a main guy.

"Once upon a time, before this happened, Vince McMahon, the most ruthless man in the world, named me The Chosen One for a reason. I bring these attributes here. And when I use them to the best of my abilities, I am the fucking business.

"Now I'm getting rolling, I'm getting fired up, stay with me now and we'll get drunk. Now when I get drunk, oh my God, I'm an even better lover and an even better dancer. Trust me.

"So, if I'm going to be the business, let's see the business cash me a big reality check.

"Let's talk about what I just did tonight. I took out the N.A.K., the bad guys—I have a problem with them, I'll explain later. I also took out one of my best friends, Jack Jester. Trust me, I asked him to stop . . . When I was in America rising in the ranks of WWE, he was here, rising in the ranks of Scotland, and I'm sorry, but I'm not sorry whatsoever . . . he will understand when he comes to . . . that I want what he's got. I need what he's got. When I get my hands on this title, I can take ICW to the next level. I'm not a good guy, I'm not a bad guy. Drew Galloway is an entertainer and a wrestler. If I want to do that to one of my best friends, what the hell will I do to everybody else?

"I see people texting, sending videos, tweets. I said, you're part of a moment. This is a moment for professional wrestling, not just Scotland. This is going to go across the world and I want you to tell everybody—tell the people in the street, tell your sisters, tell them to tell the dogs to tell the cats, tell their cousins . . . I don't care.

Put it out there: right now, we're taking a stand for professional wrestling. It doesn't have to be the machine. I'm planning to get it to the next level. I'm Drew Galloway. Tell them I'm coming. Tell them ICW is coming and tell them Hell is coming with us.

"World, look into my eyes. When you see me on a show, when you see these fans, you know you've got the best in the damn world. We are ICW and you are going to know our name. Here we, here we, here we fucking go!"

It was suitably "insane," one of the top five moments in my entire career. And it went viral. It was just an explosion from the get-go. The whole riotous, foot-stomping cheering scene.

And Dad of course was in tears. I was back!

I heard that WWE Hall of Famer Mick Foley saw the promo and messaged Triple H: "Hunter, I know he just left here, but you need to keep an eye on Drew McIntyre. He's almost like an entirely different human being."

The promo went on "Stone Cold" Steve Austin's podcast, which put more eyes on it, and it went on Chris Jericho's podcast, and he recommended people should check in on me.

From that moment in the heart of Glasgow, everything started steamrolling forward. And it was vital, now, to keep up the momentum, to stay relevant. I had seen a lot of good wrestlers go back in the indie scene and never be heard of again. I knew I would have to work harder than ever before to make it happen for me all over again.

CHAPTER 21

I'LL SLEEP
WHEN I'M DEAD

After the past couple of years mucking around doing air guitar stuff, it was a huge transition to get back in the ring with serious intent to kick some ass. In fact, it was terrifying. I remember a couple of weeks after the ICW night in Glasgow, debuting for Evolve, a company in Philadelphia, which was tiny but had a great reputation, and friends were urging me not to do it, to get out now. But I knew this was part of the journey. Evolve had a lot of buzz, and there were some incredibly talented people involved, like Johnny Gargano, Ricochet, and Kota Ibushi, to name a few. Founded by Daniel Bryan and Gabe Sapolsky to take professional wrestling in a fresh direction, the name said it all. Evolve. The concept was to focus on producing spectacular action in the ring, to entertain through more of a sports feel, rather than use the in-ring action to embellish a storyline. It was pacy, athletic, and spectacularly acrobatic.

I was originally going to make my Evolve debut against Trent

Beretta, my old buddy from FCW. He was injured, but Gabe called and asked if I was willing to take on Chris Hero—who was Kassius Ohno on NXT—and announced he was happy to put the title on me in my first match.

That night in August, at the Orpheum in Tampa, Chris and I were scheduled to appear as the last event of the show. I took the time to watch the matches prior to mine, and they were mind-blowing in their creativity and athleticism. I realized what a bubble the WWE Universe is: the guys on this roster were largely unknown, but you had Ricochet before everyone really knew his name, doing what Ricochet does . . . flips, tricks, incredible skills performed with off-the-chart timing and precision. You had Johnny Gargano, who has rightfully become such a megastar in NXT history, and guys like Roderick Strong turning up, just these incredible wrestlers. Today, their names are in the Who's Who of Superstars, but back then I was not exactly aware of everybody who was on the show. When I watched the full-throttle matches they put on, it struck me how little wrestling I'd done in the past few years. Getting in the ring used to be my comfort zone. This was going to be a daunting refresher. I mean, in 3MB, Heath did the wrestling.

There were probably at most seventy people in attendance on the night of my Evolve debut, but I was more nervous than I could remember ever being. Kaitlyn came along to support me with one of her best friends, Rita, and I told them to be LOUD when I walked out there. I adopted a policy of fake-it-to-make-it, kept a confident face on backstage, went to the ring, and thank goodness in that first match I was up against Hero, who helped me along when I needed help. I got through the match, won the title, and once again, I took the microphone—and this is when my confidence started growing in earnest. Whenever I got the mic, I consciously tried to feel the moment and tap into the wrestler I was deep down, that leadership figure WWE had always wanted me to be. I told the Evolve crowd that I'd just watched the show, I'd seen the talent, and I was going to put this place on the map. It was the same pledge I had made to the ICW fans. I was blown away by the talent at Evolve. It drove me nuts that the world did not yet know these wrestlers' names. Whatever words spouted from my mouth that night came straight from my heart.

After the sophisticated front-of-house and backstage setup of WWE, I was back to the circuit of DIY rings, tiny venues, and a rougher, adult-only vibe created by small crowds fueled by a lot of alcohol. In the UK, Dad was my merchandise guy, traveling with me to flog T-shirts and key rings as far afield as Portsmouth, back where it all started, when I slept in the ring on my very first training camp at the age of fifteen.

Shortly after my Evolve debut, I was, I think, in Atlanta or somewhere in the Carolinas—and I showed up to discover that the ceiling in the building that had been booked for our show was too low. So we looked out back and figured that the ring could just about fit into this outdoor alley area enclosed by a high wall covered in colorful graffiti. That was where I first wrestled Ricochet. He was prepared to let me do what I was comfortable with—I think he was a bit worried I was coming in as this fallen "Superstar," and he wasn't sure how easy I would be to work with. I'd been The Chosen One, but also the 3MB guy—my pedigree was confusing! I asked him what he wanted to do, how we could put together a great match, and that was cool. We got on like a house on fire. Disguising my nerves, I was ready to go out there and show the guys, and myself, that I could do this. I *wanted* to do this. Ricochet thought I was crazy, not just because I wrestled him like a psychopath but because I had damaged a hamstring and the whole of the back of my thigh was a pool of black-and-blue bruising and looked disgusting.

I fell in love again with the independent scene. I was so grateful for it. We had the freedom to think outside of the box to stage the most extravagantly eye-catching matches possible and get people talking. It was so liberating for someone with an overcharged imagination like me. I had a couple of great fights with Ricochet, making the most of his superhuman acrobatic ability. In one match, I threw him like a basketball and slam-dunked him on the mat, but he jumped back up and hit a slam dunk of a Hurricanrana, with the aid of a basketball hoop, to overpower me. So cool.

I had always thrived when I was part of a close-knit group of wrestlers working to improve . . . working to make myself better, and everyone who worked alongside me too. Wrestling and me, it's been the longest relationship and most dysfunctional relationship in my life, but I love it. Not just the physical combat, the actual business side of wrestling. Whenever I could step up and help the sports entertainment business, it meant the world to me. In WWE, it is the WWE "names" that sell the product. Back on the outside, I was looking in, and I saw I had this unique opportunity to create myself from scratch. I could make a difference to the new names scrawled in my new bookings diary, just by coming in with a social-media bang, growing my brand, and attracting attention to the indie scene I was now a part of. I was operating at 120 percent. Every title I won, I'd take it around the world, accepting challengers right, left, and center. After defeating Roderick Strong in January 2015, I held up the Evolve belt and declared it a world championship because *I* was holding it. At one stage I held five championship titles and used to travel with two suitcases—one for my stuff, the other just for the title belts. You needed to be a heavyweight champion to lift that suitcase off the ground!

John Cena was legendary for the demanding schedule he maintained. I wanted to top that. Everywhere I went, my aim was to guarantee the fans the show of a lifetime. I wanted to be the top independent dude in the world.

With my WWE experience, people started to look to me as this leader, the role that all along my career trajectory, even in my younger years, everybody wanted me to play. I'm naturally shy, an introvert who used to be comfortable only in the suspended reality of the ring, but I was ready now to step up and be The Guy. Not Thee Drew Galloway, not The Chosen One, certainly not the guy in 3MB. Just *me*. I wanted to help the rosters, I wanted to teach them what I knew, I wanted to step up and bring everyone working alongside me up a level as well. I wanted all the new generation of young wrestlers to be as inspired as me. And that became my priority wherever I worked. I'd look around and give motivational talks and say we can do this, let's do this. And it was such an important time for me—to watch ICW flourish, to watch Evolve grow, to watch the other companies I've worked with all across the world stand taller, all while I was growing into a leadership role. My diary at the time looks like alphabet soup, with dates booked for matches for various indie companies and championships around the globe: ICW, PWG, IWF, SWA, PCW, ROH, RPW, wXw, AAW, WCPW, IPW:UK, TNA . . . The list goes on! If they had a title, I was taking it, and then spreading the word so that when I defended it there were more butts on seats. I didn't just want to win, I needed to win. I worked my way up the ladders and became TNA Champion . . .

With ICW, I had a lot of fun with my old buddies from Scotland. It was cool to be hanging out again with Craig, Traps, and Lee

Greig, who wrestles under the name of Jack Jester and is an integral part in the success of ICW. We'd scheme and come up with mad plans. I'd always kept in touch with Lee. A trained hairdresser with a Goth look, he had always been a really hard worker. People would joke that we looked like twin sisters with our long hair and clean-shaven faces. He's also famously stubborn. So much so, he and Kaitlyn didn't speak for a year over some tiny issue and I had to get them both to have it out! When I was in Scotland, I stayed back at home and took a lot of advice from "Granny," a sixty-five-year-old wise man in the opposite apartment who has long been considered part of our family. Larry Gillespie had been our neighbor from the get-go. He used to tell me tales of his wheeling and dealing in London and Europe (though I can't go into the details!). My brother, John, hung out with Larry for a bit. Larry was disabled and couldn't work, so he spent a lot of his time just sitting with Mum to keep her company when she was ill. He considered my dad his little brother. Now that I was back from WWE, he would sit up until all hours with me (which can't have been good for his health), giving me motivation, dreaming up big plans. He called me "World Champion" and encouraged me to think big. Ever the wheeler-dealer, he was the force behind the badges and T-shirts in my new range of merchandise. He was always keeping an eye on us.

Evolve shows tended to be in Florida and New York and shared my agenda to create BUZZ. PWG, or Pro Wrestling Guerrilla, in Southern California, was also on my list. As a super indie putting on underground shows for crowds of no more than four hundred that sell out in seconds, it chimed with my mission. PWG has a reputation as the wrestlers' wrestling show, bringing in the likes of AJ Styles and Samoa Joe, with matches subsequently available only on DVD. That exclusivity is maintained by its loyal, knowledgeable following. Unless you got the "Please come back" chant after your first match, you didn't. Thanks to a recommendation from Roderick Strong, who I'd wrestled with a couple of times at Evolve, and who was buddies with the promoter, I was asked to be part of their 2015 Battle of Los Angeles event, which would take place over two nights. BOLAs, as they are known, also attracted Hollywood celebrities, like Sofia Vergara from *Modern Family*. I was aware that instant crowd approbation is what makes you, and I got that in a great match with Speedball Mike Bailey.

The bush telegraph worked wonders. Through an introduction from Dolph Ziggler's younger brother, Ryan (who wrestled in WWE as Briley Pierce), I was invited to Australia to appear in an Outback Championship Wrestling match in Melbourne. The promotion had been conceived in 2011 and began full operations from 2013 to 2016. I knew a couple of ex-WWE guys who had gone over and had a great time. In return for the excruciating experience of flying economy for nearly twenty-four hours—six feet, five and a half inches contorted into a tiny space, agony, even with extra room in the emergency exit row—the organizers showed you a good time, taking you around to see the koalas and kangaroos. They saw what I'd been doing with ICW and Evolve and asked how I would feel about winning the title. I agreed, renaming it the Australian Title, and packed it in my suitcase when I left, with plans to defend it in the UK and America. The Melbourne event was great, almost like a holiday in my frenetic schedule. The second time I flew to Melbourne, I took Kaitlyn and we spent almost a week there, exploring the region.

In Australia that first trip, I had also taken another booking from a different promoter, in Perth, which probably ranks as one of the worst experiences in the ring I've ever had. The poor guy who was selected to be my opponent was not only inexperienced, but really ashamed that he couldn't match me and put on anything like a show. When there's such imbalance in ability and experience, there is literally nothing you can do. "I'm sorry. Sorry. I'm sorry," the poor guy kept saying over and over again. To give the crowd the entertainment they deserved, I had to pick up the mic and do a long routine. Backstage, I slammed doors and kicked walls. To put someone so green in the ring was dangerous for my opponent and myself. I let the guy know it wasn't his fault; it was the organizer who was to blame.

Wherever I went, with whoever I worked—the Scottish Wrestling Alliance, Lucha Libre AAA Worldwide, Ring of Honour, wXw Westside Xtreme Wrestling, AAW Professional Wrestling Redefined, WrestleCade, Revolution Pro Wrestling, Independent Pro Wrestling UK—I stuck to my plan. And my principles. My buddy Adrian, who wrestles as Lionheart, put me in touch with Steven Fludder, who in 2011 had founded Preston City Wrestling (PCW). His manner is blunt, though I didn't realize that was just his way, and he rubbed me the wrong way at first. He invited me to take part in one show, which I thought would be kind of cool, but I had a very specific image of how I wanted to be in the ring. I didn't want to dilute the buzz I was making. We were negotiating and he said, "You've just been in 3MB and you expect me to pay top dollar?" So I said, "Fuck you, I'm not coming." But Adrian said once I got to know Steve, we'd get along and be friends. Finally, I went there and worked for him. We chatted, had a drink together, and got on great. I had such a good time there. He brought in a bunch of the guys from Scotland and some of the American guys I was friends with. I started off with a one-shot main event deal, but I enjoyed it so much and the crowd was so responsive that it turned into a long-term thing, and the only regret I have is that I didn't do it sooner.

The sheer number of promotions and companies on the independent scene proved how much wrestling had grown since those days in my late teens when I sought long and hard to find opportunities to train and try out my developing skills in shows around the UK. New ventures seemed to be mushrooming everywhere. I became quite excited about 5 Star Wrestling, an ambitious company set up in Scotland by Daniel Hinkles in 2015, which seemed to have money behind it, because they flew me down to the Sky Sports studios to make a commercial for the first tournament.

They released the ad, and it looked as professional as hell. No independent company had achieved that WWE-style of presentation on TV. There were high hopes for it; it was billed as a game-changer. Rey Mysterio, John Morrison, Chris Masters, and Carlito were among the top wrestlers recruited, and I was honored to be asked to be the face of the new program. I remember my dad and Jane came down and stayed in Dundee and made a weekend of it while we filmed one or two episodes, but I was dismayed to see the production was not geared for wrestling. As I'd learned at OVW and then more rigorously at FCW, the televising of wrestling requires camera specifications like no other action sport, even boxing or mixed martial arts. The production crew hadn't factored in the importance of the crowd dynamic in our shows. There were a couple of thousand people there, but you wouldn't have known it the way it was set up. In hindsight, I should have pushed harder to go for better camera angles, because it didn't look good on camera. Perhaps partly because of this, 5 Star Wrestling never took off.

Nevertheless, I had collected championship honors and title belts like they were going out of business. ICW, Evolve, the Outback Championship Wrestling, the Danish Pro Wrestling Heavyweight Championship, and the TNA title . . . ICW in particular meant a lot to me, because I was the first champion, and it was cool to have it back and take it to new heights, to try and make this great promotion a more mainstream part of Glasgow culture. People would go for a drink and a laugh and be part of the show. The Evolve title meant a lot to me in terms of building credibility and attracting bigger crowds within the wrestling bubble for the roster of incredible in-ring performers.

However, the Total Nonstop Action title (TNA) was probably the most prestigious I won in that three-year period, when I was out of WWE, just because of its history and the people who had held the title before me. Sting, Kurt Angle, AJ Styles . . . the TNA Champions were a roll call of top talents. I had a deal that I would be the same guy as I was in all the other companies, and that was great because I had turned fully bad and was embracing it, playing each company's fans off against the others'. I'd take the TNA title to ICW, and the crowd there didn't like the fact that I, their champion, was on TNA television. It was like I was fighting for the opposition almost, even though wherever I went, and the bigger name I got, it helped ICW. They would chant "FUCK TNA!" Grado, who was the great good guy—and who was also a main player at ICW and on television with TNA—even he would get booed. Initially, I was supposed to be the good guy, but they were crapping all over me. I had to get on the mic and spell it out. "I worked for WWE, I came back to ICW, and, yes, I'm working at all these other places. I am not just coming in and taking the glory; I'm killing myself to raise the profile of *me*, which in turn raises the status of this place!" I was in London to cut a promo one time. I had the ICW belt out of the bag and the crowd was going crazy. At the end, I pulled out the TNA title and raised it and pretty much said, *Fuck you all!* Someone threw a beer bottle in the ring, and someone jumped into the crowd to go and attack the guy who threw the bottle. I had one leg over the barricade ready to join in, and I stopped myself. I was thinking, You do this and there'll be a riot. I got back in the ring and singled out the person who had thrown the bottle and he was thrown out. It could have been a full-scale riot. Allegiances ran high. Mind you, reaction equaled social media traction, and that was exactly what I wanted.

My dad always says he's prouder of me for the work ethic and commitment I showed during these years than almost anything else in my career. I didn't want to sit back and be that ex–WWE wrestler who gets paid for cheesy promotions. Backstage, I probably appeared confident and knowledgeable, but as much as I was just nodding and agreeing, in the back of my mind, I was consumed with anxiety for the majority of that time. When you've hit rock bottom, it takes a while to shake off the vestiges of that humiliation. I'd been fired by WWE at the age of twenty-nine, but my confidence started to grow again, thanks to the people around me, who helped lift me up. Because of their belief in me, I started believing in myself again.

The stories that unfolded in the ring were what first drew me into wrestling, and through all my colorful adventures on the independent scene, I started to realize that my own personal story had value, it was relatable. Who hasn't thrown away a big opportunity? Who hasn't been thwarted in achieving their goal? Who hasn't struggled to deal with the curveballs life throws at us? Who hasn't felt misunderstood and cast out? Or been potentially derailed by events in their personal life? My story was a struggle with so many elements that fans could empathize with. It was *real*. Thinking back to the days when I worshipped Bret Hart, I realized that if I was to raise my currency, I had to continue to build on this tale in the ring.

Who knew what doors might open? Or reopen?

My life was rewarding as hell, but extremely challenging, during that period, and logistically very fraught. I was jumping from country to country by the week. Every three weeks I was flying internationally from home in America to the UK, which was my main base with the companies and the wrestling scene that I was trying to build up. "No" wasn't in my vocabulary. I accepted every offer, flying to Germany, Denmark, Ireland, even Australia, where I was also the champion.

Working on TV was not part of my Drew Galloway 2.0 Mission Statement. I was doing so well in the small, non-televised venues on the independent circuit. That success came with a certain integrity. TNA, when I was champion, had two weekly shows—*Impact!* and *Xplosion*. I wasn't looking to go there. When I was asked to go there, I said up front I wasn't keen on being on television. They wouldn't take no for an answer and accompanied that with an offer of good money. I agreed to do it if it could work around my other commitments, if I could be the same guy, with the same music. They said yes to everything, they were that willing to do whatever it took to get me on board. So we would film three months of TV over five days. Whether that was wrestling, doing interviews, advancing feuds, whatever, it was pretty intense, but great for my schedule. I'd jump from that taping straight to Scotland, have a show there, maybe go to England, maybe jump to Ireland if they had a show there, go back to America before heading off to Australia to defend the title. It was nonstop. I was so scared, but also angry for a long time about being fired, and I used that as fuel to motivate me to keep going and going. I took on more and more; I just could not take on enough.

The guys would tease me about my new catchphrase. Each place I landed, someone would say "Hey Drew, how you doing?" and the answer was always "I'm so tired, so tired."

I'd answer a call from Mark Dallas, "Bro, I'm in Australia. Call me tomorrow." The next day I'd tell him, "Uhh, I'm in . . . Finland."

He'd say, "Mate, that doesn't make sense," and I would say, "I know, I'm so tired!"

I never took a day off. I hardly rested. Everyone said I looked as white as a sheet. Sometimes I didn't sleep for three days. "I'll sleep when I'm dead" was my joke.

Dad said I lost my smile, but I was fired up. We had terrible hours, traveling across the UK for ten-, twelve-hour stretches, or the bus would break down and we'd be stuck on the side of the highway, worried we'd be late, but I just looked forward to getting in the ring and smashing it. With ICW, we'd be traveling around Britain in a tour bus that slept twelve, and all six feet, five and a half inches of me would squeeze into a tiny ledge of a bunk to sleep. On top of the travel and the actual training and wrestling, I was doing interviews as often as I could—I would schedule my own media commitments because in the back of my mind I knew, in order to be the most complete wrestler I could be, I had to get better in the ring, I had to keep up with these like super high-level indie guys, and establish my own niche. To do that, I had to get better at projecting *myself* verbally, which was subtly different from projecting a ring character. Speaking from my heart was a skill that improved with each promo I cut. I was determined to become comfortable being interviewed, because that's what makes a top guy. I would be scheduling interviews in the airport, in motel rooms, at home. Ever since my mission statement at ICW, I was burning with an incredible desire to prove myself; I was a man obsessed with rubbing it in WWE's face. There was a point when I couldn't fit all my titles in my bag, and then I allowed myself to think, Okay, I'm doing all right.

CHAPTER 22

A LIFE-CHANGING
ULTIMATUM

For all that I loved the camaraderie, the visceral thrill of wrestling, the euphoria that came with each milestone success in my campaign, it was a dark time. The most difficult thing of all was trying to maintain my relationship with Kaitlyn, because I was never there. As successful as my career now was out of the ring, this period was significantly hurting my personal relationship. Success demands a single-minded approach. For almost eighteen months, we would be lucky to spend five days in a month together. I don't know how Kaitlyn coped with that period. There have been many times throughout our relationship when I wondered how she put up with me. But it was particularly problematic when I was never home. She was working full-time to help pay the rent, so she didn't have the time (and we didn't have the money) to accompany me on my travels. On the road I would call her as often as I could, we'd text all the time. I made sure we always had the chance to talk, but being a physical presence, that just wasn't happening. My plans would change day by day, as I accepted bookings on the hoof. It was difficult to keep her up to date.

All the while I was seeing my old wrestling buddies who I hadn't spent time with for a long time, so there were Big Nights Out. I would spare her some details. I was pushing myself to the limit with my wrestling schedule and then running my immunity into the ground with the nights out on the constant catch-up with friends in each place I landed for the next show. Kaitlyn was at home, not having much fun, and I was living the life of Riley. On the indie scene, the business gets done in the bar—that's where we'd cultivate ever crazier storylines, critique the most recent shows, plan for the company's future. We'd stay up to stupid o'clock, and the next morning we had grand plans formulated for the next stage.

In my own way, I was trying to make Kaitlyn a part of the team as much as possible. We'd written my impassioned mission statement together; she knew my goals. She was my backup team rolled into one person; her goal was to keep me on track to be the best version of myself. She was patient and supportive, but long absences are very trying on a relationship. In my mind, she was a big part of the team, but she found it hard to see how she fit into my future plans. When I was home, I was so worn down and my mind was still on the job—monitoring how I was doing, checking the feedback, setting up the next plans, booking my travel. She put up with so much. She didn't like seeing me wearing myself down, but she knew I was doing what I needed to do. She knew wrestling was all I was ever going to do, so she didn't question what I was doing. But she didn't like the effect it was having on our life together— because we were so rarely in the same country or time zone.

As a wrestler, I was doing everything I could do. As a man and a partner, I was not available. Even when I was at home, I would be exhausted and emotionally withdrawn. Drinking had become an issue. I wasn't an addict. Drinking for me was not an insane compulsion, more a deeply entrenched habit. I'd always gone out with the guys for a beer or, in the US, a Jack Daniel's and beer, to unwind after a show. I didn't necessarily drink every day, but when I did, I couldn't stop. Worse than that, going out drinking became more important than anything else. I wasn't around for Kaitlyn when she needed me.

The lowest point was in December 2015, when her mother was diagnosed with colon cancer. She had received a phone call with the news and told me about it when she got in from work—it was one of my rare "at-home" days. She was obviously devastated and scared and just needed me to be there for her physically and emotionally. But I had planned on going out on a guys night, and even though she asked me not to go because she didn't want to be alone with her thoughts, I walked out of our apartment and didn't come home until much later the next day.

I was way out of control. I don't know how Kaitlyn put up with me, driving around the next day looking for me, making sure I was okay. Physically and emotionally worn down, she hit her breaking point and told me something had to change or she had to leave. She couldn't continue a relationship with someone who behaved like that.

Kaitlyn called my family in Scotland and let them know the extent of my issues—not an easy thing to do. She told them, just as she had said to me, that unless I made some lifestyle changes, I was likely to crash and burn, or she was going to be gone, or both. They were shocked, but immediately everyone rallied to make sure I got back on the right track. I simply cut out drinking. When I was back in Scotland, which was a lot during the ICW phase, I would say *don't* grab me a drink when people offered. When I started sticking to non-alcoholic drinks after a show, I realized drink was not a necessary way to de-stress. I discovered the joy of not being tired or hungover, of operating with clarity of thought. It was a group effort, my family and Kaitlyn, who said she would stop drinking too, and we've stuck with it. So much of my bounce back is thanks to Kaitlyn, who stepped in when I looked set on a path to self-destruction, and said, "Okay, this is what's going to happen."

We adapted, we sat down and talked everything through whenever I was home, and we tried to make it work. We had to change our expectations, our lifestyle, our work schedules, and make compromises like every couple has to do. But, with us, those compromises were on a high scale.

Kaitlyn's not the biggest wrestling fan in the world, let's say. She doesn't like it, which is great for me, because I'm so obsessed that it helps balance me out, and when I need an objective opinion, I can't ask most of my friends because they're all wrestlers and have wrestling minds. She won't watch wrestling on TV unless I'm on, but she contributed so much in terms of keeping my interviews and promos relatable to a wider audience. She introduced me to a bigger life . . . I slowly started to see my dream to return to the top in a larger context. If I wanted to be a top guy, I needed more of a business, a marketing, mind. I was able to ask Kaitlyn what would attract eyeballs outside the committed wrestling fan base. What did she like? What did she not like? Instead of using my narrow wrestler's mind to assess a situation, I relied on Kaitlyn to help me rethink it with an outsider's eyes.

I've said it before and I'll say it again. Without Kaitlyn, there is no Drew McIntyre, World Champion.

CHAPTER 23

FROM MRIs TO MARRIAGE

I was hurtling around the world at such speed, it was inevitable that it would all come crashing down. Literally, as it turned out. When you get into the ring you are putting your life in another person's hands. All it takes is one microsecond, one unguarded moment, and you can get horribly hurt. Guys have died wrestling, or been paralyzed, or suffered career-ending injuries. Ninety percent of the time people have got hurt doing something they've executed a hundred times before, but they land slightly the wrong way, hyperextend their leg, or mistime a move. In WWE, you feel safe, doing the moves, taking the moves, knowing that everyone has been rigorously trained to a certain standard—and that the ring is engineered for safety with padded posts and a well-sprung floor under the foam-covered mat.

Every single match I contemplated on the independent scene, I was holding my breath. Some characters are there to fill a role; some are very inexperienced. Every wrestling match was a huge act of faith for me. When I was on the fly, traveling all over the world on a schedule that would shame an airline inspector, it was hard to find the time to warm up properly. There were no well-equipped training rooms with qualified trainers to help prepare you; no medical center to pop into for advice on addressing the latest complaint.

In September 2016, I was wrestling for WCPW (What Culture Pro Wrestling) in Newcastle, and my opponent dropped me on my head. This guy, the champion, was really good, but the mechanics of the move he proposed can look dangerous at the best of times. My gut told me it was a bad idea. I expressed concern, but he convinced me he could deliver the move safely and it would work well for the story—which was about him beating me, leaving me with a concussion. Reluctantly (and it was my own fault not to trust my instinct) I agreed. The thing that made me hesitate was my height. It is one thing lifting a large man, but lifting a large, very tall man and executing a maneuver with him requires timing and strength. This guy was sixty pounds or so lighter than me, not ideal for acrobatically wielding my long, heavy frame. But he seemed confident, and it worked well for the story—and we all know, I'm all about the story. We had played out the match to the point where I was clearly out of it, then came this devastating finish move. It was meant to be devastating in the effect it created for the crowd, not in terms of physically cracking my vertebrae. As soon as he dropped me and I smacked onto the mat with the full force of all my 266-pound weight plus gravity, plus the force of him delivering the move, I heard a snap.

"Don't fucking touch me," I said as I lay there, wriggling my fingers and toes to reassure myself I still had feeling. There was no ambulance or medical attendant at the venue, which of course there should have been. I gingerly picked myself up, but I knew

I had been hurt badly. This weird, dull feeling spread across my upper back and into my neck. I asked if someone could please call an ambulance. I had never, ever left a wrestling venue in an ambulance before, but I was seriously concerned. Self-preservation and instinct took over. The ambulance took a few hours (seriously) to arrive. After an examination, they said the protocol was to strap me onto a stretcher. But there was no way I was going to go out, through the crowd of fans at the stage door, on a stretcher—and see that go live online. That could derail all the effort that had gone into Drew Galloway Phase 2.

I came to an agreement with the paramedics. I would walk myself out, allow the fans to take some pictures, then hop into the ambulance, which was parked around the corner. So that's what happened. Finally, I arrived at the hospital, where I waited in a hallway for a long time.

My anxiety levels were off the scale. I needed to distract myself, so Kaitlyn got a text in the middle of the night with a picture of me lying on a spine board in Accident & Emergency in Newcastle wearing a giant neck brace. And then I scrolled through every social media site I knew, trying to distract myself from my fears of the extent of the injury. I knew a long list of wrestlers whose careers had been curtailed by serious neck injury, not least my childhood heroes "Stone Cold" Steve Austin and Edge. I didn't call Dad, though he later berated me for not letting him know, but I knew he'd have just jumped in the car and raced from Ayr to Newcastle, and I didn't want him doing that.

Eventually I had an assessment and X-rays and they discharged me and said I'd been lucky, it was fine. I knew it wasn't fine: I'd heard the snap. But I still had a few commitments in the UK, so I drove to two shows. I was sensible enough not to wrestle but gave extensive interviews instead to give the crowd some value for their money. Then I flew straight back to Florida and arranged for an MRI scan. There was some confusion over whether it was my neck or my upper back, so I ended up having two MRI scans back to back, and the specialist confirmed I had non-displaced fractures of the T2 and T3 vertebrae.

To heal, I would have to wear a neck and upper back brace for eight weeks and do nothing. That meant taking time off wrestling for the first time ever. I missed the TNA pay-per-view, where I was supposed to win the newly created title, and I missed all of the following day of TV, which meant missing pay for that entire time. Eight weeks, two months, fifty-six days: however I looked at it, if felt like an almightily unwelcome press of the pause button on my career.

The concept of staying at home and taking time out of my schedule was difficult to accept, but I had to. I couldn't do anything for myself, not even go to the bathroom. I spent a lot of time on the sofa with Chaz the cat. I was never, ever home, so the one shimmering silver lining was that I was at home with Kaitlyn. After getting her bachelor's degree in Biology and considering biomedical sciences and cellular biology, she had gone into medicine—the perfect partner to nurse me back to health! For the first time, I had to depend on her to do everything for me and help me through. She had to get in the shower with me to wash my hair. That's not easy, I'm such a big guy. With her medical background, she researched healing supplements and mixed concoctions like a witch. It was the turning point in our relationship. We had quality time together. We fell more in love than ever. I could see she'd been through hell, and yet here she was, patient and loving, doing everything in her power to help me get better. After a few weeks, a CT scan showed the healing process was way ahead of schedule.

There was extra incentive in regaining fitness too. Seven months earlier, on Valentine's Day, I had taken Kaitlyn to Las Vegas with an engagement ring in my pocket. Having cleaned up my act, I was finally on the right track to be the partner she deserved. We traveled by helicopter to the Grand Canyon, and it set down in a private landing area of the Hualapai Native American territory. There were five other passengers on board, so we walked away from the group to find a private spot. I went down on one knee. I was really, *really* nervous. I started to talk about my mum. I became overwhelmed by tears. By this stage, Kaitlyn had guessed what was coming, so I asked her if she would marry me and be with me forever.

And she said yes!

We had planned a wedding for December, and I did not want to be in a neck brace then, though I was still wearing it for our Halloween-themed wedding shower in October. Kaitlyn planned my costume around the neck brace, LOL!

Under Kaitlyn's guidance, we started going for calming walks along nature trails and just enjoyed hanging out with our cats. I am, as you know by now, pretty intense and driven, and she tried to get me to relax, to live more in the moment.

With that, I found space to get a perspective on my life. Kaitlyn encouraged me to look into a better diet. I organized meal plans with a nutrition company that now calculates all of my macro- and micronutrients based on my goals. They send packaged meals weekly to the house in dry ice containers. Each prepped meal is calculated by grams of protein, carbohydrates, and vegetable servings. They are very clean, meaning no sauce and minimal carbs. I start each day with a five-egg cheese omelette, then I'll eat about four or five packaged healthy meals a day. They're usually the same meals every week, which you would think would get very boring, but I don't mind. Food is fuel. It is a rotation of beef, steak, bison, and salmon with a carb—rice, potato, or sweet potato—and three vegetables. I always pick asparagus, green beans, and Brussels sprouts. If I really want to spice it up, I'll double up on Impossible Burgers, which are vegan. In the evening Kaitlyn will tend to make something more delicious, such as pizza or tacos. It turns out diet is 80 percent of the battle in maintaining a healthy equilibrium.

Gratifyingly, I saw a huge change in my body almost instantly after starting the plan. The biggest difference of all was cutting out the partying, the drinking, the erratic sleeping habits. Cleaning up my act took self-discipline. I was learning to take responsibility, be trustworthy, and with that came confidence. I felt so much better mentally. I had assumed that brain fog was a normal thing because I was shrouded in it most of the time. Without that funk, I was able to think clearly. With the change of diet, I was in better physical shape than ever—and, best of all, my relationship with Kaitlyn was a lot healthier for it.

Some people need crazy things to happen to them to get a wake-up call. I don't recommend a broken neck, but it certainly put me on the right path.

And up the aisle! On December 9, we held a small private wedding ceremony in the Sunken Gardens in St. Petersburg. With its meandering paths and cascading waterfalls, the historic botanical garden is like a secret in middle of the city, a show-case for thousands of the oldest tropical plants and flowers in the region. It looks magical there around Christmas, beautifully illuminated, and they have a perfect private area for weddings. We had originally booked it for New Year's Eve, but three months beforehand we had to change the date so that Dad, who works now as a prison guard manager, would be able to take some time off. It was an awesome day, perfect; the family were all there, the wrestlers that I was worried about causing a scene at the free bar kept their promise and kept it together, at least for the wedding party. A group of friends from school in Ayr came too—the guys who had no interest in wrestling and who I hadn't seen much of between the ages of eighteen and twenty-one. Stuart, Cameron, Ian, Raymond, and Andrew (aka Millar, Cammo, Magoo, Fishy, and Mass Boy) were the friends I had gone to dances with—and on a rite-of-passage lads' trip to Magaluf—and always kept in touch with via social media groups. It was a perfect day in pretty much every regard, so that period of my life was definitely very, very happy.

I had tried to hide my neck injury from the world. I didn't want anyone to know. I didn't want sympathy. During this period, I was a heel in the UK. In fact, I'd turned heel in *Impact!* and everywhere else. Bad guys do not want sympathy! It's not good for business. Audiences might feel sorry for me. I mean, who wants to boo the poor guy who just broke his neck? I carried on doing interviews, reinvigorating my mission to reach the top of wrestling, but I'd learned to integrate a healthy personal life with my ambitions. I was now confident enough on the microphone to appear and just speak on the mic.

One event I didn't want to miss, and I could make an appearance work, was ICW. Mark Dallas and I had this angle going, where we hated each other on the shows, it was sort of a gang warfare about who would have control of the company. With my neck still healing, I couldn't perform, and because I'd been advertised on their tour, I flew in, and each night he and I would have this ongoing verbal battle—pretty much full-on improvisation, and it would get so heated that people in our respective gangs would charge into the ring, and the crowd was so enthralled by the action we set up they never realized I hadn't actually wrestled.

Getting the crowd in the palm of my hand—that's what I was working on, and we pulled it off time and again. When my neck had healed, I emerged super-fit. My new healthy eating regimen made a huge difference to my body and how I looked. The guys would look at me and ask me to let them in on my secret. What was I taking? What new supplement?

"Diet," I'd say. "Yes, it works."

And it wasn't long after that that I eventually ended up back in WWE.

CHAPTER 24

WILL YOU JUST TAKE A CALL FROM TRIPLE H?

The wheels kept turning in wrestling, and it was thrilling to see the ICW audience swell. There was one big show at the Scottish and Southern Energy Hydro in Glasgow that I was desperately trying to make after my neck injury, and thankfully I was cleared for it. When I first proclaimed my manifesto at ICW back in July 2014, the company was drawing crowds of maybe fifteen hundred people for a big show. When I first showed up, they were booking places like Barrowland Ballroom, a world-famous venue, and selling out sixteen to seventeen hundred. Then we moved to the Scottish Exhibition and Conference Centre (SECC) and sold out with four thousand people. When you factor in how small Scotland is, and the fact that people had to be over eighteen to gain entry (so none of the WWE family crowd), it was a testament to how strong the wrestling scene was becoming.

The next show, at the Hydro—a blockbuster venue where WWE star Nikki Cross remembers going to see Blue and Justin

Timberlake concerts—was expected to break the British independent attendance record, and to match the biggest event in European wrestling since Big Daddy fought Giant Haystacks at Wembley Arena in 1981. Newspaper headlines rolled out lines like "How the Scottish Wrestling Company that started in front of 30 people is now on the 'European *WrestleMania*.'" To be part of that beautiful moment in front of more than six thousand fans was a huge professional and personal milestone. When I was traveling around the world, wrestlers would ask me how they could get on an ICW show, and I rarely told them because I took pride in the fact we had raised the standards so high, it was difficult to get booked on an ICW show. I wanted it to be the best of the best independent talent. I'd give Mark the heads-up if I saw someone who really impressed me. I'd call and tell him this guy in this country or that country was incredible, and he could cherry-pick the best raw talent. It was a magical time. If you looked at the ICW roster during that time—Noam Dar, Aleister Black, Killian Dain, Joe Coffey, before the introduction of NXT UK—these people went on to become stars in the wrestling world and stars in WWE.

In early 2017, my television contract with *Impact!*, which had evolved from TNA, was up, and my wife—I loved saying that—and I elected not to stay. The management had changed. It was a crux time in contemplating my future direction. I had achieved everything I set out to do in the independents. I had slugged it out, grateful to all the companies that gave me a platform while making sure that everything that happened was on my terms.

It was time to move on, but where next? I was on fire right now. Thanks to people believing in me, giving me the platform, I was a top-level consummate star, and at this point I was so confident in my abilities. Miraculously, things had worked out the way I'd planned. Kaitlyn and I sat at the table at home and laid out all the options. I knew I could make a difference wherever I went right then. I believed in myself like never before. I looked the part. I acted the part. I knew that any company could give me an assignment outside the ring and I would grow their product.

So what was the next move?

When I was fired, my initial reaction was to go off and prove everyone wrong. The goal was all about getting back to WWE, but once I saw I could make a success of wrestling under my own name and earn well, that changed. It didn't escape my notice that with WWE, I had been struggling to pay the mortgage on our original apartment, but when I wrestled in front of four hundred people at PWG, I was paid well enough to close on a house. What the hell? I can buy a house now that I'm actually outside the company.

My great mate Jinder, fired at the same time as me, who after a year of being a bit lost outside WWE, worked hard, got in shape, and answered a call to be "a body" for WWE, kept telling me I had to call them. They needed experienced guys, and I'd tell him, "It's not where I'm at now. They've got to call me. They're going to have to come begging."

Where next? I figured Japan. I'd had a chat with a couple of the guys who worked in New Japan Pro-Wrestling, and they asked if I wanted to come over. I was keen to sign a part-time deal: I'd fit in there perfectly with my style and I'd learn a lot. That meant I would work a set number of dates in New Japan Pro-Wrestling, one of the top promotions in the world, while also getting to keep up my indie dates and general UK presence. It would cause such a buzz, it was the next logical move. And that's what it's all about, creating that buzz. And it was sensible: I'd enjoy the best of both worlds with stability, good pay, excitement, and prestige.

I was at Dad's house when William Regal called. He has always been a mentor, and had been keeping an eye on my work, monitoring my progress since I left WWE. I told him I was weighing my options and leaning toward Japan. There was a pause, and he asked if I'd just take a call from Triple H before I made any decisions . . .

Dad said, "They have to be watching you. You're on everywhere!"

I had said from the moment I was fired that I would only ever consider going back if WWE management contacted me personally. I've always respected Triple H. He's a great guy. So sure, I would be happy to catch up with him.

Triple H's call came when I was busy making a documentary for Evolve, so there is actually footage of me getting the phone call. We had a conversation. And it was a long one. It was pretty cool to hear some of the things he said. He was someone who had believed in me when I was younger, and he'd followed up on Foley's text and kept an eye on me. He said he was very proud of what I'd achieved within wrestling, but more importantly of all the good things he'd heard. He had seen me at a couple of shows and he said he could see the man I had become. That meant a lot to me.

As we continued to chat, it was clear that the clouds had parted and the WWE landscape of my childhood dreams was back in my viewfinder. Hunter said there was one thing he needed to put to me. I said, actually, there was one thing I needed to put to *him*. I made it clear that I wasn't looking to come back to *Raw* or *Smack-Down*, but I did have my eyes on NXT. If I were to come back, I wanted to prove myself, build myself back up from scratch. NXT was the hardcore audience I was used to from the independent scene, and I wanted to build on that to earn a place on the main roster. It was the combination of both worlds: story and action. I could tell a great story in the ring or on the mic, but equally I was very happy to go out there and have a barn-burner match. At NXT I could see myself as a leader and helping bring people up because it's such a revolving door of top talent there. The other huge appeal of NXT was that I would be working with Shawn Michaels at the Performance Center, and that would be great.

It turned out Hunter had been thinking the same thing.

My mind was made up after that conversation. I double-checked with Kaitlyn. She was on board because I was going to be based at home, in Tampa, which was insane.

CHAPTER 25

YOU KAYFABED ME, YOU BASTARD!

On April 1, 2017—April Fools' Day, I know—the idea was for me to appear in the crowd at the *NXT TakeOver* special in Orlando, which was streamed live on the WWE Network. It was the eve of *WrestleMania* 33, with excitement levels palpable across town like the night before Christmas. The plan was for the cameras to pan over at a certain point in the show to reveal me sitting in the front row of the main event. The first I heard of it was . . . yep, that morning. I was still running around tying up the ends of various commitments on the independent circuit.

So that weekend was crazy. *TakeOver* was going out at the same time as Evolve, and my slot on that was already going to be my fifth appearance of the day. I needed to speak to Gabe Sapolsky, the promoter and writer who cofounded Evolve, to figure out a way of making this work. I had mentioned to Triple H over the phone that wherever I had gone it seemed WWE became involved, like I was in ICW and suddenly WWE was involved. I was a champion in

Evolve and luckily WWE was now working with Evolve, so I knew my double-booking shouldn't be an issue. It was just a logistical complication. One of many. I remember the rising panic of the morning. In my mind, there was a certain finality in deciding it was time to come home and actually win a world title in WWE, but my return was going to start off with chaos! Luckily, I had Gabe in my corner to help navigate the waters. Gabe and I, along with WWN owner Sal Hamaoui, always had an incredible partnership, and I owe them a debt of gratitude. Gabe was a protégé of Paul Heyman, whose wisdom would later serve to unlock my true potential, as fate would have it.

We started the day thinking Evolve was my last appearance, so we had to figure out with Gabe Sapolsky how I was going to get from Evolve to NXT. WWE negotiated that with him while I wrestled a show somewhere I can't even remember, then raced to do a radio interview, followed by a signing and then a further media commitment. It was the eve of *WrestleMania* 33 "weekend," which I always call *WrestleMania* "week" because every company in the world comes together for a string of satellite events, because it brings so many wrestling fans together in one city. If you drew a Venn diagram representing *Mania* week, a big circle in the center would be WWE, with hundreds of little circles just overlapping the edge of the big circle representing all the other wrestling promotions with some sort of tangential connection to the mother ship.

Understatement of the year: it was a very busy day. Like my entire indie years in microcosm.

And in the middle of the whirl, I realized I didn't have a suit with me for my NXT appearance (what is it with me and suits?). I just hadn't had time to think it through. I wasn't prepared. I frantically called Kaitlyn. Thankfully, as we live in St. Pete, just an hour's drive away, she was able to shoot back home, grab my suit, and head back to Orlando while I was making my last appearance downtown. We rendezvoused near the Amway Center, and she jumped out of the car with my suit. From the back door of the Amway, we literally ran to Talent Relations, me trying to keep my head down so nobody saw me.

I jumped in the shower, then dressed as quickly as I could, with Kaitlyn's help. I was sweating my butt off. Aaargh, I didn't want to be a sweaty mess on camera, but I wasn't really processing it too much. I was nervous. My brain was racing so fast. I was saying to myself, Drew, you just have to look the part. You don't have to get in the ring. You don't have to cut a promo. You just have to sit there. Man in the Crowd.

Kaitlyn got the spray tan on. We were in a private locker room and it was so dark. She said she couldn't see how much tan she was spraying on my face. She was worried she'd overdone it. Then the crew were bustling in, rushing me out to my seat in the crowd. I slipped into the seat vacated earlier by Edge.

Phew! I had made it. Normally I have a little montage in my head, visualizing any on-camera stuff, but I hadn't had a chance to contemplate this moment or process my thoughts about how the fans might react . . . A mobile camera zoomed in on me, close up, and I thought, Oh God. What if they don't remember me? I look so different. Am I sweaty? Am I *orange*? What if they don't know who I am? What if there's silence? What if they put me up and there's just complete silence from the fifteen thousand people in this arena?

The camera hovered. I put a big smirk on my face. The crowd gave me a huge cheer. They knew who I was, all right. At least I think they did, or they were cheering for the sake of cheering, or for the Seth Rogen lookalike, who was sitting behind me; he was looking pretty happy too.

After that cameo appearance, I felt my phone popping with messages. One in particular confirmed this milestone moment.

Fancy Seeing YOU Here.

Those words on Twitter represented my official welcome from WWE.

It was pretty cool. I was back.

And, of course, it was straight back to business. Outside the main hall, the WWE.com interviewer expressed surprise at my appearance, and I was ready to deliver my message.

"Why would I not be here at *NXT TakeOver*?

"If you'd been following me in the past few years, you'd know I've traveled the world, won every championship there is to win, grown brands, become a bit of a franchise player. What is the next logical step? Where the best Superstars in the world are. And with the top prize, the NXT Championship. That is exactly what I want, and if that's not clear enough for you . . .

"Drew McIntyre has signed with NXT."

It was so cool because I'd kept the whole plan under wraps— good pro that I was (I hadn't forgotten those early insider secrets from Dennis Brent and Percy Pringle). Backstage, one of the first people I saw was Killian Dain, who I'd spent a lot of time with on the indie circuit.

"You kayfabed me, you bastard!" he swore amicably in my face.

The key thing about my return was that I was starting on NXT as a good guy, myself, the real Drew, albeit with the volume cranked up. I wanted to do the very same on TV as I had done as a franchise player. I had boosted the profile of many other companies, and I wanted to do it for NXT as well. I had made it clear I had other options, but this was where I wanted to be. In my first promo, I said I had the raw talent and I could lay the *SmackDown* on anyone. That was a cryptic way of saying I could have gone to *Raw* or *SmackDown*, but I didn't want to piggyback over anyone. I wanted to come to NXT and work my way from entry level to WWE Champion—but the path would be the very opposite of the Chosen One scenario.

I returned with new music—I think it had been Roderick Strong's at one point, we called it "Generic Song no.7," which he had inherited from someone else, it was the pass-on song—but we added some bagpipes to make it mine. I had to find a new finishing move because my DDT, or something very similar, was being used by Dean Ambrose, so Triple H suggested I pick a new trademark killer move. I had my kick, which I was calling the Claymore Kick before I came back to WWE. It first came about when I was wearing the tight leather pants we all wore in 3MB. I went to execute the Big Boot finisher, but my pants were so tight that the force of my right leg going up nearly caused them to split at the crotch. I kicked my other leg up in the air—and I fell on my head, which was really freaking stupid. Someone who saw it suggested if I could figure out a better way (e.g., probably not wear such tight pants), it could be a really cool finish. I worked hard on modifying it—and put it into action spectacularly against Ryback in 2013 (look up the video clip—it's cool!).

In my time with the indies, I used my DDT "Future Shock" as a primary finish, and my Claymore as a secondary trademark killer move. I like my Claymore Kick because most of the bigger guys like me have a power-based signature move. It's the smaller guys who tend to go for the running kick, but I am known for being big and strong, but also fast and agile, and with my long legs I can deliver a devastating kick to anyone of any size at any time. Roderick Strong (yep, him again) had a similar one called the Sick Kick. We had battles in our matches—the Sick Kick and the Claymore Kick we'd use as false finishes, where we'd one, two, then kick out. I went to him because he's a friend and said, "Hey, are you cool if I use this kick as a finish now that I'm in NXT?" Thankfully he was cool with that.

The look is always an important part of a wrestler's package, but I was determined that my physical appearance make a statement in itself on my return. I once said on Corey Graves's podcast that "I went from this boy who threw away his opportunity, his dream, because he wasn't giving his all, to finally growing up and becoming a man who's doing what he was supposed to do all along." When I reentered the WWE Universe, I wanted to show that I was the grown-up version of me. It was like the *Lion King* story: Simba the cute cub who is trained to become king, but gets sent off to the Badlands, where he meets his cool friends and comes back to Pride Rock as a big badass with a mane ready to roar! And he can't wait to be king. He topples evil Scar and that's the happy ending. My WWE journey was coming full circle. The circle of life and all that.

A wrestler's look is a personal thing—there is no input from the company—and with Kaitlyn's help we settled on the long, darker hair (no more ponytail in the ring) and the beard. We accidentally went too dark with the hair, leaving the dye on for too long, but I liked it and it accentuated the imposing, formidable look I was going for. Instead of having the smooth, oiled chest, I grew my chest hair. Someone joked that I had finally hit puberty in my time away from WWE.

CHAPTER 26

STARTING ALL OVER AGAIN

had been away for three years. And I returned to prove a point. I had to go back and achieve what I had set out to do originally. I would do whatever it took to get to the top. I came back humble, determined to work my way through the ranks, up the ladder, to get to where I felt I deserved to be. As well as the WWE faithful to whom I was introducing a reinvigorated Drew McIntyre—the Phase 2 Drew, bigger, meaner, with a rapacious appetite to fight—there were three years of new viewers who weren't familiar with the old Drew McIntyre. On April 12, 2017, I made my NXT re-debut as a good guy against Oney Lorcan. I couldn't be a bad guy. The fans found it hard to hate me because I had been through such a torrid journey. I had earned their sympathy, but much more importantly, I wanted to earn their respect.

My first opponent was key to my new NXT adventure; the match had to set the tone. There would be a lot of eyes on my debut match, and I knew Lorcan was an awesome combatant. He was someone I'd wrestled with outside the company, and I knew he'd bring a savage and technically jaw-dropping physicality into the ring. Just like me, he is not afraid to be hit or to hit somebody. In fact, he encourages it. He would rain upper cuts on me, run at me with a jumping cross-body move . . . I knew he would be brutal, the perfect foil for me to show the fans how aggressive I was, and agile with it. I knew we'd just smash the hell out of each other.

It was a short match, but as everyone says—when you have a match with Drew McIntyre, you don't want to time check it because you spend the entire time beating the crap out of each other. At one point, he jumped off the top rope and I caught him on the outside, which demonstrated my strength, and then pulled off a gut-wrench suplex on the outside of the ring. We did some cool flips from the top of the turnbuckle. I eventually hit the Claymore and he took a crazy bump. It was entertaining, ruthless . . . the perfect introduction for fans new and old alike to see what the new Drew McIntyre was all about. I defeated Lorcan with an emphatic statement of intent. The commentators were saying things like "Drew McIntyre fights like he wants to separate your head from your body." Music to my ears.

The locker room at NXT was a bunch of young, hungry guys coming in who just needed exposure and elevation for the world to recognize their talent. With a lot of coming and going, I became the de facto leader in that if anyone wanted advice, I was there to give it. The role was perfect for me. It was the role I'd been doing for the past few years outside WWE. And the talent who were on the roster were more or less the same guys who were in the independent scene that I'd been around as I traveled the world. I had met most of them multiple times, almost all of them at least once.

Having said that, it wasn't in my character to stalk in and declare myself the leader, William Wallace himself! A locker room finds its own dynamic, its own core figures. The thing was, I knew everybody, and I really fed off the collective passion because again it reminded me of all the other places I'd been working outside the company. I slotted back into WWE like I hadn't been gone. The majority of the crew around me were the same. It honestly didn't feel like I'd been away for three years.

The real Drew was back, but also a much more polished Drew. I came back fully aware that it is difficult to maintain 100 percent passion as a WWE Superstar, because it's a non-stop lifestyle. I knew only too well that you can get jaded inside the bubble. I found people gravitated toward me for all sorts of advice. Nikki Cross, for example. So I would watch the ladies' matches too and help them out where I could. In NXT, everybody was up, everyone was excited, everyone was so happy to be there, looking for an opportunity. I was happy to add a spark to that intensity.

My own attitude was, Okay, wow, there are a lot of talented people here. My plan to be the champion isn't going to come easy. I am going to consider every day as Day 1. Every day I have to start as if it's my first day and set out my cards.

That included my next key match against Killian Dain. To defeat him on July 19 would leave me as the number one contender for the NXT Championship, with the right to challenge Bobby Roode at NXT *TakeOver* in Brooklyn for the title. It was cool to wrestle Killian. He was someone I'd wrestled a lot in Scotland in ICW and really wanted to help bring up. He was the guy I singled out when I came back to Scotland and was assessing the lay of the land in terms of who I wanted to work with. For ICW and BCW, he was the one I wanted to wrestle. As such a giant hairy guy, he was an opponent who could credibly beat me up. When he hit me, I could convincingly go down. I also discovered he was a really nice guy who wanted to learn, to improve. We were on the same wavelength. I recall thinking Killian was freaking perfect, you know, he has the passion for the business outside the ring, and he's *gigantic*. And our work together really raised his profile.

In this match, he returned the favor. Two giant guys going at each other. He made me look like I *should* be champion. It was the last match at the end of a long taping schedule, and a fun one. And that set me up to challenge Bobby Roode.

I had never gotten to wrestle Bobby in TNA. A match was set up and it fell apart for some reason. He was one of the original TNA guys, a tag team and world heavyweight champion, and someone whose work I have always admired. He's such a good wrestler. He dresses the part, looks the part, talks the part, and he had certainly mastered the big, crowd-thrilling entrance to his "Glorious Domination" music after more than two hundred days as NXT Champion when I made my challenge. As they say, he's the man who puts the vain in vainglorious. Now I was finally going to get to work with him on the big stage in NXT. The promos were cool leading up to it, and I had a lot of fun taunting him on Twitter with lyrics from "Broken Dreams," the song from my first run that the fans loved.

Out of time, so say goodbye. What is yours, now is mine!

The words were so applicable to my story—though I was intent on flipping it round so that it was Bobby Roode whose end was drawing near . . .

Everyone was so obsessed with my old music that a short segment of the song was used in one of the buildup videos. Everyone latched on to that, it helped generate more excitement. It is the only time I've used it since I've returned to WWE, but people always ask me about it, going freaking crazy. When are you going to use the song again?

Our characters pitted against each other well to create the perfect rivalry. Since winning the title by defeating Shinsuke Nakamura, Bobby Roode's line was that NXT belonged to him and not the fans. Here I was, the real Drew, acknowledging the mistakes of my past, determined to stand up for everyone who despised complacency and entitlement. And there was Bobby . . . vain and glorious! His entrance music is so catchy it's a head start on winning the crowd over, so I devised my own way of aligning the crowd with me. A month before our championship match, I cut a promo and spelled it out pure and simple.

"I don't have a backwards button. I only go forward. And I learned the hard way.

"Once upon a time I was not the man who stands before you right now. When I showed up in WWE, I was known as The Chosen One. And I expected all these opportunities to be presented to me on a plate. I felt entitled. And when I wasn't the hardest worker in the room, that's when I failed.

"Away from WWE, I realized it was my life, my dream, my responsibility. I had to wake up and become the hardest worker in the room, and not just that, the hardest worker in the damn world!

"We all walk side by side as equals around here at NXT. Everyone except one person. The champion. Bobby Roode. When I look into his eyes, all I see is entitlement. Well, Bobby Roode, this is NOT your NXT."

Me as a baby with my mum, Angela, at my christening celebration. Mum and I always loved each other's company.

Here we are at home on Annpit Road, Ayr, the street I grew up on.

Me as a toddler with my mum and dad, Andy. I grew out of that sailor outfit fast!

I'm on the left with the teddy I had until about the age of ten (though it might have been buried in the closet). My brother, John, is on the right.

Mum congratulates me on a soccer award (I'm wearing the colors of my favorite team, Glasgow Rangers). In the background you can see Dad's fishing trophies and a doll that always freaked me out!

Some early mic skills! John and me singing for the family at Christmas, when it was a tradition for the kids to perform.

"Stone Cold" Steve Austin merchandise for Christmas when I was thirteen or fourteen.

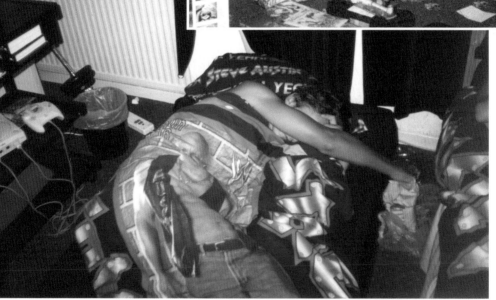

My brother was jealous of my sheets! You can see a Sega Dreamcast in the background, which we got just to play the *Royal Rumble* video game.

Yokozuna poses with (from left) our friend Blair, me, and my brother, John, at an event in Irvin, Scotland. It was the first time I saw a pro wrestler in the flesh.

A rare picture of Sheamus with short hair, with me next to him looking fresh faced, in about 2005–2006, before we signed with WWE.

Me with my wrestling buddies in Scotland. From left: Barry "Wolfgang" Young, Craig Ogston, Jack Jester, and me.

Backstage in Manchester at our WWE tryout in November 2006. From left: Ray (Sheamus's manager), Mikael Vierge, Stu Sanders, me, and Sheamus.

Enjoying my time in Irish Whip Wrestling, circa 2006, dancing with the Scottish flag. Look at those moves!

Battling with Sheamus at an Irish Whip Wrestling show. This submission hold is inspired by Japanese wrestling legend Jushin "Thunder" Liger.

Irish Whip Wrestling—Unathletic Sheamus tries to duck a leapfrog!

My debut on *SmackDown*, October 12, 2007. Anyone see the hard cam?

I defeated Brett Major, who would achieve greater fame as WWE Superstar Zack Ryder, in my debut match on *SmackDown*.

Picking up the mic after Vince McMahon introduces me as his Chosen One on *SmackDown*, September 22, 2009. No pressure!

Just twenty-four years old, winning the coveted Intercontinental Championship at *TLC: Tables, Ladders & Chairs*—December 13, 2009. I didn't know it yet, but success would not always come this easy.

Sharing the joy of winning the Intercontinental Title with Mum, Dad, and Papa (my mum's father). In the background are Papa's soccer trophies and war medals.

Returning home to a hero's reception at a *SmackDown* live event in Glasgow—April 10, 2010.

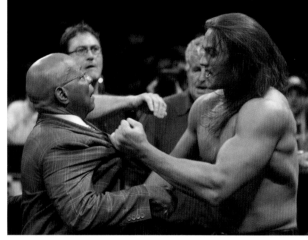

General manager Teddy Long was the perfect foil. Here he is getting a piece of my mind after stripping me of the Intercontinental Title on *SmackDown*—May 7, 2010.

Flashing a smug grin as Mr. McMahon overrules Teddy Long and returns the title to "The Chosen One." *SmackDown*—May 14, 2010.

Having a great time with Mum during a family visit to America the week of *WrestleMania XXVII* in Atlanta, 2011.

WWE's resident "rock band," 3MB (Jinder Mahal, Heath Slater, and me), playing a mean air guitar on *Saturday Morning Slam*, February 2, 2013.

At my brother's wedding with the love of my life, Kaitlyn.

I proposed to Kaitlyn at the Grand Canyon. She said yes!

Our wedding took place in the Sunken Gardens, St. Petersburg, Florida, on December 9, 2016. From left: Danielle (Kaitlyn's cousin), Angelica (friend), Rita (maid of honor), Ashley (Kaitlyn's sister), Kaitlyn and me, John (my brother), Sheamus, Traps, and Jinder Mahal.

Above: Officers from the NYPD Pipes & Drums play me to the ring at *NXT TakeOver: Brooklyn III*—August 19, 2017.

Below: My WWE comeback gets off to a rousing start with victory over Bobby Roode for the NXT Championship at *NXT TakeOver: Brooklyn III*. The emotion on my face is as real as it gets.

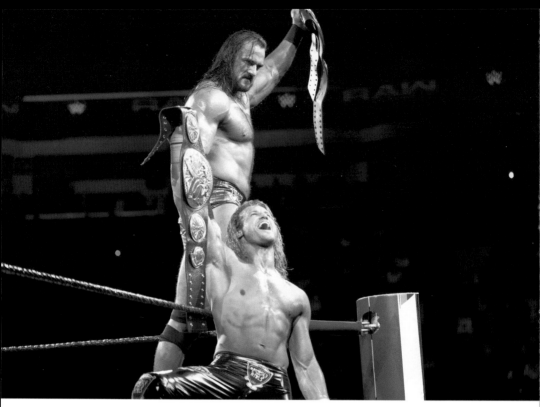

Dolph Ziggler and I may be different in style and stature but could not be more alike in our passion for sports entertainment. Here we are hoisting the Raw Tag Team Titles on *Raw*—September 3, 2018.

Taking the fight to Roman Reigns in the lead-up to our *WrestleMania* clash. The Claymore Kick gets the job done inside the ring and out. *Raw*—March 11, 2019.

Above: Soaking in the atmosphere of over eighty thousand spectators.
Left: Dropping Roman with a powerful spinebuster. *WrestleMania* 35—April 7, 2019.

Another homecoming, an entirely more focused and hungry Drew McIntyre. *WWE Live in Glasgow*—November 11, 2019.

Above and right: My "Star Is Born" moment, winning the annual thirty-man Royal Rumble Match. *Royal Rumble*—January 26, 2020.

Below: More determined than ever, taking on Luke Gallows and Karl Anderson on *Raw*, with *WrestleMania* 36 and a date with destiny squarely in my sights. *Raw*—January 27, 2020

Brock Lesnar has a menacing stare, but I'm no slouch myself. *WrestleMania 36*— April 5, 2020.

Adrenaline surging through every fiber of my being, I show The Beast who he is dealing with.

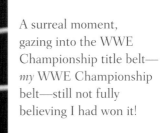

A surreal moment, gazing into the WWE Championship title belt— *my* WWE Championship belt—still not fully believing I had won it!

My signature pose looks so much better with that beautiful title in my hand. *Backlash*—June 14, 2020.

Defending my title inside the WWE ThunderDome against then thirteen-time World Champion Randy Orton. *SummerSlam*—August 23, 2020.

Motioning to the crowd, I repeated, "This is not your NXT. WE ARE NXT!!"

We started to work on the non-televised shows so I could see what he was like in the ring. Sure enough, he was awesome. When it came to the match itself, he was adamant we were making it as good as possible to set me up as the next guy because he knew he was moving to *Raw* or *SmackDown*. And we had Shawn Michaels helping us put it together. It was surreal, sitting with Bobby, this guy I respected so much and had always wanted to work with, with Shawn Michaels as our agent. Awesome. We would go to visit Shawn at the Performance Center, where he held a skull session with a select few people in NXT. It was a video-review class. The first rule of Shawn's class is that you don't talk about Shawn's class. So I can't say much about the magic that goes on behind closed doors, but I think I can reveal that we would watch the non-televised matches that Bobby and I were having, and dissect what was working and what wasn't, so we could apply that to our big match. We were totally candid and honest with our input, particularly Roderick Strong. "That was rubbish." "Don't do that." Roddy and I had always agreed that he would give me his frank opinion and I would do the same for him.

Bouncing ideas around was fun. I never let myself forget this was my second opportunity, and I wasn't going to let it fall by the wayside. I was very driven, back in student mode, very keen to take advantage of all the assets available—and Shawn Michaels's wrestling IQ was a top asset.

The match itself on August 19 in Brooklyn, New York, was a lot of fun. I emerged covered in bruises and ached for days, but I loved every minute from the moment Drew McIntyre the Savage Scot was ushered into the ring by two columns of the New York City Police Department's Pipes & Drums (a band made up of police officers with links—whisper it—not to Scotland but to the Irish American Emerald Society). The stadium lights went out as my music kicked in, the war drums resounding around the packed walls of Barclays Center. I flicked back my hair with menace (no more sleek ponytail) and stepped through the ropes, the Celtic Colossus striding out to fulfill his destiny.

I'd had my cool entrance, then Bobby's famously popular music struck up. A lot of tinkling piano and clouds of smoke, and there he was, utterly "Glorious" in a scarlet-and-gold version of his robe, wearing the huge NXT Championship belt. He stood with his arms aloft, looking up to the sky, soaking in the adulatory words of his song, with the crowd singing along. *"Glorious! No, I won't give in, I won't give in till I'm victorious. And I will defend, I will defend, and I'll do what I must until the end, until the end."* I waited in the ring trying to keep warmed up, enjoying the spectacle and the big fight feel ramping up.

The referee introduced me as the challenger. I put my hand out and touched the metal plate on the belt, as if to remind myself what was now within my grasp. I had a considerable height, weight, and power advantage, so my strategy was to intimidate Roode, the reigning, defending, and—many would say—defining NXT Champion. But he is such a wily, crafty fighter. For longer than I would have liked, he kept the contest on the outside of the ring because he knew he couldn't lose the title on the outside. The match looked like a violent confrontation between two guys who were prepared to go beyond their physical limits and beyond their tactical approach to tap deep into wells of motivation. It was pretty much a string of some of the most eye-popping moves you will see in the ring—hangman's neckbreakers, midair catches, kip ups, DDTs, spinebusters, powerbombs, belly-to-belly suplexes, sleeper holds . . . At one stage, he had me in the Tree of Woe position, suspended upside down on the turnbuckle. At another stage, I caught him by surprise with a Tope Con Giro. The momentum swung backward and forward. He got three glorious DDTs in before I got my final Claymore in . . . and pinned him for three.

I was the NXT Champion—and Brooklyn was buzzing.

As Mauro Ranallo, the commentator, declared, "Drew McIntyre has gone from The Chosen One to Number One."

I so, so enjoyed those minutes of soaking up the rapture. I kissed the belt. I roared from the top of the ropes. I felt so privileged to be the champion at a time when NXT had such an incredible roster.

And then the night got even cooler as Bobby Fish and Kyle O'Reilly climbed into the ring followed by the debuting Adam Cole, who dropped me with a huge superkick to signal the end of the show. It was the launch of the Undisputed Era, a stable comprising Fish, O'Reilly, Cole, and my old friend-cum-ring-foe Roderick Strong. That little bit of taster action was sure to keep people talking as they ambled out into the Brooklyn night. The Bobby Roode era as NXT Champion was over; the fans could expect an intriguing new web of rivalries and antagonisms as I defended my precious title.

I basked in the afterglow of those incredible scenes. Back in my hotel room, I remember having a special moment holding the title belt and trying to let it all sink in. I was musing, *Wow, what a crazy journey . . . I'm sitting here as NXT Champion now, less than five months after coming back into the WWE fold,* after all these ups and downs. The things I had said were going to happen were really happening. I had harnessed the power behind my mind to fast-track me to my goals. Talk about re- demption.

Shortly after I returned to NXT, Jinder had defeated Randy Orton and sensationally won the WWE Championship. The 3MB boys were back in town! My triumph was not (yet) the WWE Championship, but the NXT Title meant as much to me to win at that time. In many ways, it further validated my 2014–2017 spell on the independent circuit because NXT had that same hardcore fan base. It wasn't so much a diffusion brand for WWE as a niche showcase for wrestling aficionados, fans with an appreciation of the physical art of wrestling rather than fans looking for more mainstream entertainment.

As I sat there, in the quiet-ish of the night in the City That Never Sleeps, I had a private moment, lost in my own little world behind the closed doors of my hotel room. Wow, this is crazy. Everything is on track and I'm feeling on top of the world. I rang Kaitlyn and she was so pleased for me, even if I did have to explain the significance of winning the NXT Title!

When you win a title, you get to cart it around with you. I took so much pride in being the last on the show. I drove all my WWE colleagues crazy. They would all be waiting on the bus ready to leave, but because I was last, I'd get on the mic after the show and be talking to the fans, having a laugh, because I felt it was my responsibility to send them home happy. I'd ba- sically always have the Big Drew Microphone Time after every show, and I knew it drove my fellow wrestlers crazy, but I didn't care because I wanted to make sure the fans got their money's worth and then some. That was my thing. Different champions have different things . . . Some run out of the ring and pose for pictures, but I would talk for ten minutes after a match and then shake hands and have pictures taken with the title. And then go to shower and change afterward. By the time I got on the bus, everyone was moaning!

CHAPTER 27

INTRODUCING . . . THE CLAYMORE CATS

I came to NXT with renewed vigor. I treated every match as if it were my first, or last. I may have come back to WWE as a more polished and ring-sharp performer, but I was never, ever, going to let my focus drop. I learned a lot about myself traveling around the world during my time away. A new dawn, a new day, and all that, and that's the way I thought in NXT then, and it's how I think right now. In each appearance, I have to get over with the new fans who've never seen me before; I have to get over as a person and as a champion.

What makes NXT so inspiring is that that is everyone's mentality. As I well knew, it is keeping that mentality as you go along that is the challenge. Every single time I was doing an interview, every single time I stepped into the ring or cut a promo, there would be people who had never seen me before—or maybe didn't even know about WWE, like my brother, John, and me seeing it for the first time from behind the furniture at our cousins' house—and my mission was to win them over. I was never going to take no for an answer, never going to let a setback become a permanent obstacle, never forget that I had once thrown away my golden opportunity, my dream, by becoming complacent.

After winning the NXT title, I was unstoppable. I took on Roderick Strong and retained the title. Next up, I collided with Andrade "Cien" Almas, which led to William Regal posting a championship match between the Mexican and me at *NXT TakeOver: War Games* on November 18, 2017.

I was riding high . . . and being Drew McIntyre, that inevitably meant I was heading for a fall.

Literally, a fall. Toward the end of that match against Andrade, I tore my left bicep. As a setback, it was like toppling off the peak of the mountain. I had won the NXT Championship. Things were going as well as they could go. In contrast to the stress and anxiety in my first period at WWE, after The Chosen One pronouncement, I was comfortable about living up to my billing in NXT, excited and working hard to improve. I was ready for whatever came next and absolutely not prepared to be derailed by anything.

A bicep tear is a serious injury, and I was infuriated that I had gotten myself into a position where it happened. It wasn't Andrade's fault. We had talked about me taking his hammerlock DDT off the top rope before the match, and I had an instinctive fear that there was a chance I could get hurt because of the huge difference in our size and weight. Of course, there is always a chance that a move can go wrong, but I knew, with this, that there was a chance I could get seriously hurt. In my head I wasn't comfortable with it, and yet I still did it. That was my mistake. It was a stupid idea. I should have just said no. You know, you can't turn back time, but you can learn from your lessons. And why hadn't I learned from the incident that caused my broken neck?! That is pretty much the story of my life.

The thing was, I was thinking about the integrity of the match, and I wanted a spectacular finish. I knew Andrade could handle my weight, just maybe not my long body. I had misgivings. I told myself, If we just do it the right way, I will be fine. I emphasized to him that we were not going into the move until I was up there and settled. A little bit of time would pass before I would be completely comfortable. I told him, "Buddy, I'm probably up there for ten seconds before we even go." So he was expecting ten seconds, but the second I got up there, I tried to go, and he wasn't ready because I had told him to wait, and when he went to go, I reached my arm out and grabbed the top rope, which jerked my arm on my way down. Youch!

We still did the finish. He won the match, which was the plan.

It's just that my bicep was torn off the bone.

How stupid did I feel? I had known something could go wrong and it went wrong. I was so pissed off, so mad at myself. There is probably footage, somewhere, of how angry I was when I got back to the training room. I was sitting there anticipating that I would be out for months. In ignoring my instinct, I had just flung a massive roadblock in my path. I was thirty-two years old. It was ten years since I had originally signed with WWE. I really did not need any prolonged absences from the ring.

Very quickly I had an MRI scan, which revealed the extent of the damage, followed by surgery to reattach the muscle. Luckily, there was no swelling, so it was a straightforward operation. The prognosis was for a long recovery period. The doctors warned me I could be out until the summer of 2018, though personally I targeted April. I was not going to let this derail me. I put in 100 percent effort to rest, rehabilitate, and maintain my fitness, ready for a move to *Raw*. And I consoled myself with the thought that I had done more than enough in NXT to show that Drew McIntyre was a force to be reckoned with. That gave me a chance to relax and concentrate on healing.

The only time I had ever taken off was for those weeks when I broke my neck and was pretty much immobilized in a brace. This time, however, I was mobile. Anticipating a good few months of not being in the ring, and not featuring in any capacity at shows, I could use the time to focus instead on areas I needed to improve. As well as concentrating on rehab, I made a point of driving to the Performance Center to work with Shawn Michaels. There was no obligation for me to go to training classes, but I got such a lot out of Shawn's classes. I used that period to really raise and expand my wrestling IQ. It was back to working on the psychology of storytelling in the ring. I was a graduate with a degree in Criminology from Glasgow Caledonian University, and courtesy of Shawn, I earned the equivalent of a PhD in wrestling know-how.

It was a great period in one respect, spending all that time at home, taking stock of where I was in terms of my wrestling, spending time with Kaitlyn and our cats. If you're familiar with my social media output, you'll have seen that the cats play a big part in our day-to-day life. I like to call them the Claymore Cats. (We all love a bit of alliteration in WWE.) Chaz—the big black one I had on my lap when I became WWE Champion, the one who walks on the desk when I am on a video call—was the cat Kaitlyn got from the shelter a couple of years before she met me when she wanted a companion while studying so much in college. At twenty pounds, he's a healthy, muscular creature these days, but when Kaitlyn was directed to him at the shelter, having asked which cat had been there the longest, she saw a very skinny, ratlike black cat. Once they opened up his cage, he put his front paws around her neck and wouldn't let go. The rest was history! Chaz has a huge personality and is extremely intelligent. It took him all of five minutes to learn how to give us high fives for treats—and he also learned how to flush the toilet from watching us push the handle.

Then there is Hunter—and *no*, he is not named after Triple H, whose ring name was originally Hunter Hearst Helmsley. Hunter is a Maine Coon mix we picked up from the shelter together just after we moved into our first apartment. Kaitlyn and I were in the pet supermarket, which has rescue cats, and he jumped into my arms. I was holding him like a baby when another guy came over and expressed an interest in adopting him. I didn't like this guy's tone of voice; I started imagining he had a cat dungeon. I was telling Kaitlyn this on the way home, and she said, "Shall we go back and get the cat?" And we did, and that is Hunter. He is very shy, a gentle soul, and a good cat to have around when you're injured or feeling a bit below par because he's so intuitive to your emotions. We like to say he is our little nurse when we feel sad, because he loves to play, and he will open up his mouth when he is excited so it looks like he's giving you a big smile. Together they are a ruthless tag team. I just leave the living room for a second to go to the bathroom, and when I'm back, whoa, they've stolen my place on the sofa. They play with my championship belts, make look-at-me appearances when I'm live on camera from home. So the cats rule the household.

For a short time during lockdown we had a third cat—a two-year-old little gray cat we brought in from outside named Piper. Someone in Kaitlyn's mom's neighborhood abandoned her when they moved away after the pandemic kicked off. Left to fend for herself, she would sit outside the neighbor's empty house and meow at the door to be let in. It broke Kaitlyn's heart, so we took her in. It took a good month before she trusted us. And then we noticed that her front fang was missing and she was having difficulty eating. Kaitlyn took her to the vet, and they decided to sedate her in order to take a better look and clean the rest of her teeth. Unfortunately, she never woke up from the anesthesia. It was heartbreaking.

Today I wear my The CatFather T-shirt (styled like *The Godfather*) with pride, but I have not always been a cat person. We didn't have pets growing up in Ayr, and I used to be allergic to cats when I was younger. I took an antihistamine pill every day when Kaitlyn and I started living together with Chaz, until one day I forgot and realized I wasn't suffering any symptoms.

Even though I was technically indifferent to cats when I met Kaitlyn, I quickly fell in love with Chaz, and she would catch us taking naps together when she got home from class. And this was a pose I often took up while giving my bicep time to heal. Kaitlyn had researched essential oils to help accelerate scar healing. It was a team effort at home to keep the dream alive—and the scar on my arm was scarcely visible.

By the time I was ready to come back, *Raw* was the best step. It felt right, and physically, I was in fine fettle.

CHAPTER 28

MORE KILLER, LESS FILLER

R*aw* was the ideal next platform. As the longest-running epi-
sodic TV show of all time—with fourteen hundred original
shows since 1993, at the time of writing—*Raw* was the platform
on which all the Superstars had built their reputation. Compared
to the hardcore followers of NXT, *Raw* and *SmackDown* fans look
more for entertainment-based wrestling than wrestling per se, so
I knew my rise up the ranks would not happen overnight. I had to
put the new Drew McIntyre over to a larger, more casual fan base,
who would not have known me from outside WWE. Over time, I
would have to work hard to educate the audience about who I am.

When I came back to *Raw*, it was Day 1 again as far as I
was concerned, trying to prove myself all over again. In the three
years I had been outside the company, the lay of the land across
the board had changed. For a start, it was cool to see that the incredibly talented WWE women's roster had massively grown and
their matches were positioned on the top of the card alongside

the guys'. When I left, Randy Orton was WWE Champion, and initially the title changed hands between him, John Cena, Daniel Bryan, and Brock Lesnar, all established champions. I could not fail to notice that the people who had been starting out alongside me at FCW, and getting on a roll when I left, were now established top-of-the-card performers. Guys like Roman Reigns and Seth Rollins, both WWE Champions in 2015, were in a prominent position. Sheamus too was briefly World Champion that same year. It was interesting to see how far they had come not just on-screen, but backstage as well, and register how much their confidence had grown as they stepped up into dominant roles. Back in 2014, Roman and Seth were going places as a group, The Shield, but they had quickly developed into individual Superstar attractions while I was rebuilding my name on the independent circuit.

Roman was now the main star in the company, and—talk about different journeys into WWE—I remembered being aware of him before he even embarked on wrestling. He comes from an extended family of Samoan wrestlers—the Anoa'is, which includes his father, Sika Anoa'i; his late brother, Rosey; and his cousins Umaga, Yokozuna, Rikishi, and The Tonga Kid. The Usos are his cousins, and through his grandfather, The Rock is a family member. But Roman wanted to pursue football as a career, in the NFL. Unlike me, WWE stardom was never his goal. When it didn't work out in the NFL, he was doing nothing, just working as an installer for a furniture store that his family owned. When I was twenty-two, and was first on the road with OVW, Vince specifically put Umaga with me to see what I could do. And he was a little frustrated to be in a "dark" match that was non-televised, because he was a significant character on the show. In fact, he was genuinely upset, but he clearly thought, Screw it, I'll have some fun with the kid here.

The Usos were there; they weren't signed to WWE, but Umaga had brought them along hoping to get them into the scene. I learned all this later! To amuse them as much as himself, he thought, I'm going to mess with the kid because he's nervous—and I was nervous as hell. This was big scary Umaga, this huge guy who had been around forever, playing this brutal character on TV. I kept trying to ask him what he wanted to do in the non-televised match, which is the very first match the crowd sees before the show goes live. I kept hovering near him, always in the background, popping my head around the corner to see if he was busy. He knew I was there, he knew I was eager to talk, but he'd pretend I wasn't there. He was doing this to entertain the Usos, and it went on all day long. He could see I was sweating buckets. It reached the point when we were literally counting down to the start of the match, and I thought, We still haven't talked about it and I'm going to go into the ring and get killed. Finally, he grabbed me just as we were about to walk to the ring, and said, "Here's what we're going to do, this, this, this, this . . ." And he made sure that I was going to look good. He could have run right through me if he wanted to: he was a significant character up against an unknown twenty-two-year-old who had not been on TV. He won, of course, but he made sure I looked good because Vince wanted to take a look at me. A few years later, I was sad to hear of his death in December 2009 at the age of only thirty-six.

The Usos remember how Umaga had fun at my expense, messing with me all day, but in the end, he made sure I was at ease and looked like a good combatant in the match. Not long after that, the Usos were signed by WWE and came to FCW, where they developed into an awesome tag team. And Roman Reigns, their cousin, followed suit. The Usos helped him out. When I moved from OVW to Florida, and I asked Steve Keirn if I could come down and do some matches because I needed to improve for TV, I did a couple of smaller shows around Florida and in one of them, I was introduced to Roman. It was a six-man match, with three in each team, and Roman was on the other team very, very early in his career.

I remember the coaches telling me to make sure I got in with this guy because they thought he was going to prove to be a huge success. Dr. Tom Prichard told me, "He's this enormous guy, his family are in it, he's really good . . ."

So I made sure I had a little action with him. He already had that imposing presence that's more than a look, it's an aura— something you can't teach. He seemed pretty good in the ring as well! I saw him so early in his development, and then I was with 3MB when The Shield took off. I disappeared, and when I came back he was the top guy.

We all have funny old journeys to where we are today. Roman came in from a football background, and thought he'd give the family business a try and became The Chosen One, whereas I always wanted to be a WWE Superstar, never had family in it, and dedicated my life to doing it, was The Chosen One, messed that up, and had to come the long way around. Now we're both sitting on top of the card.

But I get ahead of myself . . .

Back to 2018.

I could not have dreamed up a better reintroduction than teaming with Dolph Ziggler, a great talent who was well known to the *Raw* fan base. He was always close to the top, there or thereabouts, a talent who had not yet got his due reward. We knew each other from way back, and in my mind there was no better scenario for my return than to work with him. He does his own thing, but he's a quiet, go-to locker-room leader. So smart. We had very similar views on our industry and were well matched in our passion for wrestling. I was the giant half of our pairing (he's six feet and weighs in about 215 pounds), and the dynamic was that I was his badass sidekick, helping him to win. The way I contributed to his story would help me reveal more about Drew McIntyre's character and capabilities.

Amazingly, my bicep had healed so well I easily met my target date for a return to the ring. On April 16, during the Superstar Shake-up, Dolph—who had previously been on *SmackDown*—walked out in front of a lively crowd on *Monday Night Raw* and announced himself as the "Everywhere I go, I steal the show" guy, but *one thing had changed*.

Interrupting his address on the microphone, Titus Worldwide (Titus O'Neil and Apollo Crews) turned up in the ring to offer their managerial services in his future antics.

Dolph turned down their offer, pushing O'Neil's business card back in his face, and repeated that one thing had changed. "And that . . . was that I didn't come back to *Raw alone*."

Cue my arrival in the ring. I would have been a familiar face to fans, but Drew McIntyre Phase 2 looked like he'd eaten a previous version of himself. As the hired muscle, I launched in, taking Titus O'Neil and Apollo Crews out with a punch, and the crowd went crazy. The commentators played along.

Who is that? It is? Drew McIntyre! The prodigal son has returned!

It was cool to be back—and hear the fans' reaction. I had turned heel in the process, and a week later, Dolph and I defeated Titus Worldwide.

I was up and running again.

When a new Superstar comes in, you can always detect that initial buzz from the fans. Oh my goodness, this person should be World Champion . . . They should be in the ring with this person or that person . . . They should be doing this. It was cool to feel that level of engagement focused on me. If I threw myself in, I thought, this really might work out. It hadn't worked out for me the first time, almost ten years ago, but I was now a different person. Being a little older and wiser, I realized that patience is key. WWE provides entertainment fifty-two weeks a year. Sometimes we can be on two shows on television a week, with a big pay-per-view every month. There is time to build up a solid, long-term, deep-rooted relationship with the fans.

The first stage for me was to reintroduce myself to the wider audience and establish my credentials, and I was prepared to ride with that for a year or two, if necessary.

With Dolph, I had the chance to be an integral part of some great matches, many memorable moments, all the while reinforcing my character to the point where fans were really starting to invest in me. We had a great run. It was satisfying helping him win his sixth Intercontinental Championship by defeating Seth Rollins. And then Dean Ambrose emerged to help Seth Rollins against me and Dolph. We had a fun journey together. By September, Dolph and I were *Raw* Tag Team Champions, competing against The Shield. We pretty much imposed our will on *Raw*.

When I came to *Raw*, I felt the show needed "more killer and less filler." Dolph and I both wanted to "eradicate complacency," that was the phrase we used. I had worked my butt off in my time away from WWE, and through NXT. I was disappointed to find on my return that some of the guys in the locker room were content to rest on their laurels and did not have a great attitude. I spoke out in the media and said I'd spent a lot of time backstage, and after shows with Undertaker, Rey Mysterio, Christian, even Ric Flair when I was younger and I didn't think all of them would be impressed with the entitled attitude I detected in some corners of the locker room.

It is something I genuinely believe to this day, and I don't see it as much now, but a few people would complain all the time to anyone who would listen about being unhappy with their position on the card, about how they should be at the top, they should be champion. It wasn't like they were confiding in a friend or asking for advice; it wasn't like they were taking positive action to earn respect. They would be peacocking around saying the company was an idiot because it didn't know what to do with them. But their physique and work ethic and mentality didn't mirror their words. You could see they were not putting in the effort; they did not have a good attitude. I could speak out against complacency, not because, Hey, I look this way, and hey, I'm in a good position, but because I knew where they were coming from. I understood their frustration at feeling invisible, but the reality is you have to step back and get some perspective or you're not going to get anywhere.

When I came back to *Raw*, my philosophy toward these discontented guys was, I am trying to give you the answers here, and help you to achieve your goals within the system. You can try and do it the way I did it, and get fired, and start all over at the bottom and try to take over the wrestling world . . . but trust me, that's not easy; I think I'm one of the only guys who has done it. Or you can listen to me. When I give advice, it should count for something because it comes from experience. Not from the guy who was The Chosen One and stayed The Chosen One, but the guy who was supposed to be something and then became what you are, complacent, and then got fired and had to rebuild himself.

So what I meant was that everyone on the show, the biggest show in the world, should be fighting to be on the show and not filling a spot. To deserve to be on the show, you should have the right attitude. If you're not in the main event, then set the goal to one day be in the main event and have the tenacity and patience to claw your way up the card. Why would you give the big breaks to the people who are complaining backstage when there are guys and girls in NXT calling for an opportunity who could sub in there? In the independents, in NXT, I saw a bunch of people who have the right mentality, who look better, who work harder because they have the right attitude, and I would put them in right now if I was the coach. To this day, that's what I want: an entire roster of hungry people rather than the moaning and groaning people.

CHAPTER 29

FRIENDSHIP PAYS DIVIDENDS

I was having a lot of fun honing my craft, consolidating my character. That came to fruition at *WrestleMania* 35 when I was matched against Roman Reigns for his return at *Mania* after coming back from leukemia. It was a significant match for a lot of reasons, not just because it was my first singles match at a *WrestleMania*, twelve years after I first joined the company.

As the WWE Universal Champion, Roman Reigns was the face of WWE, the top guy. As well as being huge, chiseled, and looking the part—with his full-sleeve, chest, and back battle-warrior tattoos, done according to Polynesian tradition as a sign of respect to his ancestral culture—he has a cool, head-turning charisma. People are drawn to him when he walks into a room. But on October 22, 2018, he had relinquished his Universal Championship title and announced he was stepping away to receive treatment for leukemia. It turned out he had first been diagnosed in 2007, when he was still playing football. After treatment, the condition had gone into remission. Unfortunately, eleven years on, it had returned, and Roman Reigns left the company to deal with his illness. Less than six months later, he was cleared to return to action and ready to make an emotional return.

The big bad guy who didn't express joy at his good news? Yup, the mean, hairy Scotsman who announced his own plan to end the career of Roman Reigns at *WrestleMania*.

On March 25, 2019, he accepted my challenge for a match at *WrestleMania* 35. The fact that I was the guy that he and the top management picked to go against him at the MetLife Stadium in East Rutherford, New Jersey, was a huge honor. I was being trusted with the responsibility of making sure Roman would be okay and have a successful first showcase match back. I took it as a cool nod of approval from the company and from the big man himself to be given that slot.

Roman is such an awesome guy. I have always been fascinated by his story because he and I are almost exactly the same age (he is eleven days older) and both grew up idolizing Bret Hart. It meant so much that he was happy to work with me and trust me to get him through it.

Of course, it would have been cooler to be in a match where my role wasn't clearly to lose! Everyone knew what was going to happen. It would be a terrible ending to the happy Roman Reigns story if he lost that match on his return from leukemia. Some people were down on me being in what was going to be a somewhat dominant display for Roman, saying "Well maybe next year you can be in a match where you can shine and win." I had quite a few negative voices bending my ear. My own attitude was, Well, it's *WrestleMania* and my first ever singles match in *WrestleMania* and it's against The Guy. And The Guy is returning from leukemia and the company have said, Okay, we want him in with Drew to show he can handle the most aggressive opponent, and Roman has said, I'm okay with that. Roman could have shut it down, the company could have shut it down, so I saw this is as a huge opportunity and a huge show of faith from Roman and the company.

In the end, I was going to be in a singles match in *WrestleMania*. I was in the company for years and never had a singles match.

So any negativity that came my way, I shot down. It was going to be awesome. It might not be the match that I was hoping for, or that Roman and I could deliver free range, but we could show everyone Roman was back in a spectacular way.

We had a buildup fitting a significant match on the card, and I got the big, special production entrance. I came across as a formidable bad guy. I had to say a line that was horrible, but it had to be delivered to set the tone of the match, "Leukemia might not have taken you out, but Drew McIntyre will." (Just one of the many horrible things I've had to say as a heel, along the way.) I didn't go out there as Generic Guy 3 against Roman Reigns; it was Drew McIntyre, with the bagpipes and the war drums.

Roman had warned me that even though there would be seventy thousand people in the big stadium, it wouldn't be as loud as I'd think because the noise travels up into the atmosphere. I remember going into the match and thinking, He's right, I thought the sound would be overwhelming. A quarter of the number of fans in an indoor arena would have created a much more tumultuous surround sound. It is a weird thing, as I found in the bigger shows I did, before the pandemic. You're mid-action thinking, Man, don't they care? You look around and the fans are screaming and stamping and waving their arms, but their noise gets channeled upward.

It was a brutal match. I remember taking a big bump right in front of the crowd at the barrier. Roman gave me a Samoan Drop on the floor, and it hurt so freaking much . . . I'd taken pretty much everything I had to take—and I was at *WrestleMania*, so the adrenaline was going to kick in and I was not going to feel a thing—but that Samoan Drop winded me. I was like, Oh no, give me a second or two. I couldn't breathe. I thought I might have cracked my ribs. I wanted to make sure I was giving my part to the match, making sure Roman was looking as good as possible. So I rolled around a bit, trying to catch my wind and brace myself for Roman's comeback assault because we were at that stage in the match when he was going to be rocking and rolling pretty soon, and I was going to have to get up and down pretty fast to let him get in his killer blows. I put up a good fight, but he eventually decked me with his Superman Punch and Spear. Roman Reigns's inspirational comeback was complete and Drew McIntyre's renaissance continued apace . . . and apunch.

Dean Ambrose, who had been in The Shield with Roman and Seth, had been tasked with getting me ready, and he went out of his way to make sure I looked as good as possible. We had good chemistry with each other. Afterward, I was thanked for my role. Everyone was happy to see Roman back operating at 100 percent. For a number of years, he's been The Guy, a friend of the company and a great person for WWE to rely on as a representative. It's not just what he does on the shows, but what he does on the outside. He was back, 100 percent healthy, and everyone was super-happy to see that affirmed in the ring against me. I knew I didn't have the lead role in the movie, but I understood my role and I knew it was part of my journey. Helping Roman get back was essential for the company. Everything trickles down from the top, so we have to make sure the people at the top look as good as possible.

In the meantime, I had started working as enforcer for Shane McMahon. He was the cocky boss's son who billed himself as the Best in the World, and my role was to watch his back. Acting as his sly and villainous sidekick was all part of building me up to be a bad guy. On one occasion, we were at WWE *Super ShowDown* in Jeddah, Saudi Arabia. The story centered on Shane's determination to end Roman Reigns's comeback with my assistance (a nice continuation of our *WrestleMania* clash). It was a fun plot, and my role required split-second timing. Shane dominated much of the match, but he was struggling to finish off his assault. He's down on the canvas, trying to recover from a knock, with the referee looking at him in concern, when I surreptitiously roll into the ring, whack Reigns with a Claymore Kick behind the ref's back, and roll out unseen by the official, to let Shane jump up and steal the victory. *This friendship pays dividends*, ran the WWE tweet.

Shane taught me so much. Primarily, he would tell me to relax. He showed me how to refine my act and educated me in what he likes to call "the nuances" of the industry. He'd explain that when you get to a certain level of thinking, it just flows . . . The relationship was perfect for me at that stage.

So I was enjoying myself big-time going up against the top good guys, getting great exposure (and a lot of booing), but fans of me in NXT might say they had yet to see that version of myself in *Raw*. And *I* had yet to feel I was getting the all-round real Drew McIntyre package over. My character was still fairly limited. I played the big, savage, hairy Scot who beats people up for breakfast and was always available to join a punch-up party, but I needed to unlock the version of myself that had mesmerized the indies around the world, and the NXT faithful. I needed to let the genie out of my bottle and show the fans a version of the real me.

After the Shane scenarios, I needed a new narrative. Internally, I was impatient and frustrated to still be a stalwart in team action. I craved a singles storyline. In a classic twist to my career, however, I was about to experience another setback.

In the King of the Ring event in August 2019, I lost a match to Ricochet and felt like death. I had no particular symptoms, just a general feeling of being out of sorts, low and lethargic. I went to Mexico to do a PR tour and suddenly realized that a wound I had wasn't going away; it not only showed no signs of healing, but had started to ooze pus. And I had started to get the shivers as if I had a temperature. I got the wound checked out while I was in Mexico, and right there and then the doctors said I needed surgery to cut out a nasty infection. Frustratingly, that took me out for a few months.

After four to six weeks on the shelf, I was a bit worried about being rusty, so I found an empty ring that someone lent me to practice in privately. Kaitlyn is a fitness fanatic but had never been in a wrestling ring, so I suggested she jump in and I would teach her some basics. She was doing well, running the ropes, and—in a fit of overexcitement at having a practice partner—I ran to leapfrog her, pressing her head down as I went over. She wasn't expecting this move at all and she looked up, ending up with my 260-pound body smack in her face. She swore there and then that that was the last time she would ever get in the ring.

CHAPTER 30

YOU HAVE A GREAT PERSONALITY. SHOW IT OFF MORE!

How best to come back from another absence? Being called up by Ric Flair to be on his side in Team Flair vs. Team Hogan in the tag team gauntlet contest at the *Crown Jewel* pay-per-view that was held in Saudi Arabia. It was yet another moment when I thought, If only my childhood self could see me now! Flair must have been seventy and Hogan in his mid-sixties, both absolute legends.

Ric Flair has always been such a great bad guy—with his bouffant hair, his fine suits, designer sunglasses, and extravagant feather-trimmed sequined robes, his Rolex watch and brash materialist ego. And of course he was a superb wrestler. In the eighties, the ultra-groomed and bejeweled Ric Flair was the perfect foil for Dusty Rhodes's out-of-shape working-class hero persona. And later on, his flamboyance inspired the likes of Snoop Dogg and other hip-hop artists. So to be called out in front of a huge crowd by Ric was a milestone moment.

"We're all great athletes, or we wouldn't be wrestlers," Flair said to the crowd.

"We're great men, or we wouldn't be in WWE.

"But there's nothing like the Nature Boy's team . . . And guess what? I've got the last hand to play. The fifth man in our team.

"He's a badass. Please come out here, because he's a stylin', profilin', limousine-riding, jet-flying, kiss-stealing, wheeling dealing son of a gun! Come on out . . ."

And out I walked and joined Ric in the ring. Eye to eye with such a legend, and time spent with him outside the ring—it was beyond all my childhood dreams.

"Ric Flair, you asked for a favor and it's been granted. Things are going to get uncomfortable."

Ric already had Randy Orton, Bobby Lashley, Nakamura, and King Corbin in his team, so it was cool to be considered his ace up the sleeve. We were up against Hulk Hogan's cohort of Roman Reigns, Rusev, Ricochet, Ali, and Shorty G. Now I was no serious Scottish savage—Flair had me relaxing, strutting around, flexing, posing, and chilling out. I maximized the opportunity to do all he suggested.

As fun as it was working with Flair and Hogan for the event, what I really loved was hearing their stories. They are both generous in recalling all sorts of behind-the-scenes shenanigans, the stories that never get aired on the record. I've lived so much of my life with them looming large, either as wrestlers in the ring I'd hero-worshipped growing up or as industry elders who have both always said such positive things about me to the media. They have never lost their appetite for the business. Hogan lives in Clearwater, not far from me in Florida, and he's buddies with some people I know. They tell me, "He's asking about you, he's got his eye on you, and he says he sure wouldn't want to get hit by you."

I love hearing Flair and Hogan reminisce. You get to hear every detail of every story—which, in the case of Flair, sometimes you don't want to hear! I knew I would glean a lot of in-ring knowledge from working with the pair of them, but I really liked hearing about the way things used to be. The more they talk to me, the more they realize that I'm a bit of a WWE historian of their era. Flair said he wouldn't like to take my Claymore, and I said, "Are you kidding me? After Bruiser Brody beat you up how many times?" Bruiser Brody, with his bushy beard and staring eyes, was known for roughing everybody up back in the day. I walked away and never thought anything of it, but that caught Flair's attention. He has since said I earned his respect in that exchange because I really know my WWE history.

It was a lot of fun pulling together that match under their captaincy. Here's where I'd like to thank Paul Heyman. Before our big tag match in the *Crown Jewel* show, he pulled me aside and said he had something he wanted to tell me.

"You have a great personality Drew," he said. "Show it off more!"

Coming from an arch performer like Paul Heyman, that advice was something I was going to take to heart. It was a nudge that showed he had every confidence in me; I just had to have that little bit more confidence in myself. It was the little spark of encouragement from a master of the microphone that I needed to shrug off the last vestiges of shyness. I went out there, and I remember having so much fun in a way that I maybe hadn't previously. I wasn't involved in a significant story in the match, so if I was in there I was just going to do something signature and make sure I got some space on the camera, because I wasn't the focus. Bobby Lashley and Rusev had a silly storyline going on at the time—Lashley had taken Rusev's wife—so they were kind of the one story in the match, and I was just messing with everyone as they were trying to be serious, just as Flair was prompting me to do whatever I felt like. I was growing into being myself.

All the pieces of the jigsaw puzzle were coming together. Undertaker, all those years ago, telling me to stop playing the wrestler and just *be* a wrestler. Lessons learned from Dusty Rhodes about how to use the mic and establish a rapport with the crowd; from Shawn Michaels about maximizing every dramatic nuance from a situation. Shane McMahon telling me to relax into my character and go with my instinct. All these elements were coming together glued by my own single-minded determination. I went out there, I was jawing at the crowd, flexing at Hogan, all sorts of little things like that—still playing the heel, for sure, but doing so now in a way that suggested there was something a little more complicated here, a little more interesting, than just some evil Scottish dude with a lot of muscle.

It was at this event in Saudi Arabia that I first met Tyson Fury, who appeared in a cameo, beating Braun Strowman. He and I would subsequently stay in touch, opening the conversation about headlining a first UK pay-per-view in almost thirty years against each other.

There was a strange ending to that event. After the match, we showered, dressed, and left for the airport, still sweating as you do after a match. We arrived at the small private airport, everybody was milling around, and it took a long time to get on the plane. And once we were on it, the plane wasn't leaving . . . for hours. Moods were getting a bit testy. We couldn't get our food. The people who wanted a drink couldn't drink because we were in Saudi airspace. We were on the plane on the tarmac for a couple of hours, guessing there was a mechanical issue. Some were saying Vince was waiting to be paid! No one knew what was going on. It was weird, and a bit scary. It was in the early hours of the morning when we were told we had to stay overnight to fix an issue. Then it was a case of trying to find a hotel and waiting to be allocated a room. People were going to sleep on the floor, waiting for accommodations to be sorted out. I was lucky to know a couple of the guys who worked on the crew from TNA, and they made a point of giving me and one or two other guys who'd been around for a while the heads-up and set us up with rooms pretty quickly. It was silly o'clock in the morning by this point.

Waking up late the next day, we still had time to kill before we left for the airport again. I went to the hotel gym and worked out with Cain Velasquez, a former UFC champion who was in WWE for a very brief spell, the time it takes to drink a cup of coffee really. I was chatting to him in the gym and asking him how he was enjoying WWE. He asked if this travel scenario was normal. Yes, it happens all the time, I joked. His expression didn't change—I guess all top fighters have that kind of unreadable, impassive expression. So I put his mind at rest. "No, it's never happened before. The only other thing that's happened close to this, and I've been around for a long time, was a volcano with an unpronounceable name erupting in Iceland in 2010. And it took about sixty-six hours or something to travel across Europe to get the last plane out of Madrid. And that's the closest it has ever come to something as ridiculous as this. So congratulations, Cain, you experienced the second-worst travel hiccup there's ever been!"

CHAPTER 31

HERE WE GO, STAR IS BORN, MOTHERFUCKER

People who believe in the paranormal are convinced you can turn something into physical reality through the power of focused thoughts, feelings, and beliefs. It is tempting to think that is what was happening to me as the pieces of the puzzle started falling neatly into place.

The trigger was Paul Heyman's suggestion I let my personality show a bit more. Not long after that, I was due to appear in a non-televised cage match at the end of one of our TV events. The crew needed a bit longer to set up the cage, so they asked me to go out and work the crowd a little on the microphone. All in a day's work. No problem.

But then I went out there, and man . . . I had so much fun with it. I was just myself, the real Drew. The Drew that I was back in the independents. The Drew that I was for most of my run in NXT.

The Drew that I was when I rediscovered my love for the business. I was making fun of the crowd, I was telling dumb jokes, the whole deal. Again—nothing extraordinary. I was buying time for the crew. But it's what you make of it. I made it like I was having the time of my life. And I was.

The crowd loved it, and so apparently did the people upstairs. The first thing I heard after I came backstage was "Whoa, that was something else. Okay, okay, we have to do that on television."

And it just kind of snowballed from there. Wrestling is all about timing, and just at that point I began to show my real personality, which in turn let the fans in and really start to relate to me. Instead of beating somebody up, I'd cut a quick little promo on the mic, or do a pre-match interview (and then I'd go and beat somebody up). I was still the bad guy, but now I was a heel who was having a laugh about it. I was a three-dimensional person who people could relate to and connect with. I kept going with it—and it led to the *Royal Rumble*, the fan-favorite spectacular held every January, where the main event features thirty Superstars vying to toss each other out of the ring. Every two minutes, another Superstar joins the fray. Eliminations count only when a competitor goes over the top rope with both feet touching the floor below. To win, you must be the last Superstar standing in the ring after twenty-nine others have been ousted.

As *Royal Rumble 2020* approached, I hoped it would go well, that I would have a good showing. I didn't have an inkling of how well it might go until the day of the match in Houston, Texas, or else I'd have had Kaitlyn there with me. It was awesome to be part of that *Rumble*. I could never have dreamed that I would prove to be the ultimate eliminator in what has been praised as one of the best *Rumbles* of all time for the dramatic story it told throughout. Having the opportunity to eliminate Brock Lesnar after such a dominant performance, that would have been my night made right there. But to go on and win in front of forty thousand people—on the night Edge returned—when the crowd could have turned because they have certainly turned before if they don't get the winner they want. And the fact that Edge was eliminated right at the end after his comeback from a nine-year absence and yet the crowd stayed with me . . . And it was cool that Roman and I, who have had such history, were the last two in the ring. It was a wild, wild night, and a star-making night, and in a match that goes down as well as that with the fans, you know, we're all Superstars, all thirty of us who played our part.

Edge's return was a brilliant catalyst for the story. Somebody clued me in a day or two before, and there had been stuff online. But I didn't hear it from Edge himself. I was there when he was on the road full-time. I was there in 2009 when he snapped his Achilles, and I was there when he retired while he was World Champion in the last match of *WrestleMania XXVII*. I had spent time in the ring with him, and then he'd been gone for nine years, and I just assumed that his career was finished. When I came back to WWE in 2017, I stayed in touch with him, but he had never hinted in his text messages that he might make a comeback. A return at the *Royal Rumble*? I'd believe it when I saw it.

What made *Royal Rumble 2020* so fun? It was a brilliant piece of ensemble storytelling. The blockbuster storyline was obviously, Who the hell can eliminate Brock Lesnar? He was so dominant going in as the champion, and taking such relish in running roughshod over half the *Rumble*. A few people's feelings were hurt that they were going in there pretty much as cannon fodder and not getting the chance to showcase themselves in a significant way, but sometimes it's about the story within the bigger picture. And this was the first time that the bigger picture involved me in a starring role. The story was to present Brock Lesnar at his bestial extreme, which in turn made a hero of whoever eliminated the monster. Brock was built up to be this unstoppable behemoth . . . until I stopped him.

My appetite for that feat was gargantuan. All through my years away from WWE pounding the canvases of rings on the independent circuits, there was one image I would call up in my mind as a motivation: Brock Lesnar. Was I big enough, strong enough, aggressive enough to meet his match? I used the image of him to taunt me to work harder in the gym, to set my goals higher, to match his brand of combative fury. The taunting was over; it was time to prove a point.

For twenty-six minutes and twenty-four seconds, Brock was on the rampage, an animal tossing people out of the ring. Prowl, wrestle, eliminate, chuckle, repeat. Over the rope went Elias, Erick Rowan, Bobby (now known as Robert) Roode, and John Morrison.

In came Kofi Kingston and Rey Mysterio, two guys Brock had a beef with at the end of 2018—the person he took the championship title from (Kingston) and the person whose son he beat up (Mysterio). They survived.

In came Kofi's tag team partner, Big E. And then Brock eliminated them all.

Who could possibly put an end to his depravity? In and out went Shelton Benjamin, Shinsuke Nakamura, and Montel Vontavious Porter.

In came Keith Lee and Braun Strowman, but they started to fight each other instead of Brock, and he seized the chance to hurl them both over the ropes together.

Watching backstage, that was a heart-stopping moment for me . . . When Brock went to take out Keith Lee and Braun Strowman, he grabbed them both around the legs and hoisted them over the ropes with such momentum that he nearly eliminated himself. Imagine . . .

There have been occasions when people accidentally got eliminated. Things have gone wrong, many times. Brock went right over the ropes with those two but saved himself and bounced himself back onto the canvas.

The anticipation inside Minute Maid Park was reaching hysteria. Whoever eliminated Brock Lesnar was going to win over the fans big-time, and that person was due to be the sixteenth man in the ring: one Drew McIntyre. If Brock had eliminated himself, that would have stuffed my triumphant storyline!

A year or two before I signed with WWE, I remember being astonished by the famous botched *Rumble* finish of 2005, when Batista accidentally flipped over the ropes while attempting to eliminate John Cena with his signature powerbomb. They both hit the floor at the exact same time—and they were the last two in the *Rumble*. Who was the winner? No one knew what to do, so Vince McMahon himself stormed out, incensed that the set-piece event had gone so catastrophically wrong and Batista was on the floor instead of in the ring, arms aloft, being hailed as the winner. Worse was to come. Jumping into the ring, Vince hit his thigh on the ring apron and tore his quadriceps tendon. He then tried to stand up with his torn quad, and tore his other quad off the bone too. There's an image of him sitting on his butt in the ring shouting and pointing and instructing everyone what to do from the ground. Even though he couldn't physically stand, he was running the show.

So accidents do happen, and I was very wary of anything over the top rope. I was not up for doing anything fancy. Because I knew I was winning, I wasn't taking any chances. I was only willing to do so much, in case my hands slipped or something.

Thirty minutes in, another countdown, another buzz of the buzzer, and Ricochet was the fifteenth man in and survived his two minutes with Brock.

Then it was my turn.

All of the wrestlers on the roster are seen by fans at different levels. Sometimes you get a moment that hikes you up a level, and thanks to the story with Brock Lesnar and my role in the *Royal Rumble*, my standing was set to rise. In the 2018 movie *A Star Is Born*, there is a particular scene when Bradley Cooper is on stage, and he's about to sing the song that he and the Lady Gaga character composed together early in the movie. She's standing in the wings watching him sing the first few lines. He has asked her to join him on stage, telling her this is her chance, a now-or-never situation, and while he's on stage beckoning her to come out, you can see her contemplating the moment, you know, Do I do it? You can see the inner turmoil behind her eyes. And finally, she plucks up the courage and walks right out there and belts out her part of the duet to an incredible reception . . . Don't get me wrong, no matter what, I was going to walk right out there, but it felt like a similar now-or-never moment when I was backstage. I knew Brock was in there. I knew he was on the rampage. My career was playing like a montage through my head, and I was like, You go out there, you kill this, no longer as a potential champion, no longer as "Drew's the future." I have been the future for frickin' twelve years. It's time to become the present.

And that's when I marched out there. I wasn't nervous. I was ready. The look in my eyes showed what was going through my head.

I was saying to myself, Here we go, Star Is Born, motherfucker.

People think every match in wrestling is planned out, move for move, like a movie, but it's not. I kept going back to Brock, back to him, back to him, staring him down. I was immersed in that moment, and I was thinking, You messed up, Brock Lesnar, and I could beat you up for real. That's genuinely how I felt in that moment. And just when the fans were least expecting it, Ricochet administered a low blow to Brock—and I took advantage of the moment to knock him backward over the top rope with an almighty Claymore Kick. The Beast Incarnate was out of the *Rumble*. I ripped his head off with a flash of my boot.

It was a surreal moment for the fans. Drew McIntyre of all people had got the job done. I had walked out there and eliminated Brock Lesnar. I was now officially the biggest of badasses. I have never felt an adrenaline rush like it. Poor Ricochet got tossed like a rag doll out of the ring.

It was an accomplished piece of physical storytelling: Brock had survived the mid-carders, he had held out against the people seeking revenge for the way he had destroyed them a few months ago, he had made mincemeat of some big monsters. But he couldn't fend off Ricochet and me, two guys he may not have considered would be his main threat.

And that wasn't even the climax. Frankly, that would have been cool enough. But there were stories within the main story, and the commentary team were covering various different rivalries that were unfolding in the ring as the match went on and different Superstars walked in. In the course of the event, I think I got hit with every single person's finish at least once. I was constantly getting knocked down and had to get myself back up and continue and disappear for a while and reappear and get knocked down by someone's finish again, and I eliminated quite a few people as well—Brock, Ricochet, and The Miz, for starters.

I knew Edge was coming in at twenty-one. I was in the corner with AJ Styles, and I grabbed his foot and put it on my own throat to choke myself because for one, I knew the cameras weren't on us, and two, I really wanted to watch Edge's return! This would be cool. And I just wanted to get the view of it live, so I deliberately choked myself with his foot and stared right at the entrance.

Edge's music played, and the place went fucking insane. I thought the reaction when I eliminated Brock was something else, and the noise was an echo of that. Or was it even louder? Clocking the response to Edge's appearance, it dawned on me that the crowd might be upset if Edge didn't win this . . . If I were to win, would there be booing? It was something I had considered earlier in the day, and I had talked about it to a couple of people, but that fear hit me again as I registered the fans' euphoria when they saw Edge make his entrance. The crowd had turned on people in previous *Royal Rumbles* when they hadn't gotten the winner they wanted. I knew Edge was staying until the last three, so this could be potentially bad.

And then Randy Orton marched in. Fans who remembered him and Edge as the Rated-RKO tag team went ballistic. The ring was a busy place with bodies flying left, right, and center.

So the final four were Edge, Randy Orton, Roman Reigns, and me. It was an incredible last few minutes. Randy Orton hit me with the RKO. Edge hit me with a Spear. They both did a double RKO on me. Then Edge and Randy sauntered down memory lane, back to the 2007 *Rumble*, when Edge was about to Spear Orton . . . Could they trust each other? No. Edge eliminated Randy Orton. The message, as ever, is Don't Trust Anyone.

Down to the last three. Roman and Edge were on the apron. I was trying to be a good guy, so it would not help my cause whatsoever if I knocked out Edge. Thankfully, Roman took the bullet there, but he'd been around so long he could survive a boo from the crowd for eliminating Edge.

And then there were two: Roman and me. We'd fought at *WrestleMania* the previous year, and we were rolling into our thing in front of a crowd still upset about Edge going out. I was curious to test the fans' reaction. There was a really fast back-and-forth between Roman and me; he tried to eliminate me with a quick elbow, I hit the Claymore to quickly put him out, and then thankfully I could hear the fans explode with cheers again. They wanted me to win. A win for Roman would be too predictable, and besides, I was the hero who had expelled Brock Lesnar. Roman had me over the ropes, but I fought back, ran at him with a Claymore Kick, and I was the last man standing. *I had won the Royal Rumble.* The crowd erupted and leapt to their feet, chanting "You deserve it, you deserve it," which almost made me cry in front of the whole world. I held everything together, but the past eighteen years were rushing through my head—all the ups and the downs, the part my family in Scotland have played in supporting me, my wife and all she's endured in helping make this happen. It was an overwhelming moment to process.

Who saw this coming at the beginning of the *Rumble*?

Wow! As I soaked up the crowd's cheers of approval and congratulations, I could see Edge and Roman lying slumped against the barricade where they had been flung, watching me, and they seemed happy too.

The official WWE tweet ran *@dmcintyre is heading to #Wres-tleMania* with an emoji of a shocked face.

One response that was cool to see came from The Rock: *Very happy about his. I'm a big fan of DM.*

The pop that exploded in that split second when I eliminated Roman to become the *Royal Rumble* winner—and the winner of the right to challenge for the WWE Championship title at *WrestleMania*—was the loudest I've heard in my entire career. The one in Glasgow at ICW in 2014 was incredible, and if there had been forty thousand fans in Glasgow, it might have been even louder than the decibels that reverberated against the roof at Minute Maid Park. But it was the biggest reaction I've ever inspired for a story that people loved. Brock was such a dominant WWE Champion; he had single-handedly and effortlessly eliminated half of the *Rumble*, nonchalantly leaning on the ropes after each assault, with his customary evil chuckle, like he was having a bit of banter with a neighbor over a backyard fence. And Drew McIntyre was the one who finally put him out.

People really lost their minds. Including me. It wasn't until I was doing my media rounds after the event that I learned I was the first Scottish and the first British wrestler ever to win the *Royal Rumble*. I have always been so focused on the WWE Championship that I had no idea of that record, even though I had dreamed about playing a starring role in the *Royal Rumble* since I was at primary school. This was a dream scenario I'd pictured in my head for years, and to experience it materialize and go beyond how I had imagined it . . . I mean, my imagination can't even come up with things like that . . . It was insanity. My phone was exploding with texts and messages. To scroll through and see the reaction on social media too was mind-blowing. It was too much to take in.

Mark Dallas of ICW messaged me saying, *I can't believe that that actually happened. I can't believe that's something that happened in real life, it was so incredible.* I messaged him back, and then at 6 a.m., he got another text from me saying, *I haven't been to bed yet, I can't sleep.* His response pinged: *Man, you must be buzzing like a knackered fridge.*

The next day the madness continued when I set eyes on the footage from bars not just in the UK, but across the world, and I could see the blurred images of people going crazy. There's a particular one from Glasgow, and the reaction when Brock goes over the ropes looks like the final of the biggest soccer game, when somebody whips in the winning goal in the last minute to win the Cup. That's the only time I've ever seen a reaction like that, and the fact that it was for me winning the *Royal Rumble* left me speechless.

Is this The Chosen One at last fulfilling the prophecy? That was a line posed to me by a lot of interviewers after the event. The way I saw it, I was chosen by management back in 2009 with the hope that something would develop from that, but in 2020 I felt I was chosen by the fans who had been with me on my crazy journey. Everyone knows my story. I might not look like a typical underdog, but I've been through hell and back, and I appreciate the support of the fans who have engaged with me along the way.

It can be hard for the fans to relate to a gigantic, hairy Scotsman who is scowling all the time. Now, thanks to microphone time, and loosening up and being myself, and having fun—the fans were also having fun while I was kicking butt in the ring.

As for my family, they were almost speechless. Dad said it took him days before he came down from his cloud! He's a manager at Kilmarnock prison, where every officer is a WWE fan. For almost five years he kept quiet about the connection, but somehow someone found out, and now a large contingent of the inmates too were agog at my antics and pestering Dad for any insider news.

CHAPTER 32

WHAT WOULD MUM SAY? "I KNEW YOU WOULD DO IT!"

I was looking forward to *WrestleMania*. I knew Brock was coming for me, but I would be ready with that boomstick I call the Claymore. Was I ready for my life to change overnight? Was I ready for a barmy army of Glaswegians to invade Tampa for *WrestleMania 36*? Was I ready to seize my opportunity ten years after I let the first one slip? You bet. I had worked for this my whole life.

The *Royal Rumble* was held on the 26th of January, 2020, four days before the outbreak of COVID-19 was declared a Public Health Emergency of International Concern by the World Health Organization. By March, it was declared a pandemic. As a boy, I had lapped up articles about superbugs in my *X Factor* magazines, but the reality of a deadly world plague seemed as likely in 2020 as the alien spaceships and voodoo sorcery had in those fantasy pages back when I was ten or eleven. It was an ongoing news story, but surely one that would never develop into the scenarios predicted by the most pessimistic forecasts? My mindset was, We hear about things like this on the news all the time, like SARS, and they rarely seem to spread out of the region where they originated.

The buildup to *WrestleMania* continued against the gloomy backdrop and news reports of rising infection rates and fatalities sweeping from China around the globe. It was not until I was in the UK on a media tour that the gravity of the situation hit home: little was known about this bug except that it was extremely infectious and often deadly. Region by region, country by country, the world started closing its doors and entering lockdown. We were bang in the middle of a trip to film a commercial for BT Sports in Scotland, which involved me, the hirsute Scottish hulk, stalking across the moors near Loch Lomond wearing a kilt and lugging beer kegs on my shoulders. The shoot was scheduled across two days, and at 1 a.m., the night after the first filming session, I received a text message: *We're pulling you out.*

This was followed up with a call to explain that, as a safety precaution, the company wanted me to curtail the planned publicity activities and catch a flight back to Florida as soon as possible. The situation was serious; there was talk that President Trump was about to ban all air travel into the United States from Britain and Europe. I woke up the crew who were there for the shoot and told them that we had to finish it right now or we weren't going to get it done. Thankfully, we got it in the can and raced to the airport. Also on the original agenda was a trip to visit Glasgow Rangers, my favorite football team, followed by a precious extra twenty-four hours to visit family and friends in Ayr before I flew back to America. The trip to Ibrox, home of Rangers, was jettisoned, and I rang Dad to explain how disappointed I was not to be able to visit after all. It felt like one of those race-against-time scenes in a thriller movie as we rushed to pack up, leap in cars, speed through the airport. We caught the flight from Glasgow to London at the very time we were supposed to be wrapping up filming the commercial, and made it onto one of the last flights from the UK to Florida.

During that time in the air, I pondered moodily on this unprecedented situation but assumed *WrestleMania* was still going to go ahead. I mean, when has it ever not happened?

Not long afterward, though, an official bulletin confirmed that the world would still have *WrestleMania*, just not as we knew it. *The biggest event in the WWE's calendar will still go on as planned, but without live crowds.*

How the hell was that going to play out? How was that going to look? The setup that had looked so perfect was falling into disarray. Instead of making the fifteen-minute drive across Tampa from my hometown to the Raymond James Stadium for my career-defining match at *WrestleMania*, I was now set to make the regular two-hour commute to the Performance Center in Orlando. No crowds, no electric interaction with my fans, no fanfare or fireworks. I knew how bad it was because friends were calling and cheerily *not mentioning* the empty-arena *Mania*, certain I would be crushed by the thought that my moment of glory would now be taped in advance in a sterile studio.

One thing my circuitous route to championship contention had taught me was the power of perspective. COVID-19 was yet another example of being thwarted. But when I stepped back and considered the wider context, I found I could easily shrug off my personal disappointment. To be in a main event match at *WrestleMania*, fighting for the WWE Championship, was my life's dream, and I was lucky to be living it under any circumstances. I would get to my destination eventually, even if the road ahead still had an unsettling pothole or two to negotiate.

And I got there.

Back to that moment that seems both nicely familiar and scarcely credible. On April 5, 2020, the WWE Universe—along with myself and my wife—saw me deliver a resounding Claymore Kick (or three) on Brock Lesnar, pin him in the ring, and become WWE Champion.

To become the first ever British-born WWE Champion was a real-life version of those millions of daydream montages that I have long carried in my head. I took enormous pride in my achievement. I was overwhelmed at how so many congratulatory messages said that my feat signified something for others. Like Wolfgang, who said it was "validation" for everything we had done all those years ago to try and establish a Scottish wrestling scene, from the post office training mats to the shows in front of five people. If you follow your dreams, you can do it; Drew McIntyre standing there with the WWE Championship in his hand is confirmation. It shows if you want something, you don't just knock on the door, you kick it off its hinges.

Like Noam Dar, who was a twelve-year-old student at my old high school in Ayr when I returned for a charity match with our computer teacher Mr. McLean, and who subsequently set himself the target of following me into professional wrestling. Now he's here in WWE, along with a roll call of talented Scottish wrestlers, Wolfgang, Nikki Cross, Kenny Williams, the Coffey brothers, and Kay Lee Ray . . . And NXT UK came out of a momentum we started simply by wanting to enter the world of the WWE Superstars we worshipped as kids.

It still tickles me that I was both wrestler and fan for my *WrestleMania*. I sure as hell rolled around the ring under the cameras and lights, absorbing the full force of Brock's immense strength, outwitting a fearsome champion with resilience and the well-timed power of my running kick. *And* I got to watch the whole show at home on the sofa with Kaitlyn. Twenty years ago, I was an obsessive young fan in a small apartment in a small town in a small country who chose wrestling to be my destiny. Sharing the fulfillment of my stubbornly held dream with my family in Scotland over Zoom that night brought my story full circle. I could not have done it without their support and belief in me . . . without my mum's love, her positivity, and her selfless insistence I chase my dream, without my dad and my brother's insane loyalty to the cause, without them all being there for me through the good times and the bad. And there's no way I could have done it without my wife, who inspires and encourages me to work hard to be the best version of myself. With the WWE Title belt across my lap, emotions were running high over the web, across time zones and years of bonding memories, right up to the farewells at the end of the Zoom call, when Dad leaned into his screen and said, "Kaitlyn? Thank you for looking after my boy."

The Chosen One prophecy was fulfilled (that box checked at last!), but becoming WWE Champion was just the start. My maiden voyage as WWE Champion made me realize that my true dream never was simply to win the title. It was to keep it, which was a whole different ball game. To paraphrase Arnold Schwarzenegger in *Pumping Iron*, the next installment in my story would be all about staying on top of the mountain with the food, fending off the hungry wolves below. I had what everyone else wants—and the twists and tales of my defense, the awesome triumphs, inevitable setbacks, and marauding comebacks will all be part of the continuing story of Drew McIntyre. As WWE Champion, I would defeat Big Show, Seth Rollins, Bobby Lashley, Dolph Ziggler, twice humiliate Randy Orton, then beat Robert Roode. After 203 days of my reign as champion, it was destiny (written not in the stars but in the writers' department) that I plummeted sixteen feet off a *Hell in a Cell* cage, falling through a table and hitting the ground so hard I bit through my tongue. With blood seeping from my mouth, I was convinced I'd broken something—but that pain was nothing compared to the agony of losing my title to Randy Orton after a vicious match. I've likened my career to a Snakes and Ladders board, and it was freaking classic that I would have to relinquish my championship title to a guy known as The Viper.

He did not have it for long, however. If there's one person you would back to return vigorously from a setback? Yep, it's me. I reclaimed the title from Randy just twenty-two days later and continue to pursue my ultimate goal—to remain on the WWE mountaintop.

Long ago I fell in love with the rich complexity of storytelling in the ring. It took years for me to register that my own life story has currency. I feel strong engagement now from my loyal legion of fans. We're all a team. Each match is another turn of the page, another chance to prove a point. Everything happens for a reason, and I wouldn't change one thing about my journey. It has made me the man I am today, the performer, the leader of a company, and a wrestler who gets people talking. I may be the big hairy Scottish savage, but inside I am still that shy boy who hid behind the furniture and happened to glimpse wrestling on someone else's TV— and become mesmerized on the spot. I'm all about getting eyes on the wonderful, crazy, inspiring world of WWE. If I catch someone's attention, even if they're not a signed-up fan of our colorful variety of sports entertainment, I know I can hook them. It's like when a character said to Captain Jack Sparrow, "You're the worst pirate I've ever heard of"—and quick as a flash, he said, "But you *have* heard of me!"

When Drew McIntyre became the first ever British-born WWE Champion, that was Step One. Believe me. It was just the beginning.

DREW'S GLOSSARY OF TERMS

BABYFACE Good guy.

CHOPS Striking your opponent as hard as you can, often across the chest, with an open hand (Ric Flair special "Wooooo!").

CLAYMORE KICK My finishing move: 270 pounds running at you full speed, leaping into the air, and kicking you in the face.

DDT Jake "The Snake" Roberts innovated this move. You take your opponent's head under your arm and then fall back, driving them right into the mat.

F-5 Brock Lesnar's finishing move. He's beaten literally everyone with it . . . well, except for me.

FACE-BUSTER Landing face-first on the mat. Face = busted.

FINISHING MOVE The coup de grace—that special move that will put down any opponent.

FUTURE SHOCK My first finishing move. I won the Intercontinental Title with it.

GERMAN SUPLEX In Germany, they just call it a Suplex. A move involving wrapping your arms around your opponent from behind (also known as a "waist lock"), lifting them over your head, and slamming them down onto their upper back.

GIMMICK A wrestler's in-ring persona, character, behavior, attire, and/or other distinguishing traits while performing. It is often fabricated in order to draw fan interest.

HARD CAM The main stationary camera that captures a wide shot and close-ups of all the action during filming. You want to favor this camera with your face during matches and interviews to get your moneymaker on TV as much as possible.

HEEL Bad guy.

HURRICANRANA A finishing move in which you essentially jump onto your opponent's face, wrap both legs around their neck, and backflip off them while keeping your legs locked, flipping your opponent over. Watch out for a headbutt to the crotch on the initial jump.

KAYFABE Keeping the inside secrets of wrestling. If someone you don't trust is around, saying "kayfabe" is a call to let everyone know to keep their guard up.

KICKING OUT Getting out of a pin attempt before the three count.

LEG-BREAKERS Moves that focus on injuring your opponent's leg for an inevitable submission victory.

LEG DROP This was Hulk Hogan's finish. With your opponent on their back, you jump high in the air and drop a leg across their body.

LEGIT Legitimate. Real.

PHONE IT IN Performing on autopilot; not giving your all.

POWERBOMB A move in which you lift your opponent as high as possible, then drop them to the mat back-first. The taller you are, the more effective the powerbomb.

RKO Randy Orton's finishing move. Often striking "outta' nowhere," per se, Randy swiftly elevates and hooks his opponent under the chin. Gravity forces them down to the mat face-first.

Similar versions were used by Johnny Ace during his in-ring career and Diamond Dallas Page in WCW.

ROYAL RUMBLE Yearly event in which thirty Superstars fight in an over-the-top-rope battle. It begins with two wrestlers, and another participant enters every two minutes, until all thirty have entered. The final wrestler left after twenty-nine others have been tossed over the top rope can pick which championship they wish to compete for at the biggest event of the year, *WrestleMania*.

SAMOAN DROP To execute this move, you lift your opponent up onto your shoulders in a fireman's carry position, then drive them back into the mat as fast and hard as possible.

SHARPSHOOTER HOLD Bret Hart's famous finishing submission maneuver. Bret would tangle an opponent's leg around his own and squat down, putting agonizing pressure on both the legs and lower back. Bret's niece, Natalya, uses the move today.

WRESTLEMANIA The biggest event of the year. Up to one hundred thousand people show up to *Mania* every year, outside of there being a pandemic.

ALPHABETIC SPAGHETTI

AAW All American Wrestling. I always loved working here. The promoter had great vision and amazing talent. I made it a regular stop, and being based in Chicago, it allowed me to catch up with my mate Billy Corgan.

BCW British Championship Wrestling. Where it all started for me—my initial home company, performing on regular shows. One of the early modern British wrestling companies.

ECW Extreme Championship Wrestling. Paul Heyman's company of misfits that captivated a generation of fans with reality-based storylines, and technical and signature hardcore wrestling. My brother and I were obsessed.

ICW Insane Championship Wrestling. Mark Dallas's vision, and the company where my friends and I made the wrestling world stand up and take notice. Home.

IPW:UK International Pro Wrestling: United Kingdom. One of the first modern companies. Small shows but diehard fans.

IWC Internet Wrestling Community. The lovely fans online who make their opinions very clear. Not everyone loves their harsh, sometimes contradicting opinions, but I admire their passion.

IWW Irish Whip Wrestling. Where I met Sheamus and had the chance to perform on my first television show. (We were awful, but it was the only show in Europe, and we had a platform to learn.)

PCW Preston Championship Wrestling. FKA Preston City Wrestling. An awesome company based in Preston, England, it was run out of a nightclub and used British talent along with a couple of top imports. It had a loyal fan base, and the after parties were always fun.

PWG Pro Wrestling Guerrilla. The top independent company in the world, with the top independent wrestlers, PWG offers only four hundred tickets for each show, which sell out instantly to its cult-like fan base. Getting the "please come back" chant on my first visit (especially as a former big-time WWE Superstar) meant the world to me.

ROH Ring of Honor. Top US independent company. I never had the chance to work there but always admired their innovative style, especially in early 2000s.

RPW Revolution Pro Wrestling. One of the leading UK companies during the 2014–2017 boom period. Rabid fans and quality shows.

SWA Scottish Wrestling Alliance. My first professional opponent, Conscience, ran this company, which was eventually taken over by Big Damo, aka Killian Dain. Like BCW, it's one of the first modern companies.

TNA Total Nonstop Action. This is where I really developed into a main-event performer, from a television perspective. Without the opportunity and their belief in me, I wouldn't be who I am today. I loved taking the TNA Title around the world, whether the fans loved or hated me for it.

WCPW What Culture Pro Wrestling. This was something special for a long time. I was so proud to be WCPW Champion and of what we were able to achieve. My last independent match here was against my friend and former tag partner Cody Rhodes, with ol' Wade Barrett commentating. We got a "this is awesome" chant from just standing in the ring together. It was a very special night, and it was when I promised UK wrestling I'd be the first British Champion (which you can find on the internet).

wXw Westside Xtreme Wrestling. I wish I'd gotten to work there more. wXw was all about great wrestling, and the fans were unreal.

ACKNOWLEDGMENTS

This book, and my story, is not one that happened alone. Rather, it is a tribute, a love letter, to those special people who have supported me in making my dreams come true. To my family, who have always given their unconditional love and understanding, even when I couldn't always be there over the years. The older I get, the more I realize the real superheroes don't always wear capes, but actually are your parents. To my mum, I'll always love you. Thank you for putting my wife, Kaitlyn, in my path, and continuing to be my guardian angel through this life. To my dad, thank you for always being my number one fan and showing me how to be the humble, nice man everyone is proud to recognize backstage and in the locker room. To my nana, you were a second mother to me, John, and Michelle. I know you're forever watching (and hopefully reading), ensuring I achieve my dreams. To my friends, who have proudly stood with me during the good times but also picked me up and dusted me off during the bad times. To my brothers and sisters throughout my life in wrestling, whether on camera or behind the scenes, you have become family, and I cherish every moment of learning, growing, falling, laughing, and crying with you. To my nephew, James, I fully expect you to show this to your friends one day, and tell them your uncle was once a badass who couldn't have succeeded without the help of your dad.

To John, my original tag partner, best friend, and the best little brother I could ask for.

To my wife, you took a broken man, loved him, and made him believe anything was possible. I love you, and I can't wait to keep adding to the chapters of our life together.

Finally, to all the dreamers, whit's fur ye'll no go past ye. Slainte!